Fishing
Oregon

Help Us Keep This Guide Up to Date

Every effort has been made by the author and editors to make this guide as accurate and useful as possible. However, many things can change after a guide is published—new products and information become available, regulations change, techniques evolve, etc.

We would love to hear from you concerning your experiences with this guide and how you feel it could be improved and kept up to date. While we may not be able to respond to all comments and suggestions, we'll take them to heart and we'll also make certain to share them with the author. Please send your comments and suggestions to the following address:

The Globe Pequot Press

Reader Response/Editorial Department

P.O. Box 480

Guilford, CT 06437

Or you may e-mail us at:

editorial@globe-pequot.com

Thanks for your input.

Fishing
Oregon

by Jim Yuskavitch

FALCON®

Guilford, Connecticut
An imprint of The Globe Pequot Press

A **FALCON** GUIDE ®

Cover photo by Peter Marbach
All inside photos by Jim Yuskavitch unless otherwise noted
Illustrations by Chris Armstrong
Book design by A Page Turner

Library of Congress Cataloging-in-Publication Data is available.

ISBN 1-56044-728-1

Manufactured in the United States of America
First Edition/First Printing

Contents

Map Legend

Interstate		City or Town	○ **Seaside**
US Highway		Campground	
State Highway		Point of Interest	
County Road		Resort	
Forest Road (FR)		Boat Landing	
Interstate Highway		Fish Hatchery	
Paved Road		Park	
Unpaved Road		Scout Camp	
Trail		Lava Flow	
Lake, River, Creek		Cliff	
Channel		National or State Forest/Wilderness Boundary	
Dam			
Spring, Falls			
Bridge		Map Orientation	N
State Boundary	O R E G O N	Scale	0 0.5 1
			Miles

Overview

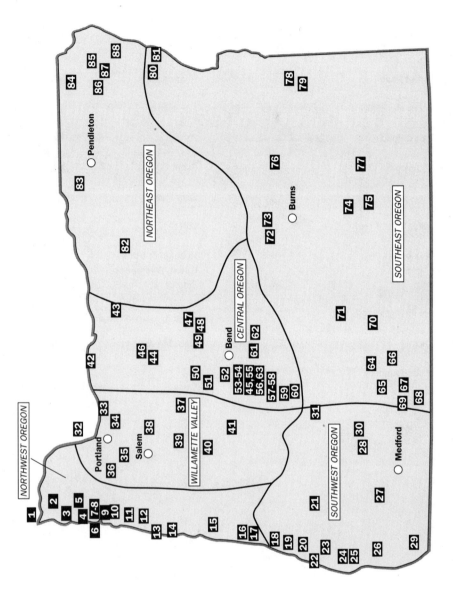

Preface

There are many hundreds of great places to fish in Oregon, from big rivers to small, remote wilderness streams. This book makes no attempt to list them all. My goal instead has been to gather and compile the most recent and most valuable information for anglers about a carefully chosen selection of Oregon waters that represents a variety of fishing opportunities and experiences. Some sites are listed because they are among the best fishing sites in the state, others because they are simply pleasant places to spend a day casting a line. Some are remote and spectacular, others are close to civilization and accessible. My hope is that, over time, you have the chance to fish them all.

In the course of writing this book, I drew on many sources of information and on the expertise of many people, in addition to my own knowledge. One group of people I particularly want to thank is the fishery biologists of the Oregon Department of Fish and Wildlife, who freely gave me their time and the benefit of their years of experience and in-depth knowledge of Oregon's rivers, streams, lakes, bays, and reservoirs. To all who assisted me in the writing of this book, thank you, and tight lines!

The Rogue River is equally known for scenic beauty and spectacular fishing.

Introduction

One could be forgiven for believing that Oregon is paradise for anglers. From its ocean bays and coastal rivers, to streams far inland, anglers pursue salmon and steelhead beneath natural backdrops ranging from temperate rainforest to desert canyon. Trout—from delicate small-stream rainbows to lake-dwelling big bruiser browns—challenge Oregon anglers throughout the state, whether they are skilled fly fishers matching wits with a wary quarry, or anglers who just like to float a worm under a bobber and enjoy the afternoon sun. And while Oregon is known for its trout and salmon fisheries, there is much more here than that. Bass, crappie, catfish, perch, bluegill, sturgeon, shad, and others all make up the mix of gamefish and fishing experiences that are here to enjoy.

And as an added bonus, Oregon offers spectacularly beautiful country to fish in, making the experience all the richer. While in quest of bottomfish or salmon in the coastal bays, you'll experience the drama of the Pacific Ocean, its rocky headlands and pounding waves. In search of winter steelhead in a coastal river? Then don your rain gear and plunge into a green, shimmering rainforest. How about trout? Do you want big lunkers fished from a glassy mountain lake or small, wily natives plucked from a rushing desert stream? Or perhaps warmwater fish are more your taste? Then cast poppers on a weedy lake or reservoir for largemouth bass, or drop bait to the depths of a muddy reservoir for the catfish lurking below.

All these experiences, and more, await the Oregon angler. So gather up your gear, put off mowing the lawn for another weekend and heed the call of the fish.

Tips and Advice

PLANNING YOUR FISHING TRIP

Planning for a fishing trip shouldn't be any more complicated than it needs to be; although how complicated that is will depend on where you are going, the time of year, and the species you are after. If you do a lot of fishing, or a particular type of fishing, you have this all figured out. If not, here are some thoughts to help you get started.

Spontaneous fishing excursions are great, especially when you are off to a nearby and familiar fishing spot. But when you are headed far afield to a new place, or are going to have a shot at fishing for a species you've never fished for before, it's good to get a little advance information.

A good place to start is with books (like this one) for ideas about where to go, and just as important, when to go. For example, while many waters have gamefish in them year-round, if you are after salmon or steelhead, you'll feel pretty foolish showing up on the riverbank two months before the run has begun, or discovering that the river is too high for fishing. So make sure you get some basic information about your intended location. (You'll find most of that essential information in these pages.) Local fishing stores and the nearest district office of the Oregon Department of Fish and Wildlife are excellent sources for up-to-the-minute information on fishing and water conditions.

A second consideration is what kind of gear you'll need for where you're going and for the species you're after. If you are not sure, you can easily get some advice on the kind of rod, reel, line, lures, bait, and other equipment you'll need from a local sporting goods shop. If you are going to try something really new, consider going to a library or bookstore to pick up some books that detail in-depth angling techniques for your target species, or better yet, get advice from an experienced angler friend. This book contains some basic information for catching various Oregon gamefish, but if you are a rank beginner, you will want to consult additional sources of information.

Other considerations include whether you need a boat (there's information in this guide), whether it involves floating a river, and if so, where do you put in and take out and how skilled do you have to be to float it. Other considerations are local travel conditions and access. Can you actually get to the river or lake? Is it surrounded by private property or are there public access points? Is it snowed in until July, or is the dirt access road 3-feet deep in mud from recent heavy rains? Calling local fishing shops or the local Oregon Department of Fish and Wildlife district office will keep you from making big mistakes. When you arrive in the area, stopping at a local tackle shop to pick the owners brain a bit and buy a few hot local lures or flies isn't a bad idea.

And once you are out on the river or lake, don't be shy about talking to other anglers you meet for advice and suggestions.

There are a couple of good ways to check out new fishing areas. One is to hook up with a friend who, ideally, already knows the ropes. The other way is to hire a guide. This is an excellent strategy for getting to know a new area and to learn some of the local tricks and techniques. It's also a good way to fish a river that you really can't do on your own because you don't own a boat or raft or are simply not experienced enough to safely float it.

And speaking of safety, always remember that water is potentially dangerous. Treat it with respect. Wearing a life jacket when on a boat or raft will do wonders to prevent you from drowning if you fall in. Keep in mind that just getting wet, especially in cold, winter weather, puts you at risk of hypothermia if you are unable to warm yourself up and get into dry clothes. Have extra clothes with you and be prepared for the possibility of bad weather—even during the summer months. Be alert while wading. Consider wearing cleats on your wading shoes in rivers with slippery bottoms. A wading staff is a great way to keep your balance.

And finally, it's always best to go on fishing outings with a buddy, especially when venturing to more remote locations or when the plan calls for boating on a lake or river. It's safer, and between the two of you, maybe you can figure out how to catch some fish. Now, dress warm, have fun, and don't forget your lunch.

Anglers get an early morning start on Upper Klamath Lake.

FISHING REGULATIONS

Oregon has complex fisheries, and naturally, complex fishing regulations. Much of this is due to two factors. One, is that Oregon has myriad runs of anadromous fish made up of different species that enter rivers and bays at different times, sometimes overlapping, sometimes not. To further complicate matters, some species of salmon—as well as trout—have been designated as protected under the Endangered Species Act, making it illegal to catch or kill them. For this reason, often, but not always, hatchery-origin fish may be kept, but wild fish must be released. In addition, these rules may vary from river to river, month to month and year to year.

Some fisheries are managed as wild fisheries; this may entail artificial flies and lures only, catch-and-release only, or a combination of the two. Often, there are different regulations for different sections of the same stream, depending on the species of fish found there, the level of fishing pressure it receives, and what the state's overall fish management objectives are.

For these reasons, and others, it is important to thoroughly review the current *Oregon Sport Fishing Regulations* handbook to make sure that you understand the rules and have all the proper licenses and tags for the type of fishing you plan to do. A separate tag is required for salmon, steelhead, sturgeon, and halibut, in addition to a sport fishing license. This handbook is available at any Oregon Department of Fish and Wildlife office, and at sporting goods stores and tackle shops.

Catch-and-Release

Catch-and-release fishing has seen an increase in adherents over the years as anglers have realized its conservation values. In some Oregon streams, angling regulations require it. Here's how to do it properly.

Wet your hands before gently grasping the fish because handling a fish with dry hands damages its protective slime. Hold it carefully, making sure that you don't put your fingers in its gills, which may cause fatal damage. Next, carefully remove the hook. Needle-nose pliers or a hemostat are excellent tools for this delicate task, especially if the hook is sunk deep in its mouth. After removing the hook, lower the fish back into the water, cradling it with your hand, or hands, depending on its size. Usually, the fish will swim away immediately. If it seems exhausted, hold it facing upstream. This lets the water run through its gills, feeding it oxygen. If you are in still water, move the fish back and forth to manually force water through its gills. If all goes well, in a moment or two even the most exhausted fish will spring back to life and quickly disappear into the depths to be caught again another day.

Telling Hatchery Fish from Wild Fish

Some angling regulations specify that only hatchery-origin fish may be taken, while wild fish must be released; this is a fairly common rule on many Oregon

A nice brown trout is released to be caught another day.

waters. You can tell the difference by looking at a fish's adipose fin—the small fin on its back just forward of the caudal (tail) fin. Hatchery fish have had those clipped off, while wild fish still have theirs intact.

Fish Identification

Coastal cutthroat trout, bull trout, and coho salmon are protected in varying degrees in Oregon rivers and lakes as their populations have declined from habitat degradation, overfishing, damming of rivers, and human development, among other problems. When fishing waters with one or more of these fish present, especially where they are protected from angling or fall under catch-and-release-only regulations, it is very important to be able to tell them apart from the other species with which they may be confused. Salmon anglers need to be able to tell the difference between coho salmon and Chinook salmon, while inland anglers should be able to differentiate between bull trout and brook trout.

Chinook salmon have a black line of pigment running along the base of their teeth and gum line, large uneven spots, and spots on both tail lobes, while coho salmon have a white mouth, small round back spots, and spots only on the upper tail lobe.

You can tell the difference between bull trout and brook trout by looking at their dorsal fins and backs. Brook trout have black spots on their dorsal fin and many wavy yellow lines on their dorsal fins and backs. Bull trout have no black on their dorsal fins, yellow spots on a darker background, and no wavy yellow lines on their backs. Coastal cutthroat trout have fine dark spots on their backs and tails, silver sides, blue-green color on their backs and a red "slash" mark on their lower jaws.

More information can be obtained on identifying these fish from the Oregon Department of Fish and Wildlife (see Appendix).

BOAT LAUNCH INFORMATION

The publication *Oregon Boating Facilities Guide* lists public and private boat launches throughout the state, including the agencies or businesses which manage and maintain them. The booklet also offers valuable tips on boating safety and catch-and-release fishing. An invaluable resource for boaters and anglers, it is available from:

Oregon State Marine Board
P.O. Box 14145
Salem, OR 97309
(503) 378-8587

RIVER/RESERVOIR CONDITIONS INFORMATION

River conditions are often a critical factor in influencing the quality of fishing at any given time, especially on coastal rivers during the winter months where water river levels can rise or fall rapidly. The following sources will help you get a handle on water conditions on many of the state's rivers.

National Weather Service Hotline
(503) 261-9246
Northwest River Forecasting Center
www.nwrfc.noaa.gov/data/streamflow/nwrfc/wo.html

The Oregonian, Oregon's largest daily newspaper, also publishes water level conditions on selected rivers in the sports section under "scoreboard."

FISHING REPORTS AND INFORMATION

The Oregon Department of Fish and Wildlife publishes a great deal of fishing and fish-related information on their website at: www.dfw.state.or.us. This includes a weekly fishing report.

Fish Stocking Reports

Call the state's 24-hour recorded hotline, (503) 872-5263, for the latest fish stocking information.

Fishing Publications

The following magazines provide useful information on fishing in Oregon:
Fishing and Hunting News
511 Eastlake Ave. E.
Seattle, WA 98109

Washington-Oregon Game & Fish
P.O. Box 741
Marietta, GA 30061

Fishing and Fish Conservation Organizations

These are just some of the groups dedicated to preserving Oregon's fish and fisheries for present and future generations. If you'd like to get involved, give them a call.
Salmon Trout Enhancement Program
Oregon Department of Fish and Wildlife
P.O. Box 59
Portland, OR 97207
(503) 872-5252

Oregon Trout
117 SW Naito Parkway
Portland, OR 97204
(503) 222-9091

Native Fish Society
P.O. Box 19570
Portland, OR 97280
(503) 977-0287

Trout Unlimited
1500 Wilson Blvd. # 310
Arlington, VA 22209-2404
(703) 522-0200

Federation of Fly Fishers
P.O. Box 1595
Bozeman, MT 59771
(406) 585-7592

How to Use This Guide

The format of this book is designed to put all the important angling information about each site at your fingertips in an easy-to-understand format. Each listing tells you the name of the fishing location, what kinds of fish you can catch there, best times to go, a general description of the area, advice on fishing there, how to get there, and where to obtain more information.

The meat of each site listing will be found in the description and fishing index sections. The description not only provides a brief overview of the river or lake's physical characteristics but includes a more detailed overview of the fish species found there, timing of runs for anadromous fish, if applicable, and the overall public access situation. Occasionally, regulations pertinent to the site are mentioned if they are notable. However, it is important that you carefully review the complete, current angling regulations before actually fishing. The fishing index tells you the specifics: where to go, the best times, and what gear and tactics are likely to be the most successful.

Directions are given from the nearest easily located town. Exact directions vary depending on the nature of each site. Some give directions to specific spots, while others take you to general areas or river reaches. The latter is particularly the case with rivers having anadromous fisheries where the fishing action takes place on different stretches at different times for different runs. Locator maps throughout the book are intended to better orient you within the state. You will need to use those in conjunction with highway maps, USDA Forest Service maps, and other maps in order to find your way around more efficiently.

Lastly, the "For more information" category lists the name of a good, reliable source or sources on angling and other visitor information for each site. Addresses and phone numbers are found in the appendix.

Oregon's Gamefish

Salmon and Steelhead

ATLANTIC SALMON *(Salmo salar)*

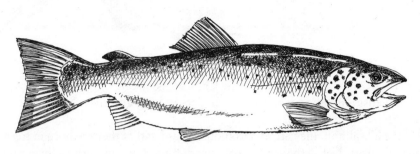

A premier gamefish on the east coast of the U.S. and in northern Europe and the British Isles, the small land-locked version of Atlantic Salmon introduced to Oregon provides excellent sport in select Oregon lakes. They average in size from 15 to 20 inches—much smaller than the anadromous version, which can approach 80 pounds—but they provide great sport nonetheless. The ancient Romans called Atlantic salmon "leaper." Anyone who has hooked one of these feisty fish will affirm the appropriateness of that name.

These scrappy fighters are usually taken with either flies or spinners. Spinners can be cast or trolled. Fly anglers find that casting leeches and nymphs, then stripping the line back in at a moderate rate is a very effective technique, as is slowly trolling nymph patterns such as a Gold-ribbed Hare's Ear. They can be taken on dry flies as well.

Best Bets for Oregon Atlantic Salmon: Hosmer Lake, Site 54; East Lake, Site 62.

CHINOOK SALMON *(Oncorhynchus tshawytscha)*

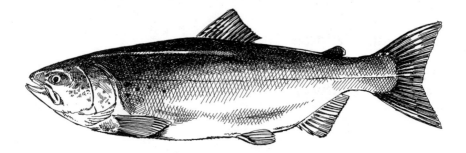

Sometimes called "king salmon," the Chinook is one of Oregon's quintessential gamefish, highly sought after by anglers in bays and rivers up and down the coast.

Like all salmon, they are anadromous, meaning that they are born in freshwater rivers, travel to the sea to grow to adulthood, then return to their natal stream to spawn. After spawning they die.

Ranging from southern California north to Alaska, and across the north Pacific Ocean, Chinook salmon tend to spawn in larger rivers, sometimes traveling long distances inland. For example, spawning runs of Chinook salmon are found in a number of rivers in Oregon's interior, which they reach by swimming hundreds of miles up the Columbia River.

Chinook salmon have two variations in their life histories. Upon hatching, some fry head out to sea within the year, while others remain in the stream of their birth one year or longer before migrating. Chinook salmon wander the Pacific Ocean anywhere from two to four years before returning to spawn. Chinook salmon are divided into fall and spring Chinook, depending on when they begin their spawning run. They generally spawn from May through January.

In Oregon rivers, Chinook salmon returning from the sea to spawn typically weigh in the 15- to 30-pound range, but they can be much larger. There are both wild and hatchery-raised Chinook salmon in Oregon rivers.

A variety of techniques are used by anglers to catch these prized fish. In bays and estuaries early in the spawning run, trolling herring as bait is a favored method, with flashers and dodgers sometimes employed to attract their quarry's attention, along with downriggers to get the bait down deep. Spoons, spinners, and other lures are also trolled slowly in zig-zag patterns to good effect. Rapalas and J-Plugs are particularly popular.

As the fish move upstream into the river main stem, eggs and shrimp are drifted from a boat or back-dragged against the current, allowing the bait to bounce along the bottom. Corkies—essentially lures that imitate a cluster of salmon eggs—are also commonly drifted, oftentimes with shrimp or eggs added to the hook. Another option is to use bait floated under a bobber, or in lieu of bait, a piece of colorful yarn added to the hook as an attractor. Jigs are another commonly employed lure.

Trolling or back-trolling Flatfish and Kwikfish plugs are commonly used, sometimes with a bit of sardine wrapped around the lure to add a touch of scent. Back-trolling Hotshots is also a favorite, and deadly, technique.

Chinook like deep water and pools, and prudent anglers take the time to fish these areas thoroughly.

Although it is entirely possible to catch Chinook salmon from the bank, bank anglers are more limited than boaters in the number of fishing techniques available to them as well as in the amount of water they can cover. In addition, a boat can be a significant advantage when fishing rivers that flow primarily through private property with little or no public bank access. You can, however, drift bait or jigs and spinfish quite effectively from the bank as well as plunk—a slang term for still-fishing.

When fishing in bays, salmon anglers use trolling rods, star-drag baitcasting reels, and 20- to 50-pound test line. In river fishing situations, for spinning or baitcasting, an 8- to 10-foot rod capable of handling ½- to 2-ounce lures, along with 10- to 20-pound test line, is a good all-around rig.

Best Bets for Oregon Chinook Salmon: Most coastal rivers in Northwest and Southwest Oregon and Columbia River, Site 32; Sandy River, Site 33; Clakamas River, Site 34.

CHUM SALMON *(Oncorhynchus keta)*

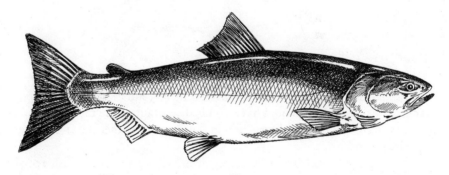

Widely distributed, the chum salmon ranges across the Pacific Ocean from the central California coast, west to the Sea of Japan and north to the Arctic Ocean. Chum salmon fry migrate to the sea as soon as they hatch, spending two or three years there before returning as spawning adults. Chum tend to spawn in the lower reaches of rivers near the ocean, usually between July and December.

Traditionally, chum salmon have been more important to commercial fishermen and to Native Americans for subsistence fishing. Historically, some popular fisheries in Oregon existed, but now, while chum salmon are the second most abundant salmon species, runs have been depressed for some time, so very limited catch-and-release fishing is available at present.

The few anglers that still pursue these fish use fly tackle and a variety of traditional salmon flies. When the fish are still in saltwater, they are more likely to gulp baitfish and squid patterns. Once they have moved into the estuary, and then upstream into the river, they may go for anything from a baitfish pattern to a colorful attractor. Since chum spawn lower in the river than most salmon, they begin to darken and become sluggish early on. For that reason, they provide better sport if they are caught very early in the run. A 9- or 9½-foot rod for an 8-weight line is a good all-round rig, although you will want something in the range of a 10-foot rod for a 9- or 10-weight line if you intend to fly fish for salmon offshore. The current state sport fishing record chum salmon weighed 23 pounds.

Best Bets for Oregon Chum Salmon: Kilchis River, Site 7.

COHO SALMON *(Oncorhynchus kisutch)*

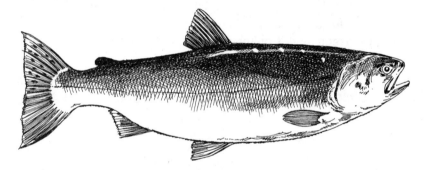

Once a mainstay of the Oregon commercial fishing industry and a very popular sport fishery as well, cohos have declined substantially in recent years due to over fishing and habitat destruction in the coastal streams and rivers where they spawn and rear.

Coho spawn in smaller tributary streams, where the young fish remain after hatching for up to two years. They spend one to two years in the ocean before returning to freshwater as spawning adults. They generally spawn in late fall and early winter. Coho salmon in Oregon waters are often in the 5- to 15-pound range.

Coho salmon angling techniques are generally similar to Chinook fishing. A notable exception is that coho tend to swim closer to the surface—typically less than 50 feet deep in bays—and they're less likely to be skulking in the deep holes while in rivers.

Best Bets for Oregon Coho Salmon: Nehalem River and Bay, Site 4; North Fork Nehalem River, Site 5; Trask River, Site 9; Salmon River, Site 11; Umpqua River and Winchester Bay, Site 19; North Umpqua River, Site 20; Coos River and Coos Bay, Site 21; Coquille River and Coquille Bay, Site 22; Lower Rogue River, Site 26; Upper Rogue River, Site 28; Sandy River, Site 33; Clackamas River, Site 34.

KOKANEE SALMON *(Oncorhynchus nerka)*

Kokanee are a land-locked version of a sockeye salmon, meaning that they live in waters with no outlets to the sea. They have adapted to these circumstances by spawning in streams and rivers while living their adult lives in lakes, which effectively become their "ocean." Kokanee spawn in the fall when they are anywhere from two to four years old.

Although they grow nowhere near the size of their ocean-going counterparts, kokanee are a very popular gamefish and veritable armies of dedicated anglers pursue them in mountain lakes and reservoirs. Although native to Oregon and other western states, kokanee have been introduced to other areas as well, due to the excellent fishing they provide.

Kokanee range the open water of lakes in schools and feed mostly on plankton. The size they reach often depends on the abundance of food and the competition for it among the kokanee population. Kokanee in Oregon lakes and reservoirs are commonly anywhere from 9 to 16 inches.

Although there are a number of methods used to catch kokanee including bait under a bobber, casting spinners, and jigging, trolling is probably the best way to fill your creel with them.

Kokanee prefer water temperatures of around 50 degrees F, which in turn determines the water depth at which they will be found—typically shallower in spring and deeper in summer. When trolling, it is important to troll at the right depth. Many serious kokanee anglers consider a fish finder to be a must-have item.

In spring, try trolling at depths of 10 feet or so with a light lure tipped with a salmon egg or piece of worm. A lake troll using flashing blades such as Ford Fenders or Beer Cans combined with a Needlefish or Wedding Ring spinner will reach deeper-swimming kokanee later in the season. If a school can be located, a jig with a piece of white corn stuck on the hook will also work quite well. Buzz Bombs are a favorite jig among Oregon kokanee anglers. Light tackle with line in the 4- to 8-pound test range is perfectly adequate for kokanee fishing.

Best Bets for Oregon Kokanee Salmon: Lake Billy Chinook, Site 46; Wickiup Reservoir, Site 57; Odell Lake, Site 59; Crescent Lake, Site 60; Paulina Lake, Site 61; East Lake, Site 62; Wallowa Lake, Site 87.

STEELHEAD *(Oncorhynchus mykiss)*

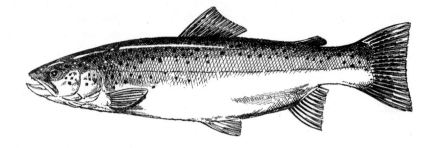

Arguably the king of Oregon's sport fish, this ocean-going rainbow trout has captured the imagination of sport anglers for decades. Notoriously difficult to catch—especially on a fly—some anglers pursue steelhead year after year with almost cult-like determination.

Although, like salmon, they migrate from the streams where they are born to the ocean, then return to spawn, not all steelhead die after spawning. Some survive to spawn a second time, and sometimes more. Steelhead remain in the stream of their birth for one to four years before swimming out to sea, where they spend a similar amount of time. In the ocean they range from off the U.S Pacific Coast to offshore of Japan and Siberia, before returning to freshwater. As with Chinook, steelhead travel far up river systems to spawn, allowing them to access numerous rivers in Oregon's interior via the Columbia River.

Steelhead have both summer and winter spawning runs, and because the timing may overlap, some streams may have steelhead in them year-round. Not all streams, however, have both a winter and summer steelhead run. There are both hatchery and wild steelhead in Oregon rivers.

Steelhead in Oregon often weigh in the 5- to 15-pound range, although they can grow much larger.

Steelheaders use similar techniques and gear as those used for Chinook and coho salmon. Farther inland, and on interior steelhead rivers, fly angling and spin fishing become increasingly popular techniques.

During their run upriver, steelhead are likely to be found resting on the downstream side of rocks and boulders lying in the river, in deep runs beneath steep banks close to the shore, and actively moving upstream in stretches of faster water and riffles. The idea is to cover as much of this potential steelhead water as possible with a fly or spinner, casting slightly upstream, then letting your fly or lure swing downstream with the current.

A typical steelhead fly fishing outfit consists of a 9 or 9½-foot rod, 8- or 9-weight sinking or sink-tip line, and traditional steelhead wet-fly patterns. Long, two-handed Spey rods are becoming somewhat popular these days as well. Fly anglers seeking a greater challenge use dry flies and floating lines. Typical steelhead wet flies include Spey flies, Green Butt Skunks, Purple Perils, Matukas, Marabous, and Woolly Buggers.

A good spinning rig consists of an 8- to 10-foot rod capable of handling $1/2$- to 2-ounce lures, along with 10- to 20-pound test line. Favorite spinners include Rooster Tails, Mepps, and Steelhead by Bud spinners.

Best Bets for Oregon Steelhead: Most coastal rivers in Northwest and Southwest Oregon; Sandy River, Site 33; Clackamas River, Site 34; North Santiam River, Site 38, South Santiam River, Site 39; McKenzie River, Site 40; Lower Deschutes River, Site 43; John Day River, Site 82; Umatilla River, Site 83; Grande Ronde River, Site 84.

Trout and Whitefish

BROOK TROUT *(Salvelinus fontinalis)*

A native of eastern North America, brook trout were introduced to Oregon— and many other Western states—around the turn of the 20th century as an additional gamefish for sport anglers.

Although commonly referred to as trout, these fish are actually a char and are related to such other northern coldwater-loving fish species such as bull trout, Arctic char, and lake trout.

Brook trout thrive in coldwater streams, both large and small, as well as in lakes, preferring water temperatures between 55 and 65 degrees F. Because so many of Oregon's streams and lakes have clean, cold water, brook trout have done well here. They are so abundant, in fact, that they may outcompete the native fish for food and habitat.

Although relatively widespread in Oregon waters, they are not heavily targeted by anglers, and most fishing for them takes place in lakes where they tend to grow to good size.

As with all trout, quite a range of tackle and techniques will work, including bait, lures, and flies—and anglers use them all. Brook trout are not particularly targeted in streams in Oregon, where they are often small. In places, however, they can provide a nice small-stream angling experience with light spinning rods or fly rods. Virtually any small spinner is effective on these fish. For fly fishers, just about any basic dry fly will work quite nicely, including Elk Hair Caddis, Adams, and Blue-wing Olives.

In some lakes and reservoirs, brook trout may reach respectable sizes of 6 pounds and more. For these fish, bait seems to be the most popular approach. The set-up is often quite simple, typically a nightcrawler or Power Bait fished under a bobber. Spinners and spoons will take them as well. Medium-action spinning rods and 6- to 8-pound test line is a good choice of tackle when going after these larger fish.

Best Bets for Oregon Brook Trout: Sparks Lake, Site 52; Elk Lake, Site 53; Hosmer Lake, Site 54; Crane Prairie Reservoir, Site 56; Fall River, Site 63.

BROWN TROUT *(Salmo trutta)*

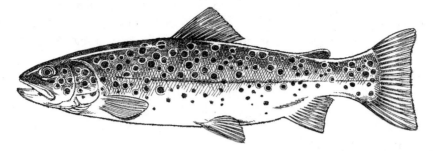

Brown trout were introduced to North America in 1883, and since then they have become a highly popular gamefish. They are natives of Europe, North Africa, and western Asia.

Although brown trout are able to tolerate slightly higher water temperatures than many other trout species, they still need good quality coldwater habitat to survive. In Oregon, they are found both in streams and lakes, and may commonly grow to 15 to 18 inches in rivers and 4 or 5 pounds in lakes and reservoirs. Monsters are also caught on a fairly regular basis; the current state record is a 27-pound, 12-ounce whopper.

Browns feed on insects, snails, freshwater shrimp, and other fish, and they're generally most active during evenings and at night. They have a reputation of being difficult to catch, which only adds to their allure.

Many fly anglers pursue browns zealously, taking them in a number of Oregon rivers with dry flies and nymphs. Trophy-sized browns can be had in some reservoirs and lakes. As with brook trout fishing, bait is often the tactic of choice, along with casting Rooster Tails, Mepps, and other spinners. Since small fish make up much of the diet of larger brown trout, trolling Rapalas and other lures that resemble minnows is one way to hook on to a lunker. Fly anglers after big browns will do well with streamers and even mouse patterns. Evenings, when brown trout are most active, can often be the best time to fish for them.

Best Bets for Oregon Brown Trout: Lake Billy Chinook, Site 46; Wickiup Reservoir, Site 57; Crescent Lake, Site 60; Paulina Lake, Site 61; East Lake, Site 62; Wood River, Site 65; Sprague River, Site 66; Owyhee River, Site 78.

BULL TROUT *(Salvelinus confluentus)*

In Oregon, native char are found in cold rivers, tributary streams, and lakes and reservoirs within the drainages of the Klamath and Columbia River Basins. Although some live year-round in streams, they often migrate to a nearby lake or reservoir to spend part of their adult lives, returning in two to four years to their natal stream to spawn. Because they prefer colder water, areas with spring-fed stream systems, such as the Metolius River Basin, often have the best populations.

Due to loss of habitat, bull trout have been eliminated from much of their original range throughout the West. In 1998, the federal government listed a number of bull trout populations—including those in Oregon—under the Endangered Species Act (ESA). For this reason, most of Oregon is closed to bull trout fishing. However, there is a provision of the ESA that does allow angling for listed fish if the fishery is well managed, so limited bull trout fishing is allowed in some Oregon waters.

In lakes, bull trout may be found along shorelines or at depths where water temperatures are in the 50- to 60-degree-F range. In rivers and streams they frequent deep pools, preferring to spend much of their time near the bottom.

Bull trout average 10 to 15 pounds in lakes, where they tend to grow larger, but they are considerably smaller in river environments. The state record bull trout to date is a tad over 23 pounds, taken from Lake Billy Chinook.

When fishing in lakes, troll large Rapalas, Flatfish, and other lures that mimic the baitfish that make up a significant part of the bull trout's diet. Nymphs and steamers are usually the best approaches for fly fishers pursuing them in streams and rivers.

Best Bets for Oregon Bull Trout: Lake Billy Chinook, Site 46; Metolius River, Site 50.

CUTTHROAT TROUT *(Oncorhynchus clarki)*

Of the four subspecies of cutthroat trout, two are found in Oregon. The coastal cutthroat trout ranges throughout rivers and streams along the coast and inland as far as the crest of the Cascade Mountain range. Some of these fish are anadromous, migrating out to sea to spend their adulthood, then returning to freshwater between early July and October to spawn in tributary streams. Other coastal cutthroats are year-round river, stream, or lake residents. The second subspecies is the Lahontan cutthroat trout which ranges throughout the waters of the Great Basin Desert portion of eastern Oregon.

Cutthroat trout may average anywhere from 12 to 20 inches on up to 7 or 8 pounds. In some areas of the West, populations of these fish have been considerably harmed from competition by introduced fish. Both subspecies have had difficulties in recent years, primarily due to habitat degradation. The problem has been especially severe with coastal and sea-run cutthroats—once an extremely popular recreational fishery—forcing the state to limit angling for them to catch-and-release only.

Spinners and bait on light-to-medium spinning tackle are typical angling approaches and are as effective with cutthroats as with other trout species. Anglers in search of an aesthetically pleasing experience stalk them with fly gear in out-of-the-way eastern Oregon streams, typically with dry flies and terrestrials. On the coast, in spite of the decline in the sea-run cutthroat trout fishery, a few die-hard fly anglers still pursue them. These traditionalists target the runs in estuaries in July and August when the fish first start showing up, using such classic fly patterns as Royal Coachman, Spruces, and Muddler Minnows.

Best Bets for Oregon Cutthroat Trout: Lower Columbia River and Youngs Bay, Site 1; McKenzie River, Site 40; Middle Fork Willamette River, Site 41; Sparks Lake, Site 52; Mann Lake, Site 77.

LAKE TROUT *(Salvelinus namaycush)*

Native to the more northerly latitudes of North America, lake trout (also known as mackinaw) have been introduced to a half-dozen or so western states, including Oregon. This char is found in a number of the deeper, colder Oregon lakes, especially in the central part of the state, creating a fishery that attracts its own special adherents.

Tending to prefer deeper water, lake trout are predaceous and opportunistic, feeding on everything from insects to other fish. Lake trout have even been known to eat mice and birds when the opportunity arises.

How big a lake trout grows depends largely on its food source. A 3- or 4-pound lake trout is a good size for one that feeds mainly on insects, while those that eat lots of fish can reach the 20- or 30-pound range. With the Oregon record lake trout to date at just over 40 pounds, it is easy to see why many anglers specifically target these fish when visiting lakes where they abide.

While it is entirely possible to catch lake trout using bait, slowly trolling large plugs such as Rapalas, Kwikfish, and J-Plugs is probably the most common and effective technique used by lake trout anglers. Keep in mind that these coldwater-loving fish will often be deep, especially in the summer when surface water in large lake bodies tends to warm, so more visible and flashy lure colors can be an advantage at these times. Some anglers use lake trolls such as Ford Fenders or Beer Cans to add an attractor aspect to their set-ups.

If you have a fish finder to help you locate concentrations of lake trout, jigging with Crippled Herrings and Buzz Bombs is a good technique. Be especially alert as you let the jig fall through the water because that is when a mackinaw is most likely to strike.

Best Bets for Oregon Lake Trout: Cultus Lake, Site 55; Odell Lake, Site 59; Crescent Lake, Site 60.

RAINBOW TROUT *(Oncorhynchus mykiss)*

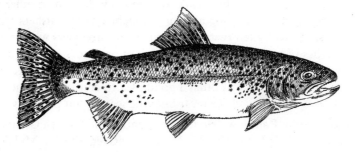

A native of the West Coast, rainbows are probably the trout that most Oregon anglers fish for, largely because both wild, naturally reproducing populations and hatchery-planted fish are so widely distributed throughout the state.

You will find rainbow trout on both sides of the Cascade Mountains in streams, rivers, lakes, and reservoirs. Stream and river-dwelling rainbows prefer faster-moving water, riffles, seams, and eddies where they wait for unfortunate insects to come drifting their way. Lake dwellers, on the other hand, do just fine in still water, providing that the lake's elevation is high enough and the water, therefore, cold enough to see them through the hot summer months.

Because of their special beauty, along with the spectacular nature of the places they live, the rainbow trout east of the Cascades are of particular interest to anglers. Called redbands, these fish evolved in an arid desert environment separated from other subspecies of rainbows. The result is a unique type of rainbow, well-suited to the hardships of life in desert streams and lakes. Fishing for these jewels in desert canyons carved by desert rivers is an exhilarating angling experience.

In Oregon, rainbow trout may range from small stream beauties, 9- or 10-inch hatchery plants, on up to 10-, 12-, or 15-pound behemoths taken from a lake or reservoir. Rainbow trout are pursued by anglers with just about every technique imaginable. In lakes, still fishing under a bobber using such bait as nightcrawlers, salmon roe, corn, Power Bait, and dragonfly nymphs will readily take rainbows. Trolling spinners and spoons is also popular. Some anglers use flasher set-ups similar to kokanee rigs. In a lake environment, rainbow trout often frequent shoals, reefs, and shallow areas near shore where there is aquatic vegetation—which provides habitat for insects on which they dine. Larger, fish-eating rainbows may be cruising in search of a meal anywhere. Medium-action spinning rods and 6- to 8-pound test line work well in lakes.

The fast-moving streams and rivers with lots of pools and riffles that rainbows prefer are generally not conducive to fishing with bait. Here, spin fishing and fly fishing take over as the primary techniques. Typical rainbow trout spinners include Mepps, Rooster Tails, and Panther Martins. A good all-around fly rod set-up for rainbow trout fishing (as well as most other general trout fishing) is a 9-footer for a 6- or 7-weight line. Fly fishers typically favor dry flies, but will often switch to nymphs and streamers when there are no insect hatches in progress or when in search of predatory lunkers. The best fly patterns to use are often specific to the particular stream you are fishing, as well as the time of year. It is often a good idea to consult with the staff at a local fly fishing shop for advice on fishing the waters you plan to visit.

Best Bets for Oregon Rainbow Trout: Most Central and Eastern Oregon lakes and rivers and Detroit Lake, Site 37; McKenzie River, Site 40; Middle Fork Willamette River, Site 41; Williamson River, Site 64; Sprague River, Site 66; Upper Klamath Lake, Site 67; Blitzen River, Site 75; Powder River, Site 80; Wallowa River, Site 85; Imnaha River, Site 88.

MOUNTAIN WHITEFISH *(Prosopium williamsoni)*

This common native resident of cold, clear mountain streams, as well as lakes, ranges across most of the West and is related to trout and salmon. Few anglers deliberately fish for whitefish, although they are often caught incidentally by fly fishers, particularly on nymphs. A typical whitefish caught in Oregon waters runs around 12 to 16 inches. They taste excellent when smoked.

Best Bets for Oregon Whitefish: Most mountain streams and rivers in Central and Eastern Oregon.

Bass

LARGEMOUTH BASS *(Micropterus salmoides)*

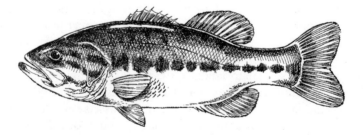

Although not known for its warmwater fisheries, bass angling in Oregon has been growing increasingly popular. A native of the northeast and southeast U.S., largemouth bass have been introduced throughout the country, including Oregon. As a result many lakes and reservoirs, along with some rivers, offer fishing for this hard-fighting gamefish.

Largemouth bass occupy a great number of habitats including lakes, ponds, and slow, deep sections of rivers. They do particularly well in reservoirs. Largemouth bass are usually found relatively near the water's surface, where water temperatures are warmer. They typically frequent areas with soft bottoms, especially where there are lots of stumps and other underwater structure. They also like areas where there is dense growth of aquatic vegetation.

These bass often hunt in schools. Their primary prey is fish, although they will eat a variety of other foods, including plankton, cray fish, and frogs.

Largemouth bass spawn near shorelines from spring into midsummer. They begin moving into these shallow areas when the water temperature gets around 60 degrees F—a useful fact for an angler in search of bass. These fish tend to become sluggish and less likely to bite as water temperatures drop below 50 degrees. Typical largemouth bass in an Oregon lake may weigh around 2 to 5 pounds.

While largemouth can be caught on bait, most bass anglers cast a variety of lures using 6- or 7-foot baitcasting or spinning rods and reels and 8- to 15-pound test line. Quite a variety of lures can be used to catch these impressive gamefish, including plastics (shaped to resemble nightcrawlers, frogs, salamanders, and other bass food), jigs, and spoons. Plugs are perhaps the most popular lures for largemouth, including stickbaits, crankbaits, minnow plugs, jerkbaits, and vibrating plugs, among others. Spinnerbaits are another favorite because they're designed to reduce snagging when fished in the weedy areas that largemouth haunt.

Some anglers pursue largemouth with fly outfits, typically using an 8½- to 9-foot fly rod and 8- or 9-weight line. Poppers and hair bugs tied to resemble minnows, frogs, and mice are favorite largemouth bass flies.

When casting for bass keep in mind that largemouth prefer eddies and backwaters, and they lurk around docks, weedbeds, and other underwater structures. They are rarely found in the rocky areas and points favored by smallmouth bass.

Best Bets for Oregon Largemouth Bass: Siltcoos Lake, Site 16; Tahkenitch Lake, Site 17; Tenmile Lakes, Site 18; Prineville Reservoir, Site 48; Crane Prairie Reservoir, Site 56; Davis Lake, Site 58; Lake Owyhee, Site 79.

SMALLMOUTH BASS (*Micropterus dolomieu*)

As popular with anglers as the largemouth, smallmouth bass prefer somewhat colder water conditions and are less likely to be found in areas of dense aquatic vegetation. They typically reside in lakes with rocky or sandy bottoms as well as in gravel-bottom stretches of rivers.

In the spring, when water temperatures hit around 60 degrees F, smallmouth bass gather in schools at the bottom of lakes to spawn, often near submerged logs. After spawning, they move out into rocky areas with shoals and other similar structure.

Included in the smallmouth's diet are fish, insects, and crayfish. Typical smallmouth bass in Oregon weigh in at a few pounds.

A good overall outfit for these fish is a medium-action spinning or bait-casting rod and reel with 6- to 8-pound test line. The same selection of lures that work for largemouth generally works for smallmouth as well, including Marabou jigs, poppers, plastics, and stickbaits. You can use essentially the same fly outfit for smallmouth or largemouth bass.

Unlike largemouth bass, smallmouth are more likely to be found in clear water, rocky areas, and off points in lakes and reservoirs. In rivers, they will be in riffles and eddies as well as around boulders and similar underwater structure.

Best Bets for Oregon Smallmouth Bass: Siltcoos Lake, Site 16; Tahkenitch Lake, Site 17; Tenmile Lakes, Site 18; Umpqua River, Site 19; Henry Hagg Lake, Site 36; Prineville Reservoir, Site 48; Lake Owyhee, Site 79; Powder River, Site 80; Brownlee Reservoir, Site 81; John Day River, Site 82.

WHITE-STRIPED BASS *(Morone spp.)*

A cross between the ocean-going anadromous striped bass and the freshwater-dwelling white bass, a population of white-striped bass hybrids provides good—if challenging—fishing in Ana Reservoir, smack in the middle of the Oregon desert. A remnant population is also in Tenmile Lakes.

Use spinning or baitcasting gear and 10- to 14-pound test line casting nightcrawlers, prawns, plastic worms, and lures that mimic minnows. Because these fish travel in schools and like to go deep, a fish finder can be a real boon.

The state record white-striped bass hybrid of 18 pounds, 8 ounces was taken from Ana Reservoir. Much larger fish are likely prowling the depths of both the reservoir and Tenmile Lakes.

Best Bets for Oregon White-Striped Bass: Tenmile Lakes, Site 18; Ana Reservoir, Site 71.

Other Gamefish

PANFISH

Oregon has a mix of panfish, all introduced, that provide good, fun fishing opportunities. Yellow perch (*Perca flavescens*), black crappie (*Pomoxis nigromaculatus*) and bluegill (*Lepomis macrochirus*) are some of the more common species sought after by anglers. All are warmwater fish. Their preferred habitat includes lakes, ponds, sloughs, and the slower-moving sections of streams and rivers.

Worms, small spinners, spoons, and jigs are used to take panfish. They can also provide great sport for fly fishers using light tackle.

Best Bets for Oregon Panfish: Siltcoos Lake, Site 16; Tahkenitch Lake, Site 17; Tenmile Lakes, Site 18; Lost Creek Lake, Site 30; Henry Hagg Lake, Site 36; Lake Billy Chinook, Site 46; Prineville Reservoir, Site 48; Lake Owyhee, Site 79; Brownlee Reservoir, Site 81.

WHITE STURGEON *(Acipenser transmontanus)*

Capable of living over 100 years, white sturgeon move between freshwater and saltwater, gathering in bays and estuaries to spawn in winter and spring. Sturgeons spawn once every two to eight years.

White Sturgeon flesh and caviar are delicious. The green sturgeon, a second, smaller species is also found along the Oregon coast, but it is not as tasty as the white sturgeon, and therefore not as sought after by anglers.

A bottom-feeder, white sturgeons may grow in excess of 200 pounds. Although there is a historical record of a 1,500-pound, 20-foot-long sturgeon caught by hook and line; a more recent record is a 394-pound white sturgeon caught in the Snake River in Idaho. The typical Oregon sturgeon is under 12 feet long.

Sturgeon anglers fish on the bottom with bait using heavy rods from 5 to 6 feet long, star-drag reels, 40- to 60-pound test line, and sinkers from a few ounces to a pound or more (depending on the prevailing currents) to hold their offering in the river current. Typical baits include eel, mud shrimp and smelt. Deep holes and channels are the places to concentrate your efforts.

Best Bets for Oregon White Sturgeon: The bays and tidewater areas of most rivers in Northwest and Southwest Oregon and Columbia River, Site 32.

CATFISH

Channel Catfish *(Ictalurus punctatus)* and brown bullhead *(Ameirus nebulosus)* are both found in some Oregon reservoirs and rivers. Both were introduced to Oregon from the eastern U.S., where they are native.

Brown bullheads live in areas of slow water and muddy or sandy bottoms, while channel catfish prefer faster-moving, clearer water. Both bottom-feeders are most active at night. Nightcrawlers and Power Bait fished on the bottom with medium spin- and baitcasting tackle is how most catfish and bullheads are caught in Oregon.

Best Bets for Oregon Catfish: Lost Creek Lake, Site 30; Henry Hagg Lake, Site 36; Prineville Reservoir, Site 48; Lake Owyhee, Site 79; Brownlee Reservoir, Site 81.

AMERICAN SHAD *(Alosa sapidissima)*

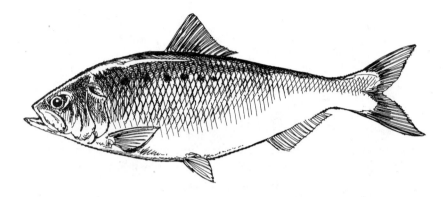

The American shad, a native of the Atlantic Ocean, was introduced to the West Coast of North America in the early 1870s; after being released into Sacramento Bay in California, they spread along the coastline.

American shad are anadromous and travel into rivers to spawn in the spring. After hatching, the young shad spend part of a year in freshwater, then move out to sea. They return to spawn in four or five years. Unlike Pacific salmon, which die after spawning, American shad may live long enough to spawn several times.

While some American shad populations are in several Oregon rivers, the largest run in the state (and on the West Coast) is in the Columbia River. This run is a good two-million strong and provides an excellent sport and commercial fishery. American shad average around 3 to 5 pounds.

As with salmon and steelhead, shad are pursued during their spawning run by anglers using light-to-medium spinning outfits, up to 8-pound test line, and small spinners or shad darts. These lures are cast across the current and allowed to swing downstream as the lure is retrieved. Fly anglers also pursue shad with 9-foot for 7- or 8-weight lines and streamers.

Best Bets for Oregon American Shad: Umpqua River, Site 19; Columbia River, Site 32; Lower Willamette River, Site 35.

WALLEYE *(Stizostedion vitreum)*

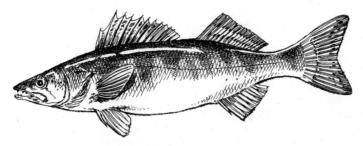

A prized gamefish, and strong fighter, there is a good population of walleye in sections of the Columbia River where there are deep, turbid pools with sunken trees, aquatic vegetation, and other underwater structure—their preferred habitat. Natives of northeast and northern North America and the Midwest, walleye have been introduced to Oregon. They feed on other fish.

Trolling plugs, such as Thundersticks and Rock Walkers, and spinner and worm combinations at a slow pace upriver, along with jigging weighted jigs—such as Erie and Whistler jigs—with a worm harness are standard approaches to walleye fishing. A fish finder can be useful as it allows you to locate the irregular bottoms that these fish prefer.

Best Bets for Oregon Walleye: Columbia River, Site 32.

BOTTOMFISH

Oregon's bays have a good selection of bottomfish for anglers to pursue from piers, docks, and jetties. Some of the most common and frequently fished-for species include rockfish *(Sebastes spp.)*, cabezon *(Scorpaenichthys marmoratus)* greenling *(Hexagrammos spp.)* and lingcod *(Ophiodon elongatus)*.

These fish are all excellent eating, although the eggs and liver of the cabezon are poisonous. They're found around offshore pinnacles, rocky headlands, reefs and jetties, easily accessible to the shore-bound angler.

Medium-to-heavy spinning outfits with 15- to 20-pound test line are generally used to take bottomfish. A variety of effective baits (fished off the bottom) include clam necks, herring, mussels, sand and ghost shrimp, and marine worms. Fish off jetties and piers where there is some underwater structure. Rockfish can also be caught at night, fishing by lantern light with spinners and spoons.

Best Bets for Oregon Bottomfish: All bays on rivers in Northwest and Southwest Oregon.

Oregon's Record Gamefish

Brook Trout	9 lbs. 6 oz.	Deschutes River
Brown Trout	27 lbs. 12 oz.	Paulina Lake
Bull Trout	23 lbs. 2 oz.	Lake Billy Chinook
Coastal Cutthroat Trout	6 lbs. 4 oz.	Siltcoos Lake
Inland Cutthroat Trout	9 lbs. 8 oz.	Malheur River
Golden Trout	7 lbs. 10 oz.	Eagle Cap Wilderness
Lake Trout	40 lbs. 8 oz.	Odell Lake
Rainbow Trout	28 lbs. 0 oz.	Rogue River
Steelhead	35 lbs. 8 oz.	Columbia River
Chinook Salmon	83 lbs. 0 oz.	Umpqua River
Chum Salmon	23 lbs. 0 oz.	Kilchis River
Coho Salmon	25 lbs. 5.25 oz.	Siltcoos Lake
Kokanee Salmon	4 lbs. 14.7 oz.	Wallowa Lake
Striped Bass	64 lbs. 8 oz.	Umpqua River
Shad	5 lbs. 13 oz.	Columbia River
Whitefish	4 lbs. 13 oz.	McKenzie River
White Hybrid Bass	18 lbs. 8 oz.	Ana Reservoir
Largemouth Bass	11 lbs. 9.6 oz.	Farm Pond
Smallmouth Bass	7 lbs. 4.6 oz.	Henry Hagg Lake
Striped Bass	64 lbs. 8 oz.	Umpqua River
Bluegill	2 lbs. 5.5 oz.	Farm Pond
Bullhead Catfish	3 lbs. 6 oz.	Brownlee Reservoir
Channel Catfish	36 lbs. 8 oz.	McKay Reservoir
Flathead Catfish	42 lbs. 0 oz.	Snake River
White Catfish	15 lbs. 0 oz.	Tualatin River
Black Crappie	4 lbs. 6.1 oz.	Small pond, Corvallis
White Crappie	4 lbs. 12 oz.	Gerber Reservoir
Yellow Perch	2 lbs. 2 oz.	Brownsmead Slough
Sacramento Perch	11.2 oz.	Lost River
Green Sunfish	11 oz.	Umpqua River
Pumpkinseed Sunfish	7.68 oz.	Lake Oswego
Redear Sunfish	1 lb. 15.5 oz.	Reynolds Pond
Walleye	19 lbs. 15.3 oz.	Columbia River
Warmouth	1 lb. 14.2 oz.	Columbia Slough

The mouth of the mighty Columbia offers a variety of fine fishing opportunities for salmon and steelhead and bottom-dwelling sturgeon.

Northwest Oregon

Salmon and steelhead dominate angling activity along Oregon's northwest coastal bays and rivers, but a variety of other fish species are taken mainly from bays—Chinook and coho are much of it but also sturgeon and bottom-fish. Steelhead and salmon are pursued in coastal rivers. Surprisingly, trout fishing isn't really a focus in this region, although there are trout fishing opportunities around. The sea-run cutthroat trout fishery was traditionally popular, but in recent years, concerns about its overall health has resulted in the institution of catch-and-release, artificial-flies, and lures-only regulations in most coastal streams. The regulations have cooled some of the angling interest in these fish, as intended, and besides, who wants to spend time catching 16-inch trout when there are 30-pound salmon in the rivers?

Although bank fishing opportunities exist along these rivers, anglers with boats tend to have the advantage of reaching good stretches of river that are inaccessible to shoreline anglers because of private property restrictions or remoteness. Typically, anglers use motorized boats in bays and lower river sections and traditional drift boats for floating upper sections. A copy of the *Oregon Boating Facilities Guide* is an indispensable reference for the north coast angler.

Unless otherwise noted, regulations for the waters listed in this section will be found in the Northwest Zone section of the *Oregon Sport Fishing Regulations* handbook.

1 Lower Columbia River and Youngs Bay

Key Species: Chinook salmon, coho salmon, steelhead, cutthroat trout, sturgeon

Best Way to Fish: boat, bank

Best Time to Fish: year-round

Description: The mouth of the mighty Columbia River, along with Youngs Bay and its two major tributaries, offers a good variety of fishing opportunities for salmon and steelhead, along with bottom-dwelling sturgeon—all popular fish in these parts.

The mouth of the Columbia is for the most part a boat fishery. Anglers prowl the mouth for fall Chinook salmon and sturgeon, Youngs Bay for the difficult spring Chinook fishery and the Lewis and Clark River for steelhead, Chinook, and coho. Excellent cutthroat trout fishing can be found in the upper, out-of-the-way sections of the Youngs River.

A variety of fishing rules are in effect in this area, so be sure to consult current fishing regulations. Regulations for coastal streams draining into the Columbia River may be different from other coastal streams.

Fishing Index: On the Columbia's mouth, fall Chinook salmon angling is from early August into mid-September. The peak is from mid-August through early September. Trolling with cut-plug herring is the standard approach, and the north side of Desemona Sands is a favored location. Sturgeon fishing is best here from April into October or November. They are caught by fishing shrimp, smelt, and anchovies on the bottom. The best tack to take on the Columbia is to watch where the charter fleets are fishing and which boats are catching fish. The charter captains are very knowledgeable about where the sturgeon are most likely to be and watching them will save you a lot of trial-and-error time. Fall Chinook and coho can also be caught by trolling off Tongue Point about 15 miles upriver. This salmon fishery, from the jetties at the mouth of the river to Tongue Point, is known as the Buoy 10 Fishery.

Just south of Astoria is Youngs Bay and its two tributaries, the Youngs River and the Lewis and Clark River. The Youngs River is 27 miles long and has steelhead, Chinook, coho, and cutthroat trout. The salmon are in the river from late August into late October. But because most of the lower river banks are in private hands, getting permission to trespass is difficult. The steelhead run, however, goes further upriver into lands owned by Willamette Industries, a timber company. Roads onto its lands are gated; however, the company allows anglers access on foot or by mountain bike.

The Youngs River has a large waterfall on it at river mile nine, which blocks the upstream movement of salmon and steelhead. But there is excellent cutthroat trout fishing above the falls, and also on Willamette Industries land, where the public is allowed to walk in. Only fin-clipped cutthroat trout may be kept.

Lower Columbia River and Youngs Bay

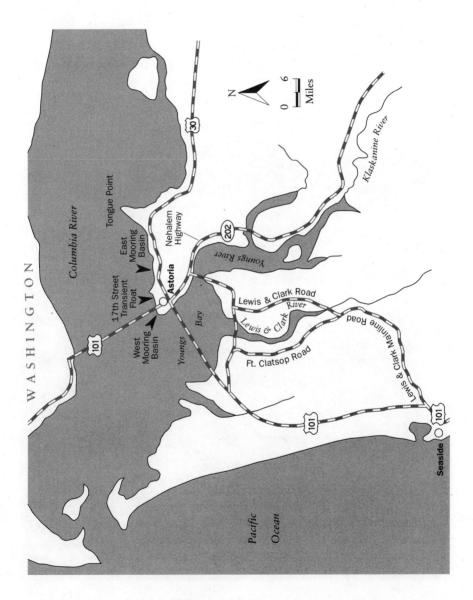

The Buoy 10 salmon fishery, as well as sturgeon fishing, are major attractions for anglers on the lower Columbia River.

Youngs Bay proper has a run of spring Chinook from mid-April through June. Raised in netpens in the bay and area hatcheries, this fishery has proved a difficult one for anglers. The bay is shallow, and the clear water makes for skittish fish. In addition, standard salmon trolling techniques have not proved to be especially effective here for reasons not entirely known. During the open season, this fishery is open to commercial fishermen on weekdays and recreational anglers on weekends. There is a good jack salmon fishery—salmon that have only spent a year in the ocean before returning to freshwater—for both coho and fall Chinook from August through November, peaking in September. Anglers cast bait and small spinners around feeder streams at high tide from the bank on the east side of the bay off the Nehalem Highway.

Directions: The lower Columbia River can be accessed via the West Mooring Basin, 17th Steet Transient Float, and East Mooring Basin public boat ramps at Astoria off U.S. Highway 30, which runs through town along the bay. To reach the jack salmon bank fishing area on the east side of Youngs Bay, go east from Astoria off U.S. Highway 101 onto Oregon Highway 202 (Nehalem Highway) for about 6 miles. Access to Willamette Industries lands on the Lewis and Clark River can be reached by driving up the drainage east of Seaside on the Lewis and Clark Mainline Road to the Warrenton Water Treatment Plant. Park at the lot on the east side of the road, walk past the gate and down the first road on your right to a good fishing area.

For More Information: Oregon Department of Fish and Wildlife, North Coast Fish District Office

2 ▶ Klaskanine River

Key Species: Chinook salmon, steelhead

Best Way to Fish: bank

Best Time to Fish: Chinook salmon, late July through December; steelhead, late November through February

Description: Not to be confused with the Clatskanie River in adjacent Columbia County, the Klaskanine is composed of a short mainstem and longer north and south forks. It offers good winter steelhead fishing, along with some opportunity to catch Chinook salmon as well. The Klaskanine empties into the Youngs River, a broad finger of Youngs Bay, south of Astoria.

Chinook are in the river from late July through December, peaking in late September. These fish are raised for planting in Youngs Bay, and few people pursue them on the river. The winter steelhead run goes from late November through February. This run usually peaks in mid-December. Most of the salmon and steelhead returning to the Klaskanine originated at one of the two hatcheries on the river's north and south forks.

Klaskanine River

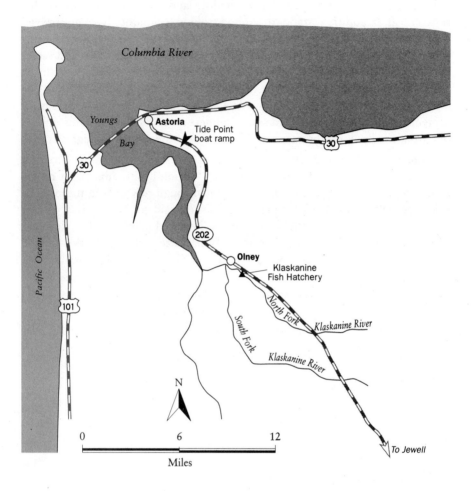

A healthy, fresh, and wild winter-run steelhead from the Klaskanine River.

At one time there was a small coho salmon fishery here—today, only an occasional stray fish can be found. If you should hook into one and want to keep it, it must be a hatchery, fin-clipped fish.

Chinook on this river run in the 15- to 18-pound range, while steelhead average about 8 pounds.

Be sure to study the current angling regulations before fishing the Klaskanine. There are bait restrictions during certain times of the year and closed sections on the North Fork near the hatchery.

Fishing Index: Standard steelhead and salmon angling techniques are employed on the lower Klaskanine, including bait, plugs, and spinners. Anglers can travel by motor-powered boat up into the tidewater area of the Klaskanine, putting in at the private Tide Point Ramp on Youngs Bay.

Upstream, the river is largely shallow with small pools that do not lend themselves well to Chinook angling techniques. For this reason, most of the river is a steelhead bank fishery. Here, drifting Corkies and eggs are the favored techniques.

There is about 100 feet of public water at the Klaskanine Fish Hatchery on the North Fork. It is also sometime possible to secure permission to fish on private property just downstream of the hatchery as well. There is is also access along OR 202, which parallels much of the main stem and its north fork. Although there is also a hatchery on the south fork that some fish return to, extensive private holdings make access hard to come by.

Sand shrimp are popular bait for salmon and steelhead anglers fishing Oregon's coastal rivers.

Directions: To reach the Klaskanine Fish Hatchery, drive south from Astoria on OR 202 for 12 miles. Public bank access is also available along this road.

For More Information: Oregon Department of Fish and Wildlife, North Coast Fish District Office

3 Necanicum River

Key Species: Chinook salmon, steelhead, sea-run cutthroat trout

Best Way to Fish: boat, bank

Best Time to Fish: Chinook salmon, late October through November; steelhead, late October through March; sea-run cutthroat trout, August and September

Description: This small north coast stream offers some fall Chinook salmon fishing along with steelhead and sea-run cutthroat trout.

Chinook are in the river from late October or early November to around Thanksgiving, peaking in mid-November. The hatchery winter steelhead run lasts from late October through the middle of January. This run peaks around the end of December. A small wild run of steelhead arrives in early February, peaking between mid-February and into March. Sea-run cutthroats move through from August to late October, with prime fishing for them early in the season before they disperse into tributary streams to spawn.

Necanicum River

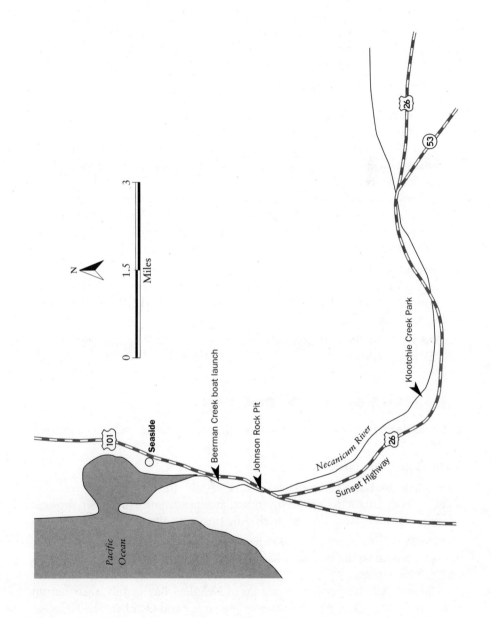

Be sure to check current regulations for the latest rules on fishing in the Necanicum.

Fishing Index: Standard techniques for both Chinook and steelhead work quite well here, including drift fishing with Corkies and Hot Shots, drifting bait shrimp and eggs under a bobber, and pulling plugs. Good drifts include Klootchie Creek Park to the Johnson Construction Company boat ramp (a private fee launch on US 101 also known as the Johnson Rock Pit, (503) 738-7328. Launch fee is $30) for steelhead and from the Johnson Construction Company boat ramp to the Oregon Department of Fish and Wildlife's Beerman Creek boat launch.

Bank anglers will find access at Klootchie Creek Park, and just upstream and downstream of the park on lands owned by Willamette Industries, a private timber company. They allow public fishing access to their lands, but you must walk in, as the access roads are gated. The Oregon Department of Fish and Wildlife also maintains public fishing access on the South Fork Necanicum, where the logging mainline road crosses the river, located off US 26 at milepost 5.

Although not as popular a fishery as it once was, cutthroat trout anglers do well with spinners such as Mepps, Rooster Tails, and Panther Martins fishing the lower river from just south of Seaside up to Klootchie Creek Park. Mornings and evenings in August are the best times.

Directions: U.S. Highways 101 and 26 follow the Necanicum River for much of its length. To reach Klootchie Creek Park from Seaside, drive south on US 101 for 2 miles. At Cannon Beach Junction turn left (east) onto US 26 and go 3 miles to the park, on the left.

For More Information: Oregon Department of Fish and Wildlife, North Coast Fish District Office

4 Nehalem River and Bay

Key Species: Chinook salmon, coho salmon, steelhead, sea-run cutthroat trout

Best Way to Fish: boat, bank

Best Time to Fish: Chinook salmon, mid-July through December; coho salmon, mid-August to early November; steelhead, late November through March; sea-run cutthroat trout, early July through September

Description: Flowing nearly 120 miles from its headwaters deep in the Coast Range mountains, the Nehalem River is a major northwest Oregon steelhead and salmon stream.

Chinook salmon begin showing up in Nehalem Bay in July, then run up the river through December, peaking in September and October. The Nehalem mainstem, along with its north fork, is one of the few remaining Oregon

Nehalem River and Bay

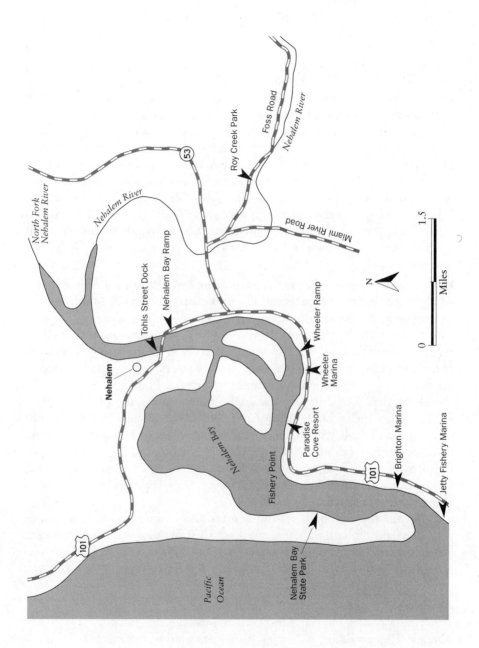

streams with a coho salmon season. These fish are available for catch-and-keep angling (hatchery-fish only, which are returning to the hatchery on the North Fork Nehalem). Only the lower river, between Fishery Point, in Nehalem Bay, to the confluence of the North Fork Nehalem is open to coho fishing.

Steelhead are present here from late November through March, with the height of the run of hatchery fish usually from January to mid-February. Wild steelhead numbers peak in February and March. Sea-run cutthroat trout begin congregating in the lower river around mid-July and run up the river through September.

Chinook salmon here average about 20 pounds while coho typically weigh about half that. An average Nehalem River steelhead runs around 7 pounds. Sea-run cutthroats commonly run anywhere from 12 inches to 16 inches.

The Nehalem River fishes best between 4 and 5 feet, so be sure and check water conditions before heading out (see "River/Reservoir Conditions Information" at the beginning of this book, page 6). As typical with all coastal salmon and steelhead streams, angling regulations vary depending on what species you are after and where you are fishing, so carefully review all the current regulations.

Fishing Index: Nehalem Bay is the focal point for most salmon fishing in this river system. Fishing for coho and Chinook usually begins by mid-July, with September and October affording the best chances for connecting with fish. Trolling with cut-plug herring or spinners are the usual approaches to salmon fishing here. The bay's narrow mouth and its east and south shores are favored stretches to troll. A total of eight public or private boat ramps (which the public may use) are in the bay and lower river.

Steelheaders back-drift eggs and sand shrimp or plugs, or drift bait under a bobber. Many anglers put in at Roy Creek Park about 12 miles upriver and drift downstream to the bay, taking out at Tohls Street Dock or Nehalem Bay Ramp. Another strategy is to put in at Roy Creek Park, motor upriver, then drift back down. Since the bulk of the Nehalem River between U.S. Highway 26 and the city of Nehalem flows through the Tillamook State Forest, fishing is allowed along this entire stretch.

You will also find both sea-run and resident cutthroat trout here, which can be caught on both flies and spinners. Most sea-runs are caught between the mouths of the Salmonberry and North Fork Nehalem rivers. Resident cutthroat can be found throughout the system above tidewater. All trout fishing on the Nehalem is catch-and-release only.

Directions: To Reach Roy Creek Park from the city of Nehalem, go south on U.S. Highway 101 for 1.5 miles. Go left (east) on the Necanicum Highway (Oregon Highway 53) for 2 miles. Turn right (southeast) and bear left onto Foss Road. Foss Road follows the river northeast to US 26 and beyond. Roy Creek Park is located off Foss Road near where Miami River Road crosses the Nehalem River. The take-out at city-owned Tohls Street Dock is on the river's west bank by the US 101 bridge. The Nehalem Bay Ramp is on the east bank at the US 101 bridge.

For More Information: Oregon Department of Fish and Wildlife, Tillamook District Office

5 North Fork Nehalem River

Key Species: Chinook salmon, coho salmon, steelhead

Best Way to Fish: bank

Best Time to Fish: Chinook salmon, September through December; coho salmon, mid-August to early November; steelhead, late November through March

Description: This productive branch of the Nehalem River offers angling for coho and Chinook salmon as well as steelhead. Both species of salmon are moving through this fork in earnest by September and October. Chinook peak here in September while coho peak in October. Although Chinook are still in the river into December and continue to be available for anglers, fishing closes for coho in November. Only fin-clipped coho salmon may be kept. Winter steelhead are here from late November through March. The run of hatchery fish peaks between mid-January and February, while the wild run is most numerous in the river during February and March.

The North Fork Nehalem is difficult to float and requires good boating skills. The best bet for most anglers is to fish from the bank just below and above the Nehalem Fish Hatchery, where public access is allowed.

The North Fork Nehalem fishes best at 3 to 4 feet. You can get current river and fishing conditions by calling the hatchery information line.

Fishing Index: A mix of eggs and sand shrimp, spinners, or jigs under a bobber are the popular techniques here; jigs tend to be the favored technique. Several holes in the immediate vicinity of the hatchery typically hold fish. You will find some good wild steelhead water just above the hatchery as well. Property above the hatchery is owned by a private timber company, Longview Fibre. They allow public fishing access on their lands.

This is a popular angling location and it can get a little busy during the height of the runs, especially on weekends. There is a handicapped fishing platform at the hatchery, making this a good location for salmon and steelhead anglers with disabilities.

Directions: From the city of Nehalem go south on U.S. Highway 101 for 1.5 miles. Go left (east) on the Necanicum Highway (Oregon Highway 53) for 8 miles to the Nehalem Fish Hatchery.

For More Information: Nehalem Fish Hatchery

North Fork Nehalem River

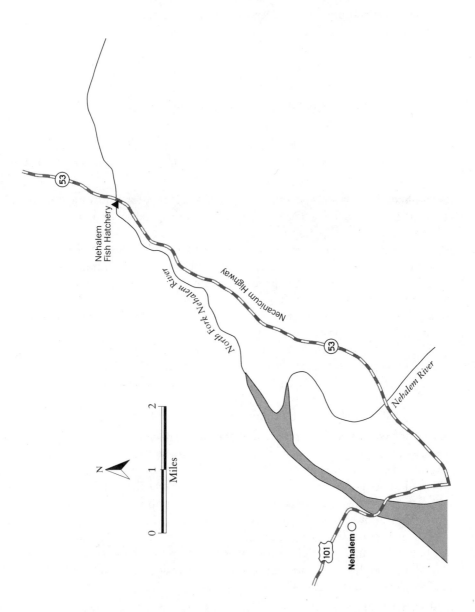

6 Tillamook Bay

Key Species: Chinook salmon, late-April through mid-June and late August to late September; sturgeon and bottomfish, year-round

Best Way to Fish: boat, bank

Best Time to Fish: year-round

Description: This large bay north of the city of Tillamook offers a wide range of fishing opportunities. It also serves as the point of entry for salmon and steelhead runs on the Wilson, Trask, Kilchis, Miami, and Tillamook Rivers, all of which empty into the bay.

Salmon and bottomfish provide the bulk of the fishing action in Tillamook Bay. Spring Chinook fishing hits from late April through mid-June, peaking in late May or early June. The fall run starts in mid-to-late August and peaks in mid-to-late September. Bottomfish including rockfish, cabezon, lingcod, surfperch, and greenling are available year-round. Sturgeon are also in the bay year-round, although most fishing for them happens from December through May.

An Oregon angling license is required to fish for salmon and bottomfish in the bay. Regulations may vary from year to year for both salmon and bottomfish, so be sure and read up on the most current fishing rules before you pack your gear. In addition, the Oregon Department of Fish and Wildlife issues fall and spring special regulation flyers each year to update anglers on the latest rules for fishing on the lower bay.

Fishing Index: Anglers after Chinook troll with cut-plug herring, sardine-wrapped Kwikfish and Flatfish along the east side of the bay from its outlet to the sea to Bay City. South of Bay City to Memaloose Point trolling spinners such as Clearwater Flashes or Teespoons is the favored approach. Another good bait trolling area is in the channel on the west side of the bay off Pitcher Point. The hole (known as Oyster House Hole) off the public boat launch at Memaloose Point is a popular spot to cast spinners. Low tide is often the best time to catch salmon in the bay as they concentrate in the deeper holes.

The fall Chinook fishery is extremely dependent on how long the fall rains last. Lots of rain will send all the fish upriver at once and fishing will drop off very quickly. A drier spell will keep them in the bay longer, making them available to anglers.

For bottomfish, go with kelp worms, sand shrimp, and mussels fished off the bottom near pilings and submerged rocks where they like to lurk. Good shore access locations include Bay Ocean Spit and along the access road to the South Jetty, North Jetty at Barview Park, Old Coast Guard Pier, and Hobsonville and Memaloose Points. Lingcod can be caught off the jetties by bouncing bait off the bottom. These fish are hard-hitting biters and have been known to take a bare hook.

Tillamook Bay

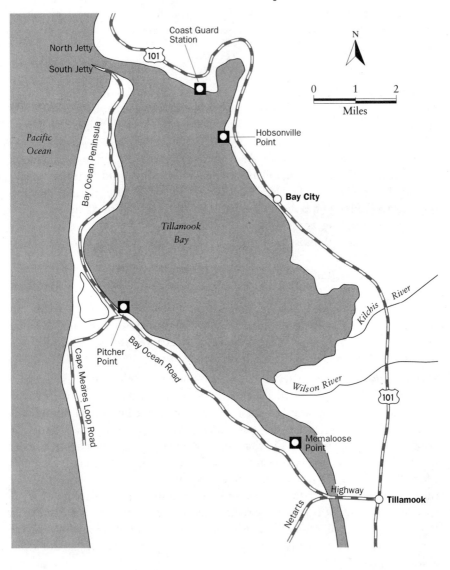

North Jetty

South Jetty

Coast Guard Station

101

Pacific Ocean

Bay Ocean Peninsula

Hobsonville Point

Bay City

Tillamook Bay

N

0   1   2
Miles

Pitcher Point

Cape Meares Loop Road

Bay Ocean Road

Kilchis River

Wilson River

101

Memaloose Point

Netarts

Highway

Tillamook

The docks and jetties along Oregon's coastal bays offer opportunities for catching a variety of bottomfish.

Sturgeon are best fished for by boat using sand shrimp, mud shrimp, smelt, and herring as bait and fished on the bottom in deep holes. Good sturgeon areas in Tillamook Bay include off Bay City and in the west channel off Pitcher Point. A low slack tide is often the best period for sturgeon angling, but be aware that you can get your boat stuck at these times.

Directions: Tillamook Bay is located immediately northwest of Tillamook, and may be accessed via U.S. Highway 101, Netarts Highway, Bay Ocean Road and other local roads. To reach the popular Memaloose Point and boat ramp, drive west from Tillamook on the Netarts Highway for about 1.5 miles, then north on Bay Ocean Road for 1.5 miles.

For More Information: Oregon Department of Fish and Wildlife, Tillamook District Office

7 Kilchis River

Key Species: Chinook salmon, chum salmon, steelhead

Best Way to Fish: boat

Best Time to Fish: Chinook salmon, early September through December; chum salmon, mid-October to mid-November; steelhead, mid-November into May

Description: This small coastal river rises in the Tillamook State Forest and flows some 20 miles before emptying into Tillamook Bay. With a good run of steelhead and fall Chinook salmon, this stream can be a popular destination for local anglers.

The fall Chinook run happens from early September through December, with the peak generally lasting from mid- to late October. The winter steelhead run goes from mid-November into May, with the hatchery fish peaking in late December. The wild fish peak in March and April.

A unique aspect of this river is its chum fishery. Once heavily fished by gear anglers, depressed chum salmon runs have caused the state to open it only for catch-and-release with artificial flies and lures. Chum are typically in the river from mid-October to mid-November. The state record chum salmon, weighing in at 23 pounds, was taken from the Kilchis River in 1990.

The best angler access to the Kilchis River is by drifting, but there is some access on public lands. Three boat ramps on the river—Kilchis County Park, County Park, and Mapes Creek—provide good put-in and take-out points.

The Kilchis fishes best between 4 and 6 feet (see "River/Reservoir Conditions Information" on page 6).

Fishing Index: Anglers use tried-and-true salmon and steelhead techniques here, drifting or back-dragging bait, floating eggs and sand shrimp under a bobber, back-trolling plugs, or casting spinners.

Kilchis River

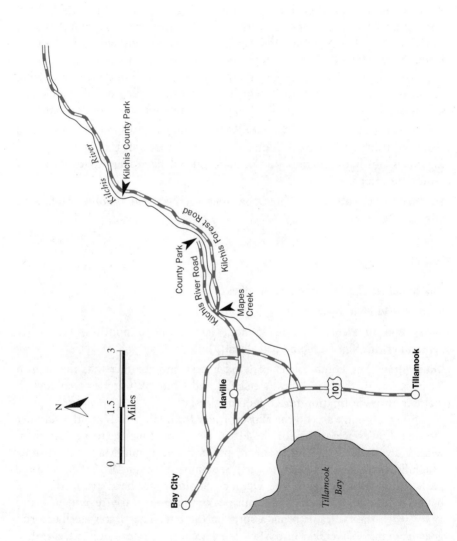

Most fishing is done downstream from Kilchis County Park. The primary drift is from the park down to Mapes Creek. Although the Kilchis is best fished by boat because so much of it flows through private lands, there is potential bank access in the Tillamook State Forest. A forest road running along the river can be reached by crossing the Mapes Bridge. The banks are steep here, but it is possible to get to the river in spots.

There is not a great deal of interest in fishing for chum salmon these days, but some fly fishers give it a try with traditional freshwater salmon flies such as Glo Bugs, Teeny Nymphs, and Matukas. Chum salmon will be in the river below Mapes Creek.

For all anadromous fish runs on the Kilchis, you will find the best angling immediately after a rainy spell, which brings fish holding in Tillamook Bay into the river—provided that flood stage (7 feet or more) is not reached.

Directions: To reach Kilchis County Park, the uppermost limit of salmon and steelhead fishing here, go north on Kilchis River Road, off U.S. Highway 101, 2.5 miles north of Tillamook. Continue on Kilchis River Road for about 6 miles to the park.

For More Information: Oregon Department of Fish and Wildlife, Tillamook District Office

8 Wilson River

Key Species: Chinook salmon, steelhead

Best Way to Fish: boat, bank

Best Time to Fish: Chinook salmon, late April to mid-June and early September through December; steelhead, June to May

Description: The combination of good access and the fact that the Wilson River is one of the state's best steelhead and Chinook fisheries combines to make it a top destination for Oregon anglers.

Spring Chinook ascend the Wilson River from late April into the summer months; however, angling for these fish closes on June 15 to protect them while they spawn. Angling for them peaks between mid-May to mid-June. The fall Chinook run is on from early September through December, with the peak fishing from mid- to late October. Summer steelhead are in the river between June and January. This run peaks twice—in early to mid-July and again when the fall rains bring a surge in the bite. The winter steelhead run goes from mid-November into May. The hatchery fish peak in late December, while the wild fish peak in March and April.

Wilson River spring Chinook average around 20 pounds while fall Chinook weigh in at 25 to 28 pounds. Steelhead are typically in the 10- to 12-pound range.

Before heading out to the Wilson, make sure you check on river conditions. The Wilson River fishes best between 4½ and 6 feet (see "River/Reservoir

Wilson River • Trask River

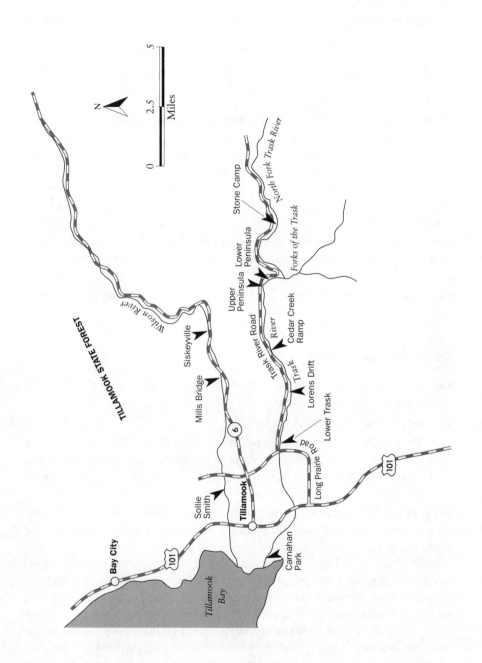

Conditions Information" on page 6). A variety of angling regulations are in effect for steelhead and salmon on the Wilson River. Check the current regulations for details.

Fishing Index: Anglers in pursuit of salmon back-troll Kwikfish and Flatfish wrapped with herring, back-bounce sand shrimp and salmon eggs or drift them under a bobber. Spinner aficionados cast Blue Fox, Clearwater Flash, and T-spoon spinners. Chinook anglers target the deeper holes and fish them thoroughly. Steelheaders drift Corkies, sand shrimp, or eggs under a bobber and back-bounce bait. Plugs and spinners work as well.

There are two major drifts on the Wilson—from Siskeyville to Mills Bridge and from Mills Bridge to Sollie Smith. All are county-owned boat launches. Because much of it is paralleled by Oregon Highway 6, the Wilson River has some of the best public bank access of all the Coast Range streams. This is particularly true of the portion of the upper river that runs through the Tillamook State Forest, offering many access points for both steelhead and salmon fishing.

Directions: Access to the Wilson River may be had along Oregon Highway 6, west of Tillamook. County boat ramps are located off the highway. The boundary of the Tillamook State Forest is about 10 miles west of Tillamook.

For More Information: Oregon Department of Fish and Wildlife, Tillamook District Office

9 Trask River

See map on page 47

Key Species: Chinook salmon, coho salmon, steelhead, sea-run cutthroat trout, and resident cutthroat trout

Best Way to Fish: boat, bank

Best Time to Fish: Chinook salmon, April through mid-June and October through November; coho salmon, early September through mid-November; steelhead, January through March; sea-run cutthroat trout, July through October

Description: With runs of fall and spring Chinook salmon, coho salmon, winter steelhead, and sea-run cutthroat trout, the Trask is a top destination for serious anglers.

Spring Chinook begin moving into the Trask from April through June, peaking in mid-May to mid-June. Runs of fall Chinook begin entering the river in October, going through November and peaking in mid-October. Coho salmon are here from early September to mid-November. This run usually peaks at the same time as the fall Chinook run. The Trask's wild winter steelhead run begins in January and ends in March. Sea-run cutthroats begin congregating at tidewater in July, moving up through the river system to spawn through October.

The Trask is managed as a wild winter steelhead fishery, although anglers often catch Wilson River–bound hatchery fish that inadvertently stray into the river from Tillamook Bay. The Trask is also one of a handful of rivers where angling for coho salmon is allowed, but only the hatchery cohos—designated by their clipped adipose fins.

Trask River spring Chinook salmon average 13 to 15 pounds, while their fall counterparts often top 20 pounds. Coho run in the 5- to 14-pound range while steelhead average 5 to 15 pounds. Sea-run cutthroat trout are typically 14 to 16 inches.

Seven public boat launches are located on the river, and although bank access is not as abundant as on some other coastal streams, it is possible to get to some good water without a boat.

As with all coastal salmon and steelhead streams, check water conditions in advance of your trip. The Trask River fishes best at water levels ranging from 5½ feet up to 7 feet (see "River/Reservoir Conditions Information" on page 6). This river also has a variety of regulations governing angling, including bait restrictions and closures on its upper reaches. Be sure to review current angling regulations before heading out.

Fishing Index: Chinook anglers drift fish with sand shrimp or eggs under a bobber, back-bounce bait or back-troll with Flatfish and Kwickfish. A favorite drift is between the boat launch at the Oregon Department of Fish and Wildlife's Lorens Drift launch to the county-managed Lower Trask boat ramp, where U.S. Highway 101 crosses the river south of Tillamook. The water just downstream from Lorens Drift launch is a hot spot for bank anglers. Hospital Hole, just downstream from the US 101 bridge also offers public access for bank anglers.

Jigs, Corkies, and plugs, along with eggs and shrimp drifted under a bobber, are all used to take steelhead on the Trask River. Keep in mind that most of the fish here are wild and that catching fish with bait sometimes reduces the option of releasing them unharmed. The float from Lorens Drift to Lower Trask is as popular with steelheaders as it is with salmon anglers. The areas around the north and south fork of the Trask River offer good bank angling possibilities. The riverbank in the vicinity of Lorens Drift and at the various other public boat launches along the river off Trask River Road is another good location.

In addition to its sea-run cutthroats, there is also a good population of resident cutthroat trout in the upper river and in its north and south forks. However, in order to protect juvenile steelhead and salmon which use these streams as nurseries, these forks are only open to trout fishing for a few weeks in late May through mid-June. Both forks are seasonally open to steelhead fishing.

Directions: From Tillamook go 2.5 miles south on U.S. Highway 101. Turn left (east) onto Long Prairie Road. Follow Long Prairie Road for about 4 miles, turning right (east) onto Trask River Road. Numerous public boat launches are located off this road, which follows the north bank of the river. To reach the forks of the Trask, continue east on Trask River Road for about 9 miles.

For More Information: Oregon Department of Fish and Wildlife, Tillamook District Office

10 Nestucca River

Key Species: Chinook salmon, steelhead

Best Way to Fish: boat, bank

Best Time to Fish: Chinook salmon, late April to mid-June and early September through December; steelhead, June to May

Description: Boasting a spring and fall Chinook salmon fishery along with both summer and winter steelhead runs, the Nestucca River is as productive a stream, from an angler's perspective, as you will find along the Oregon coast.

Spring Chinook enter the Nestucca beginning from late April into summer, although the season closes for them in mid-June. Peak season is usually mid-May until the season's end. Fall Chinook arrive by September, holding in tidewater until the first fall freshets send them upriver, generally from October through December. This run usually peaks in mid- to late October. The Chinook runs are a mix of hatchery and wild fish. Both the winter and summer steelhead runs are made up primarily of hatchery fish, although wild fish are present as well. The summer run goes from June into January, peaking in early to mid-July, then again with the fall rains. The winter run lasts from mid-November through May. The hatchery fish peak in late December, while the wild fish tend to come on strong in late March or April.

Spring Chinook run in the 18- to 20-pound range while fall fish run a bit larger at 25 to 28 pounds. Steelhead weigh anywhere from 10 to 12 pounds. There are also chum salmon in the Nestucca, but because of the run's weakness, angling for these fish is no longer allowed.

While the angling opportunities on the Nestucca River are great, it does have one drawback: not much public shoreline access is available for bank fishing along its lower reaches. For this reason, you will do much better on this river, and have more water available to fish, if you own or have access to a boat.

Be sure and check river conditions before fishing the Nestucca. It generally fishes best between 4 and 5 feet (see "River/Reservoir Conditions Information" on page 6). A variety of regulations govern fishing on the Nestucca River, including bait restrictions on some segments and closures on the upper river and tributaries, so peruse the latest angling regulations prior to your trip.

Fishing Index: Fishing for fall Chinook tends to be concentrated in the long, narrow, and shallow Nestucca Bay. If you have a boat, trolling cut-plug herring and plugs in the bay's "narrows" is a standard approach. However, because of the confined nature of the estuary, you won't find as many boats

Nestucca River

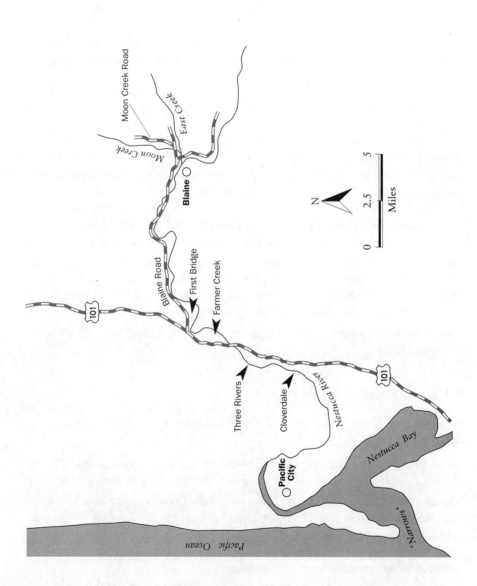

fishing here as in other Oregon bays, simply because there is not room for a lot of watercraft.

Once the Chinook are in the river, back-bouncing bait and back-trolling Kwikfish and Flatfish wrapped with sardine will catch them. As always when fishing for Chinook, it pays to spend time thoroughly fishing deep holes where these big fish like to lurk. Bank anglers tend to fish with eggs and shrimp under bobbers or cast spinners a little higher upriver where there is more bank access.

Drifting Cheaters and Corkies is an effective steelhead technique on the Nestucca. Kwikfish and Flatfish, spinners, and back-dragging sand shrimp or eggs are effective as well. Crayfish tails are also employed as bait. Although not an extremely popular steelhead stream for fly fishers, some give it a try using Salmon River MVPs, Purple Perils, and Babine Specials.

Primary drifts are from First Bridge ramp to the Farmer Creek launch (both managed by the Oregon Department of Fish and Wildlife); Farmer Creek to Three Rivers; and Three Rivers to Cloverdale. Cloverdale is also an Oregon Department of Fish and Wildlife launch, while the Three Rivers ramp is a county boat launch. The area around Blaine and the mouth of Moon Creek has some public access. Once above Blaine on the upper river, you begin to get into USDA Forest Service and Bureau of Land Management lands with lots of public access. The river this far upstream cannot be run by boat.

Directions: Access to Nestucca Bay can be had at Pacific City. U.S. Highway 101 follows the lower river north to Beaver. At Beaver, Blaine Road (County Road 7) parallels the Nestucca westward into public lands. Boat launches are located off Blaine Road and US 101.

For More Information: Oregon Department of Fish and Wildlife, Tillamook District Office

11 Salmon River

Key Species: Chinook salmon, coho salmon, sea-run cutthroat trout

Best Way to Fish: bank

Best Time to Fish: Chinook salmon, mid-August to December; coho salmon, mid-August to December; sea-run cutthroat trout, early July through October

Description: This coastal stream flows out of the Coast Range forest and empties into the sea near the Tillamook-Lincoln county line just south of Cascade Head. Although a small river, it has good runs of Chinook and coho salmon, which return each fall and winter to the Salmon River Hatchery near Otis, making it very popular with area anglers.

Both Chinook and coho salmon are in the river from around mid-August through November or December. Runs peak when fall rains cause a surge in the river level, which stimulates the fish to move upstream, so it is important

Salmon River

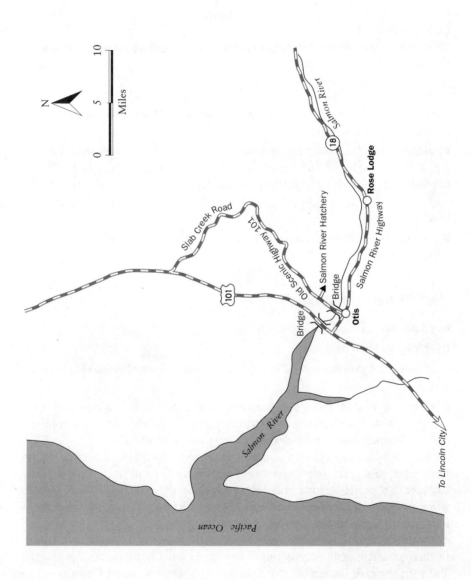

to keep an eye on the weather before coming here. This is one of a select number of rivers in Oregon where coho fishing is allowed, although only for hatchery fish, identifiable by their clipped adipose fins.

Fishing Index: Because of the rather shallow nature of the Salmon River, most anglers fish from the bank. The area around the Salmon River Hatchery, at the U. S. Highway 101 bridge and at the bridge in the community of Otis, are all favored bank angling locations. It is possible to motor a boat upstream from the bay and fish holes. The first 5 miles of river are deep enough for that tactic, so some do.

Bait fishing with sand shrimp or eggs either drifted or fished under a bobber is a standard approach for salmon here. Casting spinners offers good opportunities for a hook-up as well.

For cutthroats, the tidewater area is best from mid-July into September with flies or spinners. All trout fishing on coastal Oregon streams and rivers is catch-and-release only.

Directions: To reach the Salmon River Fish Hatchery, go north from Lincoln City on U.S. Highway 101 for about 7 miles. Turn right (east) onto Oregon Highway 18 and drive 2 miles to Otis. Go left (north) from Otis for 0.5 mile on Scenic Drive. Turn right (east) on North Bank Road and go 0.5 mile to the hatchery.

For More Information: Oregon Department of Fish and Wildlife, Tillamook District Office

12 Siletz River

Key Species: Chinook salmon, steelhead

Best Way to Fish: boat, bank

Best Time to Fish: Chinook salmon, May through November; steelhead, year-round

Description: This 70-mile-long coastal stream sports both a winter and summer run of steelhead, along with spring and fall Chinook. It is traditionally one of Oregon's top steelhead and salmon angling streams.

Summer steelhead begin entering the river in May, tapering off in November, just as the winter steelhead run begins. Its run lasts into May. The summer run peaks in June and July, with another small increase in activity when fall rains hit, typically in September or October. The winter run peaks in February and March.

Spring Chinook salmon are here from May through August with peak fishing generally in June and July. The run of fall Chinook starts in August and runs through November, with the peak in September and October.

As with all coastal steelhead and salmon rivers, water levels and precipitation affect the fishing for better or worse. Make sure you determine current river conditions before packing up your gear.

Siletz River

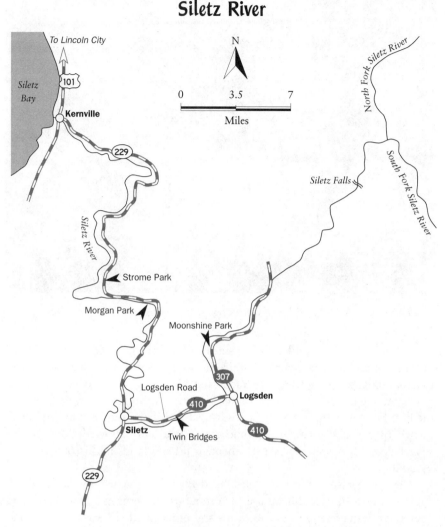

The Siletz is closed to angling above Siletz Falls. The North and South Forks and their tributaries are closed as well. Because salmon and steelhead rules are complex, check the current regulations for specifics.

Fishing Index: Fall Chinook fishing takes place primarily in the estuary areas by boat, where trolling Kwikfish or Flatfish wrapped with sardine, spinners, or cut-plug herring are effective approaches. Sand shrimp or eggs fished in holes are productive as well.

Spring Chinook and steelhead are best fished for in the freshwater sections of the river. Drifting sand shrimp or eggs under a bobber or back-dragging it from a boat are good Siletz techniques. Plugs such as Wiggle Warts are also effective.

A net ensures a "caught" fish and causes less strain on fish that will be released.

If you have a boat and are after steelhead or spring Chinook, a variety of drifts are possible. The favorites are from Morgan Park to Strome Park, Siletz to Morgan Park, Twin Bridges to Siletz, and Moonshine Park to Twin Bridges. For bank anglers, Moonshine Park and the gorge upstream from the park are the best bets. Although the forest lands upstream from the park are privately owned by a timber company, public access is usually allowed. Most of the river below Moonshine Park runs through private lands and is best covered by boat.

The gorge also has the best steelhead fly fishing water on the river. Fly anglers in pursuit of steelhead use such standard patterns as Purple Perils and Spey Flies. Fish around logs, root wads and other in-stream structures, and in pools.

Directions: Several of the roads which parallel the Siletz River allow access to boat launches and bank fishing. From Lincoln City go 4 miles south on U.S. Highway 101. Turn east at Kernville onto Oregon Highway 229, which follows the river. About 25 miles south of Siletz turn left (east) off of OR 229 onto County Road 410 (Logsden Road), which continues along the river. At Logsden go left (north) onto County Road 307 and drive about 5 miles to get to Moonshine Park.

For More Information: Oregon Department of Fish and Wildlife, Mid-Coast District Office

13 Yaquina Bay and Yaquina River

Key Species: Chinook salmon, herring, sturgeon, bottomfish

Best Way to Fish: boat, bank

Best Time to Fish: Chinook salmon, late August through early November; sturgeon, January through April; bottomfish, year-round; herring, February and March

Description: This bay, at the mouth of the Yaquina River immediately south of Newport, is a major focus of ocean fishing activity in Oregon. There's a much sought-after run of Chinook salmon and abundant populations of bottomfish.

Because the coastal town of Newport is a long-time tourist area, ample charter boat services, motels, restaurants, and other recreational amenities are available.

Fall Chinook begin entering the bay by the third or fourth week of August, moving up into the Yaquina River from mid-September to early November. Occasionally Chinook salmon that are not Yaquina River fish temporarily move into the bay from the sea as they chase schools of baitfish. Known as "feeder kings" they can provide a short-term angling opportunity if you are in a position to get out into the bay on short notice. The regular Yaquina River run provides for a more reliable fishery.

Shore-bound anglers take advantage of a local pier.

Yaquina Bay and Yaquina River

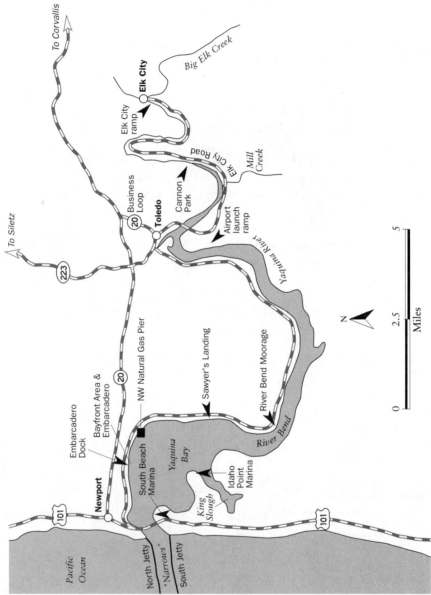

Not to be ignored is the opportunity to catch a variety of species of bottomfish including sturgeon, rockfish, cabezon, surfperch, and greenling. An Oregon angling license is required to fish for bottomfish, and since the number of fish you may keep varies from year to year, be sure to check the current regulations.

Fishing Index: All Chinook salmon fishing here takes place from the estuary to Elk City, about 20 miles upriver. Anglers on the bay do best trolling herring at the "narrows" between the North and South Jetties, and off the east side of the bay opposite King Slough. Plugs, spoons, metal jigs, and spinners also work well. A downrigger is often recommended when trolling. Boaters also fish spinners in the narrower tidewater area and up the river as far as Elk City. Casting bait and spinners from the jetties is an effective strategy for the bank-bound. There are eight boat launches along the river from Elk City downstream to the bay, offering plenty of boating options as well as bank fishing opportunities.

A small run of steelhead moves up the river from December through March, but the fishery takes place mainly in Big Elk Creek at Elk City.

Bottomfish anglers in the bay do best when fishing with such bait as sand shrimp, kelp worms, and mussels fished off the bottom near submerged rocks or pilings, where these fish tend to congregate. Fishing for rockfish at night using lures can also provide excellent sport. Some good access points include the north and south jetties, Newport Bayfront, and Abbey Street Pier and the Northwest Natural Gas Pier on Bay Road.

Sturgeon can also be caught by fishing shrimp, herring, or smelt on the bottom in deeper holes from River Bend to Mill Creek. January through April is the best time. In February and March there is also a popular herring fishery in the bay. Anglers catch them with herring jigs around moorings and docks. South Beach Marina and the Embarcadero are good locations to try.

Directions: Yaquina Bay is located immediately south of Newport. Yaquina Bay Road (County Road 533) can be accessed off U.S. Highway 101 on the north shore of the bay. Yaquina Bay Road follows the north shore of the Yaquina River to Elk City. Elk City Road connects Elk City with Toledo. Boat ramps may be accessed from these roads.

For More Information: Oregon Department of Fish and Wildlife, Mid-Coast District Office

14 Alsea River

Key Species: Chinook salmon, steelhead, sea-run cutthroat trout

Best Way to Fish: boat, bank

Best Time to Fish: Chinook salmon, mid-August to mid-November; steelhead, December through March; sea-run cutthroat trout, July through October

Description: A renowned western Oregon salmon and steelhead stream, the Alsea River flows over 50 miles from its headwaters in the Coast Range northwest of Eugene to the sea at Waldport.

Chinook salmon begin entering the estuary around mid-August, peaking in the river in September and October and ending in November. Steelhead are in the Alsea River from December through March, with the peak in December and January. Sea-run cutthroat trout begin congregating in tidewater in July, moving into the river to spawn through October.

Much of the Alsea is paralleled by Oregon Highway 34, with a number of public boat launches along its banks. A good portion of the river also flows through the Siuslaw National Forest, offering more public access opportunities. There are a dozen public boat ramps and seven commercial ramps along the river as well as one public ramp and one commercial ramp on the bay.

Alsea River Chinook salmon average around 25 pounds while steelhead run around 8 pounds. Sea-run cutthroats can go up to 20 inches, but are more likely to be in the 12- to 16-inch range.

Since the arrival of fall rains stimulates the Alsea's anadromous fish to head upriver (while too much rain may make it unfishable), be sure to inquire about water conditions before going. The Alsea River usually fishes best between 4½ to 6½ feet.

And don't forget to check the current angling regulations, since the rules governing fishing in coastal streams can be complicated.

Fishing Index: Before the fall rains begin, the first Chinook salmon to arrive from the ocean will be hanging around tidewater, making that the place to target them early in the season. As the rains arrive, the fish will begin their ascent upriver. Trolling cut-plug herring and Blue Fox spinners, back-trolling Kwikfish and Flatfish wrapped with a sardine, and drifting sand shrimp or eggs under a bobber are all tried-and-proven salmon-catching techniques. A popular drift is from Blackberry Park to Mike Bauer Wayside. Both are managed by the USDA Forest Service and have public boat launches. Fall Chinook are primarily a bay and tidewater fishery, with the best fishing from the town of Tidewater down to Waldport.

Drift fishing is the most common method for steelhead angling on the Alsea, although bait under a bobber and Marabou jigs, as well as back-trolling plugs are also good techniques to try. A favorite drift for steelhead is between the county boat ramp at Five Rivers Launch and Mike Bauer Wayside. The launch at Mill Creek County Park is another good put-in for steelheaders. There is also some good access for bank angling just below the

Alsea River

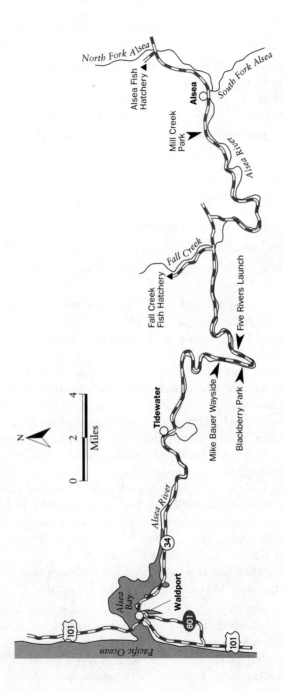

Alsea Fish Hatchery on the North Fork Alsea River. The many public boat launches to be found along the river also provide good public access points for bank anglers.

For sea-run cutthroat trout, concentrate around tidewater early in the season, later moving upstream with the fish, using streamer patterns or spinners.

Directions: The boat launches and banks of the Alsea River are easily accessible along Oregon Highway 34 on the 40-mile stretch between Alsea and Waldport. The Alsea Fish Hatchery is located on Fish Hatchery Road, on the north side of Oregon Highway 20 at milepost 43, east of Alsea.

For More Information: Oregon Department of Fish and Wildlife, Mid-Coast District Office

15 Siuslaw River

Key Species: Chinook salmon, steelhead

Best Way to Fish: boat, bank

Best Time to Fish: Chinook salmon, August through November; steelhead, November through March

Description: Meandering through forest and farmland before emptying into the ocean at Florence, the Siuslaw River offers first-class opportunities to fish for a run of wild fall Chinook salmon, as well as a robust run of hatchery winter steelhead, derived from wild broodstock.

Chinook salmon start showing up in the bay in August, peaking there in September. Over the next two months, the fish begin their migration up the river. This fall Chinook run ends in November. Steelhead are in the river from November through March, with the last two months of the run producing the largest concentration of fish. Bottomfish are available in the bay year-round.

Fall Chinook here are typically in the 20-pound range, while steelhead average around 5 pounds.

Keep in mind that it is wise to find out what the river conditions are before heading out for salmon and steelhead. High water may blow out the river, making it a waste of time to fish, while late arrival of freshets will keep the fish holding in the bay. The Siuslaw fishes best at around 5 feet (see "River/Reservoir Conditions Information" on page 6).

A variety of angling regulations are in effect for steelhead and salmon on the Siuslaw River. Check the current regulations for details.

Fishing Index: Angling for Chinook salmon is concentrated in the bay and tidewater areas of the river. Early in the season, Chinook will drift in and out of the bay with the tides. The waters at the river's mouth and the Coast Guard station area are likely places to troll herring-wrapped Kwikfish and Flatfish, or T-Spoon and Clearwater Flash spinners. As the fish enter the mainstem, anglers follow them as far as Mapleton, 20 miles upstream. In addition to the

Siuslaw River

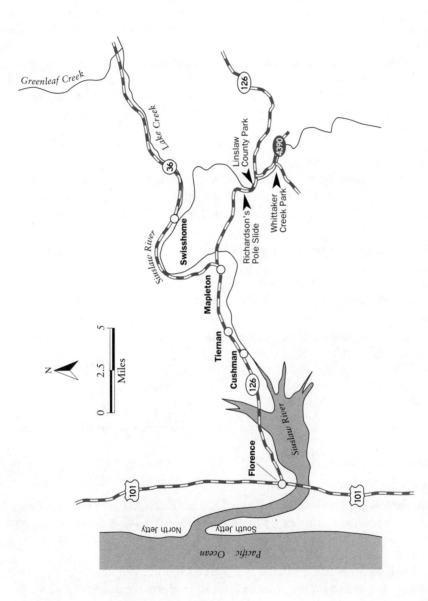

Mapleton area, other good Chinook salmon drifts in which to back-troll sand shrimps and eggs include the area around the small community of Cushman and in the vicinity of Tiernan, 8 miles and 14 miles upstream, respectively. There are public boat launches at both locations.

Bay anglers can also take rockfish, greenling, cabezon, and surfperch using kelp worms, sand shrimp, and mussels, all fished off the bottom around submerged rocks and pilings. Good locations include the North Jetty, Port of Siuslaw in Florence, and the South Jetty and Pier in the Oregon Dunes National Recreation Area.

Steelhead fishing takes place in the freshwater sections of the river, upstream from tidewater. Steelheaders drift fish with a Corky and sand shrimp or eggs, or back-troll with plugs such as Hot Shots and Wiggle Warts. The most popular river section to drift is from Whittaker Creek to the forks around Lake Creek, and in Lake Creek from Greenleaf Creek on down. Good bank fishing areas include the public boat ramp at Whittaker Creek, along with sections of the Siuslaw National Forest through which the river flows just downstream. There are also two other public boat launches just downstream of Whittaker Creek, including the ones at Linslaw County Park and Richardson's Pole Slide, the latter operated by the Oregon Department of Fish and Wildlife.

Directions: The Siuslaw River and its boat launches are accessible via Oregon Highway 126, which run along much of the river. To reach Whittaker Creek, drive 25 miles east on OR 126 (bearing right, and over the river at Mapleton). At Augusta, turn right (south) onto County Road 4390 and go about 1.5 miles.

For More Information: Oregon Department of Fish and Wildlife, Mid-Coast District Office

16 Siltcoos Lake

Key Species: largemouth bass, black crappie, bluegill, sea-run cutthroat trout, rainbow trout

Best Way to Fish: boat

Best Time to Fish: year-round

Description: At 3,164 acres, Siltcoos Lake is the largest lake on the Oregon Coast, connected to the sea by the three-mile-long Siltcoos River. Just 8 feet above sea level, the lake averages 11 feet in depth, with a maximum depth of 22 feet.

Partly because it is so shallow, the lake supports abundant aquatic plant growth. In practical terms, this biological productivity makes Siltcoos Lake a good place to grow fish, particularly largemouth bass, which average in the 2½-pound range here. It also has good populations of crappie and bluegill along with hatchery rainbow trout and some sea-run cutthroats. In the past,

Siltcoos Lake

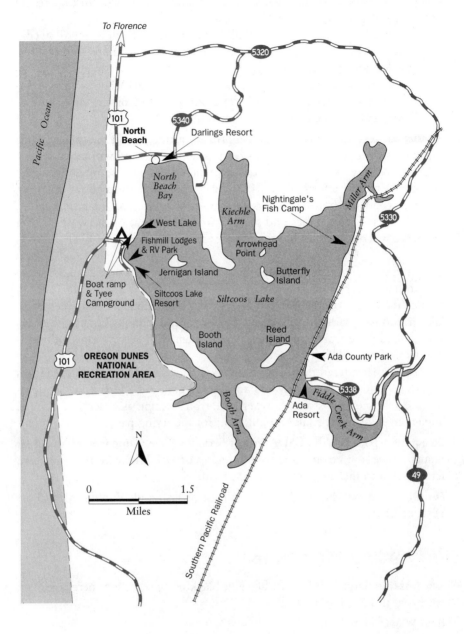

yellow perch were the most abundant fish here, but lately the perch taken are small, possibly due to overpopulation and stunting. Because of this, interest in angling for them has dropped off.

Coho are found in the lake as well, but angling for them is not allowed.

There are several resorts on the lake and seven boat ramps: three public and four located at resorts. The public may launch boats at the resorts, however, some charge launch fees. In addition, there is a USDA Forest Service picnic area and a campground (Tyee Campground) located on the west shore.

Siltcoos Lake is open to angling year-round.

Fishing Index: Largemouth bass are a primary attraction. In the spring, when the water is still a bit on the cold side, jigs with pork rind will pique a bass' interest. As the water warms during summer, plugs, spinnerbaits, and crankbaits all are effective. Plastic worms work well throughout the year. Lots of wood the bottom of this lake translates into lots of bass habitat. Look for places where logs and stumps are sticking out of the water. Those areas are where you will find underwater structure, and most likely, bass as well.

For crappie, jigs, spoons, small spinners, and bait all work. Look for these fish around underwater structure as well—a good area is around the railroad trestles that cross over inlets and Fiddle Creek Arm on the east side of the lake. To do well with bluegill, you will need to find schools. Look in the bays and around underwater brush piles. Catch them with earthworms and mealworms under a bobber.

Trout are scattered throughout the lake, but fishing near the shorelines is usually a good bet. Nightcrawlers and Power Bait, are effective, as are spinners. Unlike coastal streams, where all trout fishing is catch-and-release, anglers may keep some lake-caught trout for the frying pan.

Directions: To reach the USDA Forest Service's Tyee Campground and boat launch, drive south from Florence for 6 miles on U.S. Highway 101, then turn left (east) onto the campground access road.

For More Information: Oregon Department of Fish and Wildlife, Mid-Coast District Office

17 Tahkenitch Lake

Key Species: largemouth bass, bluegill, black crappie, yellow perch, sea-run cutthroat trout, rainbow trout

Best Way to Fish: boat

Best Time to Fish: year-round

Description: This 1,645-acre coastal lake has a rather extensive shoreline with lots of narrow arms and bays, along with a reputation as a good largemouth bass fishery. Because the water here is clearer than at Siltcoos Lake to the north, the bass can be a bit hard to catch. Anglers will also find bluegill, black

Tahkenitch Lake

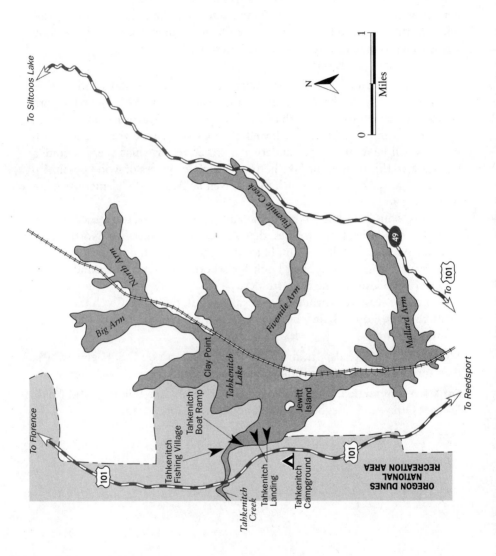

crappie, yellow perch, sea-run cutthroat trout, and rainbow trout plying these waters. The largemouth here average around 2 pounds—a bit smaller than bass in nearby Siltcoos, reflecting this lake's somewhat lesser productivity.

There is also a run of coho salmon in the lake, but angling for them is not allowed.

Because much of the shoreline is brushy, bank fishing is limited. There are three boat launches here, all on the Tahkenitch Creek arm. The USDA Forest Service maintains a campground (Tahkenitch Landing) here. Most of the lake's northwest shoreline is within the Oregon Dunes National Recreation Area, which is managed by the USDA Forest Service.

Tahkenitch Lake is open to angling year-round.

Fishing Index: Ideal water temperatures for bass here are from about 55 degrees F into the low 60s. In the spring, when the water is still cool, jigs with pork rinds elicit interest from sluggish bass. Throughout the warmer months, plugs, spinnerbaits, and crankbaits work well. Plastic worms are a year-round stand-by. Bass will be in areas with underwater structure, of which there is quite a bit scattered throughout the lake bottom. Watch for pieces of wood poking up above the water surface, and fish there. Fivemile Arm and Coleman Arm are good areas to check out.

Jigs, spoons, and bait take crappie and perch, also around structure. Try fishing around the train trestles that cross the entrances to North Arm, Fivemile Arm, and Mallard Arm. Bluegill angling can be fun with earthworms or mealworms under a bobber. Look for schools in bays and around under-water brush piles near the train trestles.

Trout are scattered throughout the lake and in the arms. Catch them with nightcrawlers, Power Bait, and spinners such as Mepps, Rooster Tails, and Panther Martins.

Directions: From Reedsport, drive about 8 miles north on U.S. Highway 101, then turn right (east) to the Tahkenitch Boat Ramp.

For More Information: Oregon Department of Fish and Wildlife, Mid-Coast District Office and Oregon Dunes National Recreation Area

The 31-mile fly-fishing-only section of the North Umpqua River is legendary among steelheaders.

Southwest Oregon

Variety is the hallmark of southwest Oregon. Here you will find great Chinook and coho salmon and steelhead rivers along the coast, while bays and estuaries provide fishing opportunities for salmon, sturgeon, and bottomfish. This part of Oregon also has some of the state's best warmwater fisheries, including coastal bass and panfish lakes, as well as an outstanding river smallmouth bass fishery.

Add to this variety of angling opportunities the fact that two of Oregon's most famed rivers are located here—the North Umpqua and the Rogue—making southwestern Oregon a first-class fishing destination.

As with the north coast, a boat is an advantage for salmon and steelhead angling on coastal rivers and on some lakes. As you move inland, there are more opportunities for bank fishing. Boaters will want to have a copy of the *Oregon Boating Facilities Guide* for reference, while an angler interested in fishing from the bank or by wading would be well-advised to have some national forest and topographical maps on hand.

Regulations for the waters listed in this section will be found in the Southwest Zone section of the *Oregon Sport Fishing Regulations* handbook.

18 Tenmile Lakes

Key Species: largemouth bass, bluegill, black crappie, brown bullhead, steelhead, sea-run cutthroat trout, rainbow trout

Best Way to Fish: boat, some bank

Best Time to Fish: year-round

Description: Loaded with easy-to-catch largemouth bass, Tenmile Lakes is the most popular destination for bass anglers in western Oregon. Bass tournaments are held here nearly every weekend through the summer months—attracting enough people to occasionally cause conflicts with others out recreating on the lake.

Referred to as Tenmile Lakes, they consist of two lakes—North Tenmile Lake and the southern lake, simply called Tenmile—connected to each other by a narrow channel. Tenmile is just over 1,600 acres in size and averages 10 feet deep, and 22 feet at its deepest point. North Tenmile Lake is a bit over 1,000 acres, and is similar in depth to Tenmile.

Because most of the shoreline is privately owned, you will do much better fishing these lakes by boat. There are a total of six boat ramps run either by the county, the USDA Forest Service, or commercial resorts. Boats can be rented at the lake.

There are two popular areas for fishing from shore. These include a large public fishing dock on Tenmile Lake and the dock at Northlake Resort. Lots of people fish from these locations.

These lakes are open to angling year-round. In addition to anglers, the lakes are very popular with a variety of other water-sport enthusiasts, including water skiers and pleasure boaters, and they can be rather crowded on summer weekends.

Fishing Index: As with other coastal lakes, anglers entice largemouth bass early in the season with jigs and pork rinds, switching to plugs, crankbaits, and spinnerbaits as the season warms. The best bass fishing tends to be in the spring and summer when they are variously found in deep water, close to shore and in weed beds.

Lots of crappie are taken on crappie jigs, while fishing earthworms or meal worms under a bobber is a great way catch bluegill. There are also a few white-striped bass in the lakes—remnants of a now-defunct fishery. Although not many are left, there are some big ones of 20 pounds and maybe more. If you want to give it a shot, try trolling Rapalas, or casting shrimp in deeper areas in the early morning or evening.

Trout fishing for both cutthroats and rainbows is best in the spring while the lake water is still cold. The best results come from trolling Ford Fenders and spinners. There is a run of steelhead in the lakes and in Tenmile Creek, which connects these bodies of water to the ocean. Steelheaders typically troll

Tenmile Lakes

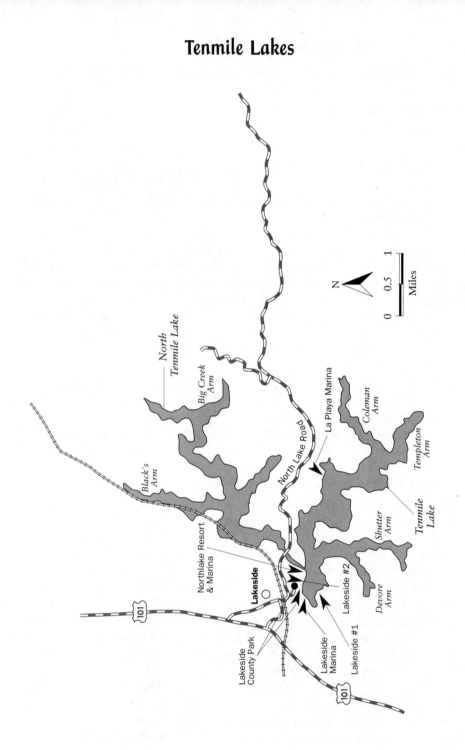

North
Tenmile Lake

Big Creek
Arm

Black's
Arm

North Lake Road

La Playa Marina

Coleman
Arm

Templeton
Arm

Shutter
Arm

Tenmile
Lake

Devore
Arm

Northlake Resort
& Marina

Lakeside

Lakeside #2

Lakeside
County Park

Lakeside
Marina

Lakeside #1

101

101

N

0   0.5   1
Miles

with Blue Fox spinners and Flatfish near the Tenmile Creek outlet, or in the upper arms as the fish congregate in anticipation of continuing their migration up these feeder streams to spawn. Trout anglers fishing lake trolls sometimes catch steelhead as well.

There are also some brown bullheads in the lakes. Fish off the bottom with nightcrawlers. The upper ends of the arms, where the water is shallower, are good spots to find bullhead. Another good tactic is to fish the channel between the two lakes at night. If you do this, though, it's important to anchor your boat off to the sides of the channel to avoid being hit by boats passing by. Take a lantern along for added visibility, and use it.

Directions: To reach Tenmile Lakes, drive south on U.S. Highway 101 from Reedsport for about 9 miles. Turn left (east) onto the access road to Lakeside and Lakeside County Park, and go about 1.5 miles to Tenmile Lake.

For More Information: Oregon Department of Fish and Wildlife, Charleston District Office

19 Umpqua River and Winchester Bay

Key Species: Chinook salmon, coho salmon, steelhead, smallmouth bass, American shad, white sturgeon

Best Way to Fish: boat, bank

Best Time to Fish: year-round

Description: Meandering over 100 miles to the sea at Reedsport from its confluence with the north and south forks just northwest of Roseburg, the Umpqua River has enough variety of gamefish in its waters to provide anglers with year-round sport.

Spring Chinook begin entering the river by the first of March through mid-May, peaking in April. Most fall Chinook go up the South Fork or North Fork Umpqua, both of which are closed to angling for this species. They are pursued in the lower river, however, and are generally there during the same time the coho salmon are: mid-August into November. Coho peak from mid-September to mid-October. The steelhead run goes from late November through mid-March, peaking in January and February. Shad are best targeted from mid-May through June.

Angling access to the Umpqua River is generally pretty good with a number of areas open to bank fishing and nine public boat ramps, along with another two on Winchester Bay.

A variety of rules govern angling on the Umpqua River, depending on what section you are fishing and what species you are fishing for. Be sure and check the most recent angling regulations before heading for the river.

Umpqua River and Winchester Bay

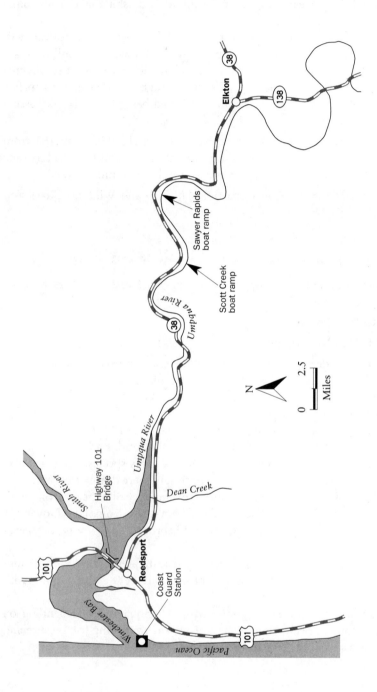

Fishing Index: Spring Chinook angling is typically concentrated on the lower river. It's a pretty laid-back fishery, where anglers anchor their boats, back-bounce eggs and shrimp, herring, Kwikfish, and spinners, play cards and take it easy while waiting for a strike. A popular put-in for this sort of fishing approach is at the Landing, just west of the town of Sutherlin, off Tyee Road by the Umpqua Store.

Fall Chinook is primarily an estuary fishery, with anglers typically trolling herring between the Coast Guard station on Winchester Bay to the U.S. Highway 101 bridge, and upstream around the Dean Creek area. A good fall Chinook salmon hole called Leatherwoods is at the first set of rapids upstream from the Umpqua Landing. Another good reach is from Sawyer Rapids boat launch to Scott Creek boat launch, and off the bank at Sawyer Rapids RV Park (where you can pay $1 for permission to fish there). Casting lures and drifting bait work well here.

For coho, most people troll Wee Wiggle Warts, Vibrax spinners, and Bang Tails from a boat, drifting along at a slow pace and casting off the side. You can catch cohos from the bank in some areas as well. Good locations for cohos include bank fishing just below the rapids at Sawyer Rapids RV Park, as well drifting from there down to Scott Creek. Another popular coho drift is from James Wood boat ramp to Osprey boat ramp. There is more bank fishing access at River Forks Park (where the North Fork Umpqua flows into the mainstem). Coho anglers often catch fall Chinook, since both fish are in the river at the same time and respond to the same fishing techniques.

Winter steelheaders mainly plunk bait from shore or from an anchored boat. The stretch from James Wood boat ramp to Osprey boat ramp is a good steelhead drift. The rapids at Sawyer Rapids RV Park is an excellent steelhead bank fishing location. Spin 'n Glos, eggs, shrimp, and plugs are all popular for catching steelhead. Side drifting bait and plugs is a popular technique on the Umpqua. Although there is a good run of summer steelhead on the North Umpqua, there is little summer steelhead fishing in the mainstem.

Shad anglers use crappie jigs, shad darts, and flies on light tackle sporting 4- to 6-pound test line. If you have a boat with a motor, you can put-in at Sawyer Rapids boat ramp, motor upstream, and troll for shad and fish for smallmouth bass at the same time.

The Umpqua River has a very good smallmouth bass fishery and you can catch them on plastics that imitate crayfish and sculpins, on Rooster Tails, and on any number of flashy, colorful lures. Flys work well, too. The smallmouth here can be pretty aggressive biters, as they often stack up in holes and become very competitive with each other, striving to be the first to grab any food (or lure) that comes their way. The area around the confluence of the North and South Forks is a good place to look for smallmouth, and so are the backwaters on the James Wood to Osprey drift. Smallmouth are also found in the South Umpqua, so it is worth exploring a bit upstream in that fork as well. Although larger fish in the 16- to 18-inch range are more often caught during

Umpqua River and Winchester Bay

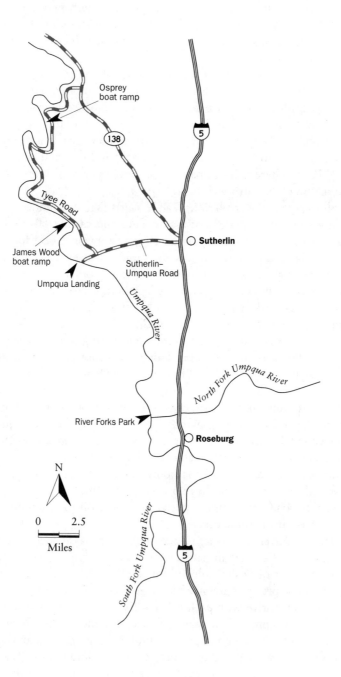

Osprey
boat ramp

138

5

Tyee Road

James Wood
boat ramp

Sutherlin

Sutherlin–
Umpqua Road

Umpqua Landing

Umpqua River

North Fork Umpqua River

River Forks Park

Roseburg

N

0   2.5

Miles

South Fork Umpqua River

5

the spring spawning period, August is the best time for smallmouth, with 100 fish in a day not uncommon for those who work at it.

Directions: Oregon Highways 38 and 138 parallel most of the Umpqua River between Reedsport and Sutherlin. From Sutherlin, river access may be gained by going west on Sutherlin-Umpqua Road for about 8 miles to Umpqua. From Umpqua, Tyee Road follows the river downstream, eventually meeting with OR 138, while Garden Valley Road follows the river upstream to the forks.

For More Information: Oregon Department of Fish and Wildlife, Southwest Region

20 North Umpqua River

Key Species: Chinook salmon, coho salmon, steelhead

Best Way to Fish: boat, bank, wading

Best Time to Fish: Chinook salmon, late March through early July; coho salmon, September through November; steelhead, July through September and February and March

Description: The North Umpqua is particularly known for its summer steelhead angling along a 31-mile fly fishing-only segment on the upper river. A gorgeous stream of amazing water clarity flowing through a deep, forested canyon, fishing this river is an experience not to be forgotten, whether or not you bag one of its notoriously difficult-to-catch (on a fly, at least) summer steelhead.

But the North Umpqua also has winter steelhead, coho salmon, and spring Chinook salmon, offering bait and lure anglers the opportunity to enjoy this classic river on their own terms.

Chinook salmon migrate up the North Umpqua from late March or mid-April through early July, peaking in May. Coho salmon run from September through November, with the last two months providing the best fishing. Although there are some steelhead nearly year-round, the best months for targeting them is July though September. There also tends to be a small peak after the first fall rains, which usually hit in October. The winter steelhead run peaks in late February.

A variety of rules govern angling on the North Umpqua, depending on what section you are fishing and what species of fish you are after. Be sure to check the most recent angling regulations before heading for the river.

Fishing Index: Plunking with bait on the bottom, drifting sand shrimp and roe under a bobber, drifting bait, or casting spinners are all standard North Umpqua spring Chinook angling techniques. Bait under a bobber is the more common approach. A favorite float for drift boaters is from Colliding Rivers boat launch to Whistlers Bend Park, both managed by Douglas County.

A happy North Umpqua angler hefts his catch.

North Umpqua River

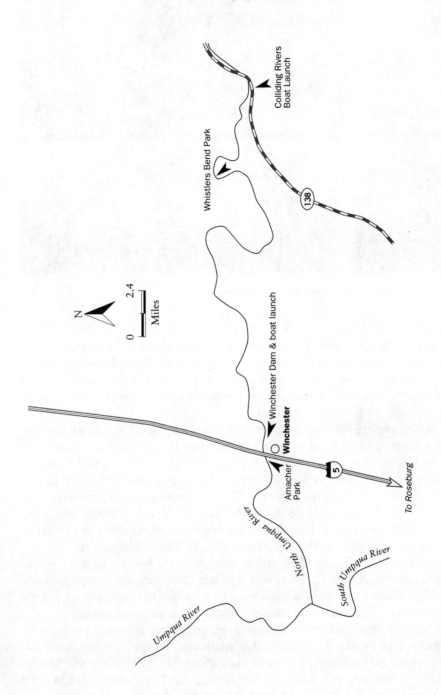

Fly fishing a deep run on the North Umpqua.

Another approach for those with a boat is to put in at Amacher Park (a county park with a boat launch just below Winchester Dam) and motor from hole to hole, back-bouncing bait. Bank anglers can find about 2 miles of public river access in the small riverside community of Idleyld Park, between Swiftwater Park and the Idleyld store. This area can be a pretty crowded place in May when the Chinook run peaks.

Coho anglers fish with spinners from the bank, casting them into pools in the Swiftwater Park-to-Idleyld bank access area. The quality and timing of the coho fishery is very dependent on the rains. If they come early in the fall, the fish will ascend the river from the ocean immediately and be nice and bright. If the rains come late, the fish may already be turning red by the time they make it upriver. About 70 percent of the coho run on the North Umpqua consists of hatchery fish, making the odds good of catching one that may be taken home for dinner. All wild coho salmon must be released unharmed.

The Colliding Rivers to Whistlers Bend Park is a favored float for winter steelheaders with a boat, where they will side-drift with eggs and plugs. Bank anglers plunk in the Idleyld Park area. Few fly fish for steelhead during the winter run, as the cold water makes them sluggish and hard to tempt.

Summer steelhead are a different story, and many dedicated steelhead fly fishers make regular summer and fall pilgrimages to the fly-fishing-only section of the North Umpqua: it's from just above Rock Creek to Soda Springs Dam. While many regulars have their favorite steelhead runs to fish, a good approach is to drive along Oregon Highway 138 as it parallels the river, pull

North Umpqua River

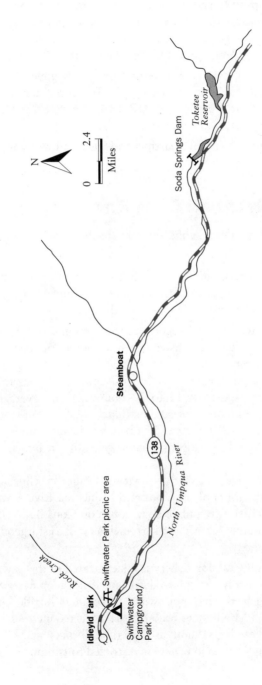

over at turnouts, and fish the water below if it looks promising. Summer steelhead angling on the North Umpqua is best at dawn and dusk. The North Umpqua has a very slick, treacherous bottom with lots of underwater shelves and unexpected drop-offs. Waders need to stay alert. Cleats for your wading shoes are highly advisable. A wading staff is not a bad idea either.

Further downstream, gear-oriented summer steelheaders drift Corkies and bait between Colliding Rivers and Whistlers Bend Park.

Directions: Oregon Highway 138 (North Umpqua Highway) parallels the North Umpqua River for much of its length. To reach Idleyld Park, drive about 25 miles east from Roseburg on OR 138. The fly-fishing-only section begins about 4 miles east of Idleyld Park.

For More Information: Oregon Department of Fish and Wildlife, Southwest Region

21 Coos River and Coos Bay

Key Species: Chinook salmon, coho salmon, steelhead, sturgeon, bottomfish

Best Way to Fish: boat, bank

Best Time to Fish: Chinook salmon, July through late October; coho salmon, October and November; steelhead, December through March; sturgeon, January through April; bottomfish, year-round

Description: Long rated one of Oregon's top salmon and steelhead fisheries, the Coos River, along with its extensive bay and sloughs, offers anglers lots of elbow room.

The fall Chinook run begins in July or August and goes through late October. Chinook average from 15 to 23 pounds. Coho averaging 6 to 8 pounds are in the bay and open for angling (hatchery, fin-clipped fish only) in October and November. Winter steelhead move through the system from December through March, with peak fishing generally in January and early February.

Overall, the lower river is fished by boat for Chinook, while steelheaders target upstream of the forks of the Coos and Millicoma Rivers, which is the head of the tide. There are six public boat ramps on Coos Bay.

Bottomfish, including rockfish and surfperch as well as sturgeon, are available to anglers in the bay.

Fishing Index: The fall Chinook fishery is concentrated in the bay up to tidewater and does not really get going until late August or early September. Anglers troll herring in the bay but switch to spinners in tidewater. At the forks, drifting eggs under a bobber becomes the preferred method. There is no in-river fishery for these big salmon, as once the fall rains hit, they disappear upriver pretty quickly. The coho fishery is restricted to Isthmus Slough, which

Coos River and Coos Bay

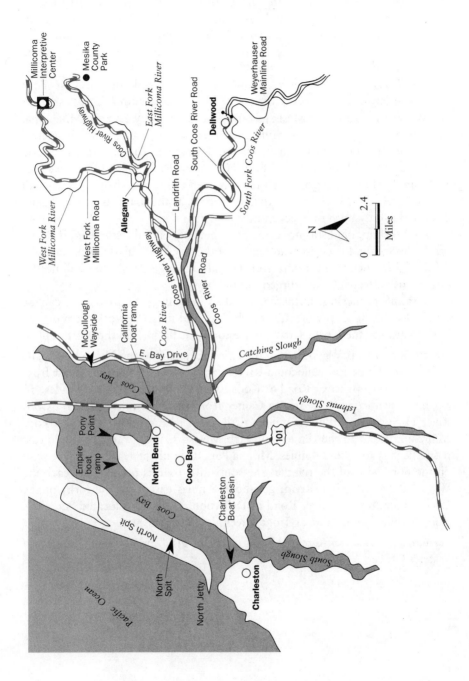

Millicoma Interpretive Center

Mesika County Park

West Fork Millicoma River

West Fork Millicoma Road

East Fork Millicoma River

Coos River Highway

Allegany

Landrith Road

South Coos River Road

South Fork Coos River

Dellwood

Weyerhauser Mainline Road

Coos River Highway

Coos River Road

Coos River Road

Coos River

Catching Slough

Isthmus Slough

McCullough Wayside

California boat ramp

E. Bay Drive

Coos Bay

Empire boat ramp

Pony Point

North Bend

Coos Bay

Charleston Boat Basin

Coos Bay

North Spit

North Spit

Pacific Ocean

North Jetty

Charleston

South Slough

101

N

0   2.4

Miles

extends south from the bay's eastern arm. Trolling with spinners is the most popular and effective technique here.

Steelheaders target the South Fork Coos River and east and west forks of the Millicoma above tidewater. Most anglers drift Corkies, sand shrimp, or eggs on these streams, but there is some fly fishing potential on the South Fork Coos. There is limited access for boats on these rivers; the bulk of the fishing is from the bank.

The Coos River Highway follows the north bank of the East Fork Millicoma River and allows a variety of bank access points. The best bank access on this stream is at Mesika County Park. On the West Fork Millicoma, the best bank access is at the Millicoma Interpretive Center, which is operated by the Oregon Department of Fish and Wildlife. You can also get good bank access for 22 miles of the South Fork Coos River off the Weyerhaeuser Company's Mainline Road. But first you need to contact their agent, North Pacific Security (541-267-5915) to get a permit, as the road has a locked gate. The road is only open on weekends.

Sand shrimp, mud shrimp, clams, and herring will take sturgeon, if fished off the bottom in lower tidewater areas of the bay, particularly in the channel off the North Bend boat ramp from January through April. You will need a boat to fish effectively for sturgeon in the bay.

Bottomfish such as surfperch, rockfish, greenling, and cabezon can be caught by fishing kelp worms, sand shrimp, and mussels; work them off the bottom around the North Jetty, Charleston Boat Basin, and the North Spit.

Directions: Coos Bay is located at the cities of Coos Bay and North Bend. The forks of the Coos and Millicoma Rivers can be reached by driving east from Coos Bay on Coos River Road or Coos River Highway for about 9 miles. To reach the Millicoma Interpretive Center from Coos Bay, drive east on Coos River Highway for about 9 miles to Allegany, then go north on West Fork Millicoma Road to the center. To reach Mesika County Park, continue east past Allegany for about 4 miles. Mesika Park can only be reached via the road on the north side of the river, as the south side road is private. To reach the Weyerhaeuser Mainline Road, go about 5 miles east from the forks of the Coos on South Coos River Road to Dellwood. The gate is located here. The next 22 miles, to the gate at Tioga Creek, is open to fishing.

For More Information: Oregon Department of Fish and Wildlife, Charleston District Office

22 Coquille River and Coquille Bay

Key Species: Chinook salmon, coho salmon, steelhead, bottomfish

Best Way to Fish: boat

Best Time to Fish: Chinook salmon, July to November; coho salmon, mid-August to mid-October; steelhead, December through March; bottomfish, year-round

Description: Formed by the confluence of its forks at Myrtle Point, the Coquille River snakes its way about 35 miles through Coast Range forest and farms to its ocean outlet at the city of Bandon.

Chinook salmon enter the bay and river in July and August, then move upriver through November. The best fishing in the tidewater and lower river is from late August to late October. Steelhead are here from December through March. Their run peaks in January and early February.

There is a run of coho salmon on the Coquille River which can be fished (hatchery, adipose fin-clipped fish only) between mid-August and mid-October on the 8.5-mile stretch from the U.S. Highway 101 bridge to Bear Creek. Such special seasons may change from year to year, based on the health of fish populations. Be sure to study the most current regulations before heading out.

The vast majority of salmon and steelhead fishing is done by boat between the forks at Myrtle Point downstream to the bay at Bandon. There are eight boat ramps along this stretch of river, allowing for a good variety of drifts. While there is a strong run of Chinook eagerly sought by anglers, the South Fork Coquille is the better choice for steelhead aficionados as it has the better combination of strong runs and good access of all the other forks in this river system.

In the bay proper, there are plenty of opportunities to take a variety of bottomfish, including cabezon, rockfish, surfperch, and greenling.

Fishing Index: Chinook fishing is good on the lower river, below Rocky Point from late August through September, with the action moving upriver as the season progresses until it culminates in late October or early November. Bait is the preferred technique lower in the river, while spinners are the method of choice further into tidewater. Steelhead anglers drift Corkies and Hot Shots, and eggs and sand shrimp under a bobber, and pull plugs.

Steelheaders should also consider paying a visit to the Middle Fork Coquille, which enters the mainstem near Myrtle Point. There is lots of good bank access to this stream off Oregon Highway 42.

For bottomfish in the bay, fish sand shrimp, mussels, and kelp worms off the bottom in rocky areas or off piers and docks. Good access for bottomfish angling in Bandon includes Bullards boat ramp, Bullards Beach, and the north jetty in Bullards Beach State Park, Weber Pier at the Port of Bandon, and South Jetty.

Coquille River and Coquille Bay

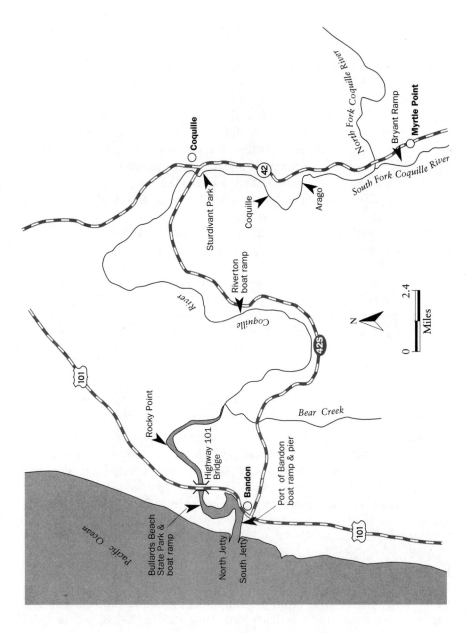

Directions: From Bandon, County Road 42S and Oregon Highway 42 parallels most of the Coquille River.

For More Information: Oregon Department of Fish and Wildlife, Charleston District Office

23 South Fork Coquille River

Key Species: Chinook salmon, steelhead

Best Way to Fish: boat

Best Time to Fish: Chinook salmon, August through November; steelhead, December through April

Description: Rising out of the Siskiyou National Forest and flowing into the mainstem Coquille River near the city of Myrtle Point, the South Fork Coquille is especially well known for its excellent steelhead fishery; it's the primary draw for anglers, although some pursue Chinook here as well.

Chinook are in the system from August through November, with the greatest numbers during October and November. The steelhead run goes from December through April. Although it tends to peak in January and February, fishing remains strong throughout February and into late March and April for large, wild steelhead.

Although Powers Highway parallels much of the river, most of the land is privately owned, making drifting by boat the best way to fish here.

Anglers work the river from its mouth 30 miles up to the boundary of the Siskiyou National Forest. From there the river is closed to angling for the next dozen miles. All wild steelhead must be released unharmed; however, the bulk of the steelhead on the South Fork Coquille are hatchery stock.

Fishing Index: Drift fishing sand shrimp or eggs, Corkies, Spin-n-Glos, or back-drifting Kwikfish and Flatfish are the most commonly used methods on this river. There is also good fly water along the river, but the vast majority of anglers here fish gear.

A common and easy drift begins at the Oregon Department of Fish and Wildlife–managed pole-slide boat launch at Beaver Creek and goes down to Myrtle Grove State Park. There is also a series of gravel pits along the river that serve as informal put-ins and take-outs. The upper river runs faster, with potentially dangerous rapids (and some impassable ones) requiring good river running skills. If you plan on tackling this river section, seek advice from experienced South Fork Coquille boaters. There is not much bank access along this stream.

Directions: To reach the Beaver Creek launch, drive south from Myrtle Point on Oregon Highway 42 for about 2.5 miles. Turn right (south) onto Powers Highway and go about 10 miles to the launch. You will pass the take-out at

South Fork Coquille River

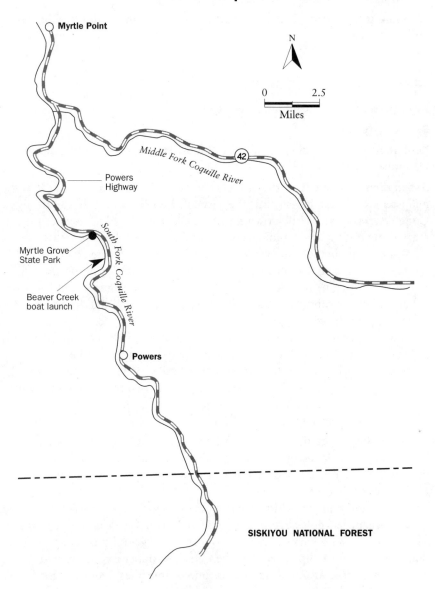

Myrtle Point

N

0   2.5
Miles

Middle Fork Coquille River

42

Powers
Highway

South Fork Coquille River

Myrtle Grove
State Park

Beaver Creek
boat launch

Powers

SISKIYOU NATIONAL FOREST

Myrtle Grove State Park off Powers Highway about 8 miles south of the intersection of OR 42 and Powers Highway.

For More Information: Oregon Department of Fish and Wildlife, Charleston District Office

24 Sixes River

Key Species: Chinook salmon, steelhead

Best Way to Fish: boat

Best Time to Fish: Chinook salmon, October through December; steelhead, December through March

Description: The Sixes River rises out of the steep terrain of the Siskiyou National Forest and flows west into the Pacific Ocean a couple of miles north of Cape Blanco. Similar in character and in the fishery it offers as the nearby Elk River, the Sixes is a popular destination when the Chinook run is on, but it sees less interest in its catch-and-release-only wild winter steelhead fishery. Fall Chinook salmon are in the Sixes from October through December, peaking in late November. The steelhead run goes from December through March, peaking in January.

Chinook average 25 pounds but may reach into the 50-pound range. Steelhead average 8 to 10 pounds up to 20 pounds.

Much of this river flows through private lands, giving anglers with access to a boat a distinct advantage, but there is some bank access.

Fishing Index: Back-trolling Kwikfish and Flatfish wrapped with sardines, as well as drifting or back-dragging eggs and shrimp are effective on the Sixes. The two most popular drifts are from the Bureau of Land Management's Edson Creek launch to the private Sixes River Store launch, or from Edson Creek to the Oregon Department of Fish and Wildlife's Mid-Drift launch. The Edson Creek launch is steep, so you will need a four-wheel-drive vehicle to put in. There is also a boat launch at Cape Blanco State Park, allowing a drift trip to within 4 miles of the ocean, although the fishing is usually better upstream. You can find some bank access off Sixes River Road, or try fishing at the two public boat ramps along the upper river.

Directions: From Port Orford, drive 5 miles north on U.S. Highway 101. Turn right (east) onto Sixes River Road (County Road 184). This road parallels the river. Edson Creek launch is about 4.5 miles up Sixes River Road. The Mid-Drift take-out is 1 mile upstream from where US 101 crosses the river.

For More Information: Oregon Department of Fish and Wildlife, Gold Beach District Office

Sixes River • Elk River

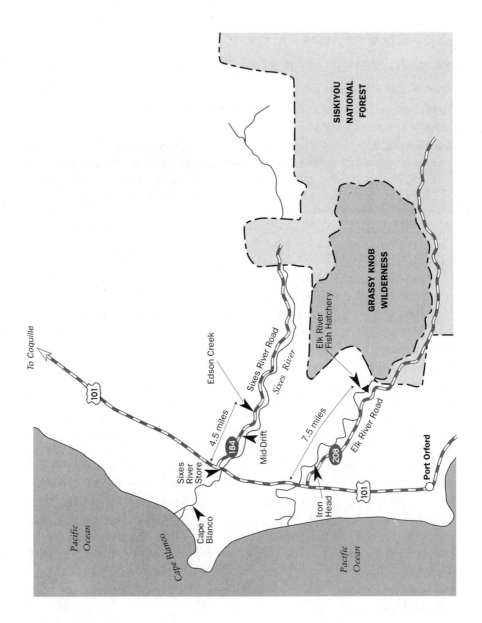

25 Elk River

Key Species: Chinook salmon, steelhead

Best Way to Fish: boat

Best Time to Fish: Chinook salmon, October through December; steelhead, December through March

Description: This small coastal stream flows out of the wild and rugged Siskiyou National Forest and spills into the Pacific Ocean between Port Orford and Cape Blanco. It is a popular and often crowded river during the Chinook salmon season. Its catch-and-release wild hatchery run attracts a smaller number of anglers in search of a high-quality fishing experience.

The Chinook run up the Elk from October through December, with late November finding the largest concentrations of fish. Steelhead are here from December through March, peaking in January.

Elk River Chinook average 25 pounds, and some may reach 50 pounds. Steelhead are typically in the 8- to 10-pound range but can get as large as 20 pounds.

Because the bulk of the Elk River—at least the steelhead and salmon waters—flows through private lands, a boat is the best bet here, although it is possible to find some public bank access along Elk River Road. There are only two public boat launches on the river.

The Elk River typically fishes well up to 7 feet.

Fishing Index: Drifting or back-dragging eggs or shrimp, or back-trolling plugs, are the two basic approaches on the Elk River. The main Elk River drift begins at the Oregon Department of Fish and Wildlife's boat launch at the Elk River Fish Hatchery; the take-out is 9 miles downriver at the Iron Head launch, which is also managed by the state.

Directions: From Port Orford, drive north on U.S. Highway 101 for 3.5 miles. Turn right (east) onto Elk River Road, which parallels Elk River. Drive 7.5 miles to the hatchery and boat launch. The hatchery is on the left. The take-out at Iron Head launch is just upstream from where US 101 crosses the river.

For More Information: Oregon Department of Fish and Wildlife, Gold Beach District Office and Elk River Fish Hatchery

Lower Rogue River

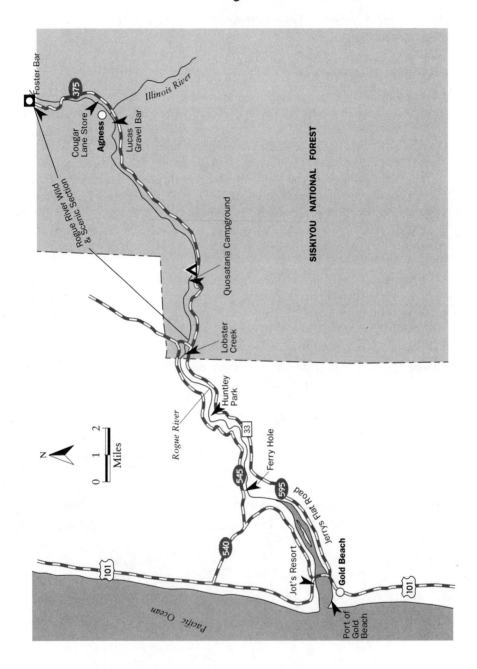

Foster Bar

375

Cougar Lane Store

Agness

Lucas Gravel Bar

Illinois River

Rogue River Wild & Scenic Section

Quosatana Campground

SISKIYOU   NATIONAL   FOREST

Lobster Creek

Huntley Park

Rogue River

33

Ferry Hole

N

0   1   2
Miles

545

595

540

Jerrys Flat Road

Jot's Resort

Gold Beach

Port of Gold Beach

101

101

Pacific Ocean

26 Lower Rogue River

Key Species: Chinook salmon, coho salmon, steelhead

Best Way to Fish: boat, bank

Best Time to Fish: Chinook salmon, March through October; coho salmon, September through December; steelhead, August through April

Description: Much of the 40-mile stretch of the lower Rogue River from its outlet to the ocean at Gold Beach up to Foster Bar, above the small community of Agness, is flatwater with numerous gravel bars.

Fall and spring Chinook salmon, coho salmon, and summer and winter steelhead are all attractions for anglers on the lower Rogue. Spring Chinook enter the river around the end of March or the beginning of April through June, with the run peaking in May. Fall Chinook are in Rogue Bay by late July, moving up into the river by September and October. Coho are caught here between September and the end of December. This is a small hatchery run of about 50,000 fish on their way back to the Cole M. Rivers Fish Hatchery 150 miles upstream. Any wild coho caught on the Rogue must be released.

Summer steelhead move into the river beginning in mid-August, while the winter steelhead run goes from late November though April, peaking in January.

Access for boaters and bank anglers on the lower Rogue is very good. There are nine boat ramps between Foster Bar and the river's mouth while a series of roads—Jerrys Flat Road, Forest Road 33, and County Road 375—parallel the river between Gold Beach and Foster Bar. At about milepost 10 from Gold Beach, you enter the Siskiyou National Forest and the beginning of the river's Wild and Scenic section.

Fishing regulations along the Rogue River are fairly extensive, depending on what segment of the river you are on and what species you are after, so be sure and review the latest angling rules before starting your trip.

Fishing Index: Anglers begin targeting spring Chinook in April in the tidewater area (there is no bay fishery here for spring Chinook). With the exception of the reach between Foster Bar and the mouth of the Illinois River, which is popular with drift boaters, the lower Rogue is primarily a power-boat fishery. Typically, the approach is to fish from anchored boats, or from one of the many gravel bars that line the river—a good half of which are accessible by vehicle. Anglers plunk with shrimp or roe or go with Corkies or Spin 'n Glos. The overall idea is that you are after fish actively moving upstream. The trick is to get your bait or lure in the "lane of traffic."

Fall Chinook fishing begins in the bay during the last half of July, but doesn't really pick up until August. At this time of year the most common and successful technique is to troll spinner blades and whole bait—usually herring or anchovy. By August, the mainstem water has begun to cool off and the Chinook start to head upstream. By September and October they have moved into the river in earnest. At this point, anglers adopt the same strategy as for spring Chinook.

Some coho are caught in the bay by trollers in September, but by the end of that month, or early October, about half the run has made its way into the river, where they are targeted by plunking from anchored boats or off gravel bars.

While there is a decent run of summer steelhead in the lower river, most anglers are after the half-pounders—steelhead that have returned to freshwater from the sea early and are usually in the 12- to 16-inch range. While the bulk of the half-pounder fishing takes place between mid-August and October, many of these fish spend the winter in the Agness-to-Foster Bar area, so it's possible to fish for them for considerably longer than most people do. Bait is allowed, although discouraged by restrictions on hook sizes (see current regulations). Fly fishing and spinner fishing dominates this fishery.

Winter steelheading gets going around the end of November or early December with anglers plunking from anchored boats or gravel bars, as with spring Chinook.

Directions: You can access the lower Rogue River from Gold Beach to Foster Bar via Jerrys Flat Road (County Road 595), Forest Road 33 (Agness Road), and County Road 375.

For More Information: Oregon Department of Fish and Wildlife, Gold Beach District Office and Siskiyou National Forest

27 Middle Rogue River

Key Species: Chinook salmon, steelhead

Best Way to Fish: boat, bank, wading

Best Time to Fish: Chinook salmon, April through September; steelhead, July through early November

Description: The 90-plus-mile segment of the Rogue River from Gold Ray Dam, near Gold Hill, to its confluence with the Illinois River near Agness, is considered the middle section of the river by the Oregon Department of Fish and Wildlife, which manages it. In addition to fishing, the middle Rogue is very popular with whitewater rafters, especially on the Wild and Scenic section of the Rogue Canyon.

The two major fisheries here are Chinook salmon and steelhead. There is both a fall and spring run of Chinook salmon as well as winter and summer steelhead. A particularly interesting steelhead fishery is for what are called "half-pounders." These are steelhead that have returned to freshwater from the sea early and are usually in the 12- to 16-inch range. They provide excellent sport during the fall. There is also a limited amount of coho angling on this stretch as well.

Middle Rogue River

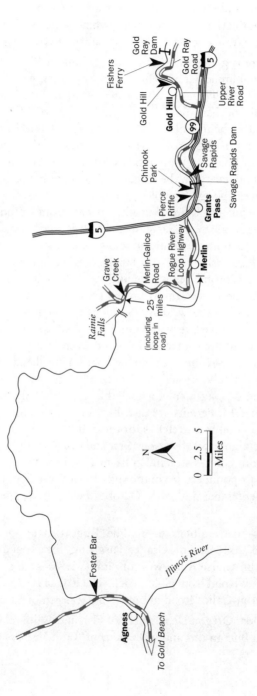

For the most part there is good public access on much of this river segment. There are around 25 public boat launches as well as numerous turnouts for bank fishing.

Fishing regulations along the Rogue River are fairly extensive, depending on what segment of the river you are on and what species you are after, so be sure and review the latest angling rules before starting your trip.

Fishing Index: There is good Chinook salmon fishing in May and early June along a 2-mile stretch immediately below Gold Ray Dam, where the fish tend to concentrate and hold. There is public bank access here for plunking, casting spinners, or drifting bait. Boaters can put in at a primitive county boat ramp at the dam (drift boats only; it is too rugged to launch a motor boat). Fall Chinook angling in this area runs from mid-May through September, with most fishing by boat. Back-pulling Kwikfish wrapped with herring is a technique gaining popularity on the Rogue with Chinook anglers.

Further downriver, spring Chinook are sought around Savage Rapids Dam in April and May, while fall Chinook angling is best from Grants Pass downstream between late August into September. There is some coho salmon fishing around Savage Rapids Dam from mid-to-late October through early November. A nice bank fishing area for fall and spring Chinook is just below Rainie Falls (angling is prohibited within 400 feet below the falls), reached by hiking along the Rogue River Trail from the trailhead off the Merlin-Galice Road on the upper end of the Wild and Scenic River section.

The river between Grave Creek and Gold Ray Dam gets good for summer steelhead in the fall and for winter steelhead between January and April.

The Wild and Scenic section is a popular float for steelhead, coho, and fall Chinook anglers from July through late August. (A permit is required from the Bureau of Land Management to float this section of the river between May 15 and October 15. Permits are distributed through a lottery system.)

But the real action on this stretch is for the half-pounders that will hit just about anything including bait, flys, spinners, and other small lures. There are some bait restrictions on this stretch, so be sure and consult current angling regulations. The half-pounders are in the river from September through early November, with September and early October being the prime time to fish for them.

Directions: Access roads along the middle Rogue River include Oregon Highways 99 and 234 east of Grants Pass and the Rogue River Loop Highway and Merlin-Galice Road west of Grants Pass. Access to the Agness area is via the Agness Road from Gold Beach. The Rogue River Trail to Rainie Falls is off the Merlin-Galice Road about 25 miles north of Merlin.

For More Information: Oregon Department of Fish and Wildlife, Central Point District Office and Bureau of Land Management/Rand Visitors Center

28 Upper Rogue River

Key Species: Chinook salmon, coho salmon, steelhead, rainbow trout

Best Way to Fish: boat, bank, wading

Best Time to Fish: Chinook salmon, May through July; coho salmon, November and December; steelhead, April through January; rainbow trout, April, May, September, and October.

Description: The 30-mile reach between Gold Ray Dam, near the city of Gold Hill, up to the state-operated Cole M. Rivers Fish Hatchery, just below Lost Creek Reservoir, is generally considered the upper Rogue River for fishery management purposes. The Rogue River extends, of course, above the reservoir where it originates deep in the Cascade Mountains.

On this segment of the river, anglers will find spring Chinook salmon from May through July, peaking from early June through early July and summer steelhead from May through January. They peak in July, then again in December. The best winter steelhead fishing is generally from mid-March through mid-April. There are also resident rainbow trout throughout the upper river as well as some resident cutthroat trout.

There are nine public boat launches between the fish hatchery down to Gold Hill, providing plenty of drift options. Good public bank access exists along much of the upper Rogue as well. The ramp at Tou Velle State Park is the last boat ramp before Gold Ray Dam. For this reason only anglers with motor-powered boats can access the several miles of fishable water between the park and the dam, because you must be able to motor back up to the park to take out.

Fishing regulations along the Rogue River are fairly extensive, depending on what segment of the river you are on and the species you are fishing for, so be sure and review the latest angling rules before starting your trip.

Fishing Index: During the run, spring Chinook will be found throughout the upper river (but below the reservoir). Boat anglers commonly back-bounce bait such as sand shrimp or roe, drift Corkies and Spin 'n Glos or back-drift plugs such as Kwikfish or Flatfish. For bank angling, there is public access on federal and state lands along a 1-mile stretch of river just below Cole M. Rivers Fish Hatchery, where you can drift bait or cast spinners.

Steelheaders use bait and lures from boats and bank, except in September and October, when regulations change to permit flies only. You don't have to use a fly rod however, and a popular technique is to drift standard steelhead streamers under a bobber. After November 1, everyone switches back to bait and lures.

Because these salmon and steelhead are returning to the Cole M. Rivers Fish Hatchery, where they were originally released, anglers begin to concentrate their fishing efforts there later in the season.

Upper Rogue River

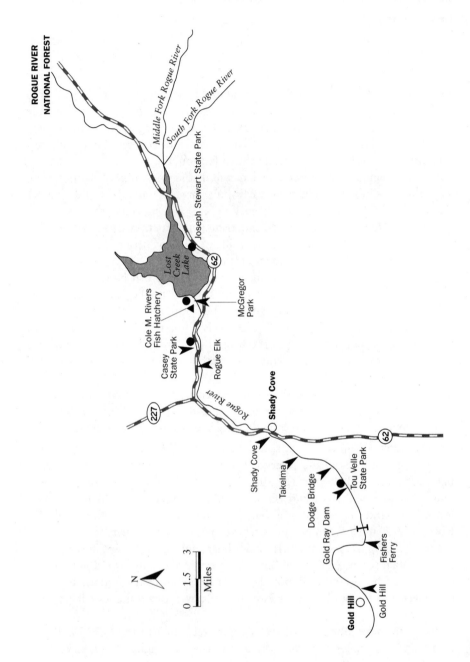

A classic riffle-run stretch of the Rogue River. The Rogue is home to Chinook and coho salmon, steelhead, and resident rainbow trout.

Of particular interest to fly fishers is the 0.5-mile section of the river between Lost Creek Dam and the hatchery, called the "Holy Water." It is a year-round catch-and-release, fly fishing-only rainbow trout fishery. Angling here is best in April, September, and October. Although it is fishable in the summer, water is released from the dam at this time of year to help migrating salmon and steelhead. So the river may be a bit higher than what is optimal for fly fishing. Try Blue-winged Olives, Elk Hair Caddis, and March Browns. There is a salmonfly hatch here that begins in late May and lasts well into June. Access to the Holy Waters is excellent, as lands along both sides of the river here are public.

Rainbow trout are also stocked above Lost Creek Reservoir. Much of this part of the river flows through the Rogue River National Forest, with numerous campgrounds and other public access sites.

Directions: The 30-mile length of the upper Rogue River can be accessed via a variety of roads from Medford and Gold Hill. To reach the Cole M. Rivers Fish Hatchery public access area and the Holy Waters, drive north from Medford on Oregon Highway 62 (Crater Lake Highway) to Casey State Park at milepost 29. Turn north (left) on Takelma Drive and go about .75 mile to Cole M. Rivers Drive. Turn right and follow the road across the river to the hatchery. Angling areas on the national forest lands can be reached by continuing north on OR 62 past Lost Creek Reservoir.

For More Information: Oregon Department of Fish and Wildlife, Central Point District Office

29 Chetco River and Chetco Bay

Key Species: Chinook salmon, steelhead, sea-run cutthroat, bottomfish

Best Way to Fish: boat, bank

Best Time to Fish: Chinook salmon, October through December; steelhead, December through March; sea-run cutthroat trout, July to October; bottomfish, year-round

Description: Located on the extreme south coast about 5 miles north of the California border, the Chetco River is a bit out of the way for most Oregon anglers. But its excellent run of hatchery winter steelhead along with a productive fall Chinook salmon run can make a long drive here well worth the effort. The Chetco River is one of coastal Oregon's best salmon and steelhead fisheries.

Fall Chinook are here from October through December, with the peak around the end of November. Steelhead push their way upstream from the sea between December and March, peaking in January and February.

Fall Chinook average around 25 pounds and may go as large as 50 pounds. Steelhead run about 8 to 10 pounds, although fish up to 20 pounds are sometimes caught here.

Chetco River and Chetco Bay

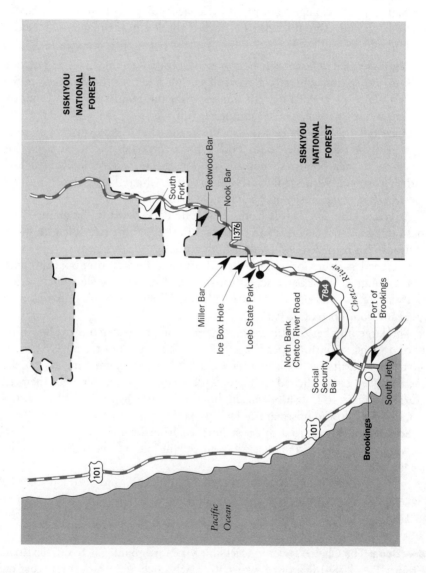

In addition to the river, there are opportunities to take fall Chinook in the bay at the beginning of the season, before the first winter rains send them upriver, as well as year-round angling for bottomfish.

There are a total of eight public boat launches between Brookings harbor and the Chetco's confluence with its south fork, offering plenty of drifts along with access for the bank-bound angler.

As with all coastal rivers with anadromous fish runs, regulations may be complex, and can change from year to year depending upon the overall health of steelhead and salmon stocks. Be sure to check current regulations before heading out.

Fishing Index: The Chinook fishery is concentrated around the head of tide early in the season where anglers troll cut-plug herring or spinners at the river's mouth, or cast bait and spinners from the South Jetty for Chinook salmon, as they gather for the fall upriver run.

Once fall freshets entice the fish upstream, the 12-mile stretch of river from head of tide to the South Fork Chetco becomes the focal point for anglers, who back-bounce shrimp and salmon eggs or back-troll Kwikfish and Flatfish wrapped with sardines. Fly fishing for Chinook is popular on this reach as well, using freshwater salmon patterns.

A typical Chinook drift is from Loeb State Park down to the unimproved boat ramp at Social Security Bar, on the south shore at the river's mouth. Both locations also provide good bank fishing access.

Steelheaders drift Corkies, Puf Balls, yarn, and Birdies from boat or bank. There is quite a bit of bank access for steelheaders on a 5-mile stretch of the river which flows through the Siskiyou National Forest, beginning about 1 mile upstream from Loeb State Park.

The large number of public boat ramps along the Chetco provide a variety of options, with the upper five offering the best and most productive combinations of drifts, as well as additional bank access. Some anglers on the Chetco River equip their drift boats with a small motor, allowing them to return upstream to re-fish promising holes and runs. Motorized boats, however, are not allowed upstream of Ice Box Hole.

Sea-run cutthroat trout are best pursued from Loeb State Park down to tidewater with flies or spinners. All trout caught in the Chetco River must be released unharmed.

Such bottomfish as surfperch, greenling, rockfish, and cabezon may be caught with kelp worms, sand shrimp, and mussels fished off the bottom at the south jetty or the fishing pier located there, and at the fishing pier at the Port of Brookings.

Directions: The Chetco River is accessible via North Bank Chetco River Road (County Road 784) from Brookings. To reach Loeb State Park, drive east on North Bank Chetco River Road for 8 miles.

For More Information: Oregon Department of Fish and Wildlife, Gold Beach District Office

30 Lost Creek Lake

Key Species: rainbow trout, Chinook salmon, smallmouth bass

Best Way to Fish: boat, some bank

Best Time to Fish: year-round

Description: Formed by a dam on the upper Rogue River, Lost Creek Lake is 3,400 acres in size and averages 136 feet deep. A deep lake, it plunges to over 300 feet in the middle.

The rainbow trout stocked here average 10 to 12 inches, but 18- to 20-inchers can be caught as well. There is also a nice population of smallmouth bass averaging 8 to 10 inches, up to several pounds. The lake has some bluegill, black crappie, and brown bullhead as well as a very small population of large-mouth bass. Chinook salmon are also stocked here as fingerlings, averaging 10 to 12 inches, but eventually growing to as large as 18 or 20 inches.

In addition to fishing, the lake is very popular with a variety of water-sports enthusiasts including pleasure boaters and water skiers. Joseph H. Stewart State Park is located on the eastern shore and has camping, a picnic area, and boat launch. There is also a boat ramp operated by the U.S. Army Corps of Engineers on the north side of the lake, by the dam. A commercial marina, Lost Creek Marina, is located on the lake, which sells bait and tackle, rents boats, and provides a boat launch and moorage as well.

Lost Creek Lake is open to angling year-round.

Lost Creek Lake harbors smallmouth and largemouth bass, rainbow trout, black crappie, brown bullhead, and Chinook salmon.

103

Lost Creek Lake

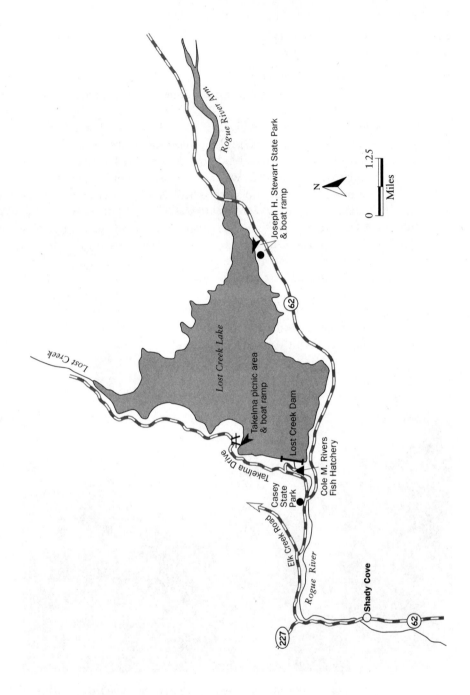

Fishing Index: Rainbow trout are best pursued along the shoreline by trolling spinners or still-fishing with nightcrawlers or Power Bait. May and June are the best months for Chinook angling. The best approach is to troll deep with small spinners. Use lead core line to get more depth. The area near the dam is a good place to prospect for salmon.

For smallmouth bass, Marabou jigs, poppers, plastics, and stickbaits all are effective. Good smallmouth bass locations include around the dam and offshore from Lost Creek Marina.

If you don't have a boat, a good bank fishing area is along the access road to the dam. But because fishing here necessitates pulling your catch straight up the steep bank, make sure you use a heavier test line than you might otherwise employ.

Because this lake is popular with waterskiers and others, in midsummer, anglers often concentrate on the Rogue River arm where the channel narrows and a low speed limit for boats is enforced.

The water level in the lake fluctuates by as much as 60 feet over the course of a year. It is full in late April through most of June, when it is then drawn down. This tends to slow the fishing down a bit, although it picks up in the fall when the reservoir is once again filled.

Directions: From Medford, drive north on Oregon Highway 62 for about 35 miles. Turn left (north) into Joseph H. Stewart State Park.

For More Information: Oregon Department of Fish and Wildlife, Southwest Region Office and Joseph H. Stewart State Park

31 Diamond Lake

Key Species: rainbow trout

Best Way to Fish: boat

Best Time to Fish: May through October

Description: This 3,200-acre jewel of a lake is surrounded by a forest of conifers in the Cascade Mountains at an elevation of 5,183 feet. A very popular recreational area, Diamond Lake has traditionally been one of the state's best trout fisherys. But recently, its rainbow trout population has undergone some tough times due to an unauthorized release of tui chub, which are hogging all the food in the lake and outcompeting the rainbow trout. Rainbow trout fingerlings have been regularly released into the lake by the state each spring. They would grow to 9 or 10 inches by the fall and blossom to a pound by the season opener the following year. But the heavy competition for food by the nonnative chubs are lowering the trout's survival and growth rate. To combat this, the state has embarked on a regular stocking program of 10- to 12-inch trout during the summer. Over the long-term, the state is studying its options that might range from poisoning the chubs out and starting over again, to leaving the chubs there and changing the mix of available gamefish

Diamond Lake

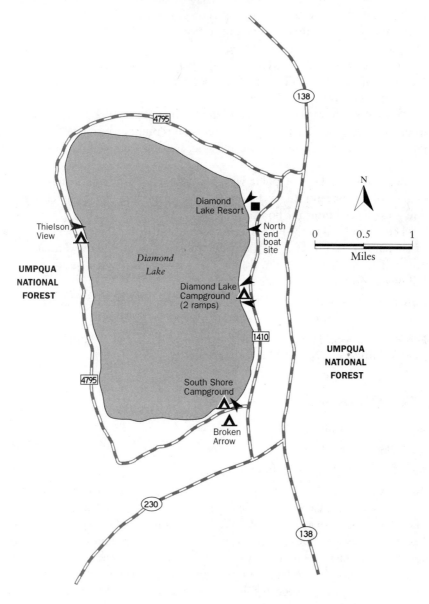

to those that can better stand the competition. In the meantime, fishing here remains decent, although it will likely take some time to regain Diamond Lake's former glory.

There are a variety of recreational amenities at Diamond Lake including a resort, RV park, and a number of USDA Forest Service campgrounds. There are six USDA Forest Service–operated boat ramps on the lake. Diamond Lake is open for angling from April 22 through the end of October.

Fishing Index: Angler philosophy on Diamond Lake is divided about 50-50 between trolling or still-fishing with bait. The trollers usually troll Flatfish and flasher set-ups or Triple Teazers. Still fishers favor Power Bait. Good trolling areas are along the east and west shorelines, while bait anglers prefer the "Cheese Hole" off the northeast end of the lake.

Fishing in Diamond Lake is usually best from ice-out, which typically happens around mid-May, until the end of June. During the warm months of July and August the trout tend to go deeper and fishing slacks off a bit. As the weather cools in September and October, the bite picks up again.

You will need a boat to successfully fish Diamond Lake.

Directions: From Roseburg drive east on Oregon Highway 138 for about 80 miles. Turn right at the sign for Diamond Lake, which is immediately on the west side of the highway.

For More Information: Oregon Department of Fish and Wildlife, Southwest Region and Umpqua National Forest/Diamond Lake Ranger District

Willamette Valley

Taking in a broad reach of Oregon including bustling cities, bucolic farmland, and mountain forest, the Willamette area provides fishing opportunities as close as your front door and as far away as the shimmering Cascade peaks.

In the greater Portland area, the mighty Columbia River along with its tributaries—the Willamette, Clackamas, and Sandy Rivers—offer urban anglers an amazing selection of year-round fishing including some of the state's best salmon and steelhead streams. In addition to the chance to catch these signature Pacific Northwest gamefish so close to home, opportunities to fish for the more unusual abound as well, including excellent sturgeon fishing along with American shad and walleye. Further east, into the foothills of the Cascade Mountains, anglers can also pursue steelhead and salmon, stalk wild trout in a mountain river, or troll away the day on a placid reservoir.

Because so much of Portland area fishing—especially on the Columbia—is boat oriented, a copy of the *Oregon Boating Facilities Guide* will be a great help here. Unless otherwise noted, regulations for the waters listed in this section will be found in the Willamette Zone section of the *Oregon Sport Fishing Regulations* handbook.

32 Columbia River (St. Helens to Bonneville Dam)

Key Species: Chinook salmon, steelhead, American shad, sturgeon, walleye

Best Way to Fish: boat, bank

Best Time to Fish: Chinook salmon, February through March and August through September; steelhead, May through August; American shad, mid-May and June; sturgeon, February through October; walleye, July through September

Description: This 55-mile stretch of the mighty Columbia River flowing past downtown Portland's doorstep offers plenty of excellent and varied fishing for most of the year, no matter what your "taste" in fish is.

Chinook salmon come through from February well into May, although the fishing season for them ends in early April. Steelhead provide good action on this reach from May into August. Shad fishing is best from mid-May through June. Sturgeon are around throughout the year, although spring and summer are the most active fishing periods. For something a little different, walleye can be caught in selected sections of the river with late summer and early fall being the prime angling time. There are also some mixed, miscellaneous warmwater fish in the Columbia, although fishing for them is not particularly popular, or very good for that matter. There are coho salmon here as well, although that fishery is concentrated around the lower river near Astoria and the mouth.

Columbia River (St. Helens to Bonneville Dam)

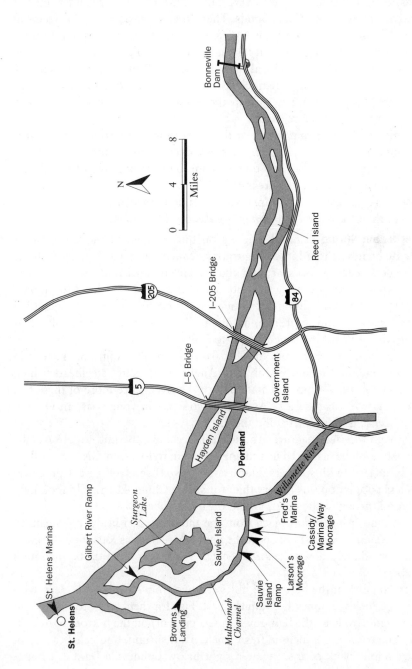

A Columbia River spring Chinook averages 12 to 18 pounds up to 30 pounds. Their fall counterparts are typically in the 15- to 30-pound range but may grow as large as 40-plus pounds. There are two basic stocks of steelhead on the Columbia. One called the "A" Run are in the 6- to 12-pound range, while the "B" Run fish grow a bit larger, from 12 to 20 pounds. "A" Run fish are headed from the ocean to local rivers, while "B" Run fish are on their way higher into the Columbia system, clear into Idaho. Shad run about 3 pounds each while "keeper" sturgeon are in the 42- to 60-inch range. Larger and smaller sturgeon must be released.

In spite of the fact that much of this river is in close proximity to large urban populations, access is good. There are over 30 boat ramps available for public use from Bonneville Dam downstream to the community of St. Helens, and a number of bank access areas as well.

Fishing regulations for this area will be found in the Columbia River Zone section of the *Oregon Sport Fishing Regulations* handbook.

Fishing Index: Spring Chinook angling on this segment of the Columbia is mostly by boat, anchored in concentrations called "hog lines" or by trolling. Boat anglers tend to focus around the St. Helens area and around Sauvie Island, while bank fishers can find some access along the Multnomah Channel. Traditional salmon techniques are used in this fishery, including spinners, Flatfish, and, more commonly, trolling cut-plug herring. March is typically the peak fishing time for spring Chinook.

Steelhead anglers fish Spin 'n Glos from the bank around St. Helens in May and June, or by boat in July and August. The better steelhead fishing tends to be on the Washington state half of the river, since more of these fish have originated in hatcheries. (As long as you stay in your boat, an Oregon angling license is valid for fishing there.)

Although the steelhead are around into December, by mid-to-late August the fall Chinook have moved in and anglers begin to focus on this run, trolling through the river with spinners, Flatfish, and Kwikfish. Trolling cut-plug herring is less popular on this fishery than for spring Chinook. Fall Chinook fishing is good through September, falling off by October.

Most shad fishing takes place from the Interstate 205 bridge upstream to Bonneville Dam. The best area is at the dam where there is lots of public bank access, immediately downstream. To catch shad, cast shad darts and small spinners.

Sturgeon lurk at the bottom of holes ranging from 45 to 70 feet deep with the 20 miles below Bonneville Dam the best. Fish for them with stout rods and heavy weights (to keep the bait down in fast current) on the bottom with bait. Good baits to use here include fresh smelt, sand shrimp, and eel. Because of its good public bank access, the area right below Bonneville Dam is a popular sturgeon fishing destination.

There is a small, but somewhat popular, walleye fishery on this river stretch from Bonneville Dam down to the Interstate 5 bridge. Troll with spinners, worms, and grubs during July, August, and September when the fish come up onto the flats and are easier to catch. Also, concentrate around island shorelines, as well.

Directions: To reach Bonneville Dam drive east from Portland for 36 miles on Interstate 84. Take exit 40, and follow the signs to the dam. From there, roads lead to public bank access points just below the dam. St. Helens is about 24 miles north of Portland off U.S. Highway 30. US 30 intersects with the Multnomah Channel about 7 miles north of Portland. There are a number of boat ramps along this channel.

For More Information: Oregon Department of Fish and Wildlife, Columbia Region Office

33 Sandy River

Key Species: Chinook salmon, coho salmon, steelhead

Best Way to Fish: boat, bank, wading

Best Time to Fish: Chinook salmon, March through June and late August through September; coho salmon, September and October; steelhead, mid-November through early February and mid-April through August

Description: A stream of glacial origin, the Sandy River begins in the Mount Hood National Forest, just west of Mount Hood, snaking its way some 40 miles to where it flows into the Columbia River near Troutdale. A long-time top producer, the Sandy offers spring and fall Chinook salmon, coho salmon, as well as both winter and summer steelhead.

Spring Chinook are in the river from early March through June, with the peak running from late April through the end of May. Fall Chinook make their upriver run from late August through September. Coho are around in September and October. There are two winter steelhead runs. The hatchery run starts around mid-November or early December lasting into January, while the run of wild fish enters the river between late December through March. The peak of the hatchery fish is generally late December or early January. The wild run peaks around late January or early February upstream, in the vicinity of the city of Sandy.

A mix of boat and bank fishing, the Sandy has relatively good access for anglers via a state fish hatchery and riverside parks.

The Sandy River has some bait restrictions and closed areas where Chinook salmon spawn around Oxbow Regional Park. All wild coho salmon must be released unharmed. Be sure and read the most current sport angling regulations when planning a fishing trip to the Sandy River.

Fishing Index: Spring Chinook fishing is mostly a bank and wading affair, with the best locations around Marmot Dam, Sandy Fish Hatchery, Dodge Park, Oxbow Park, and Dabney and Lewis and Clark State Parks. Some anglers drift by boat from the boat ramp at Oxbow Regional Park down to Dabney, or from Dabney to Lewis and Clark. Drifting sand shrimp and eggs

Sandy River

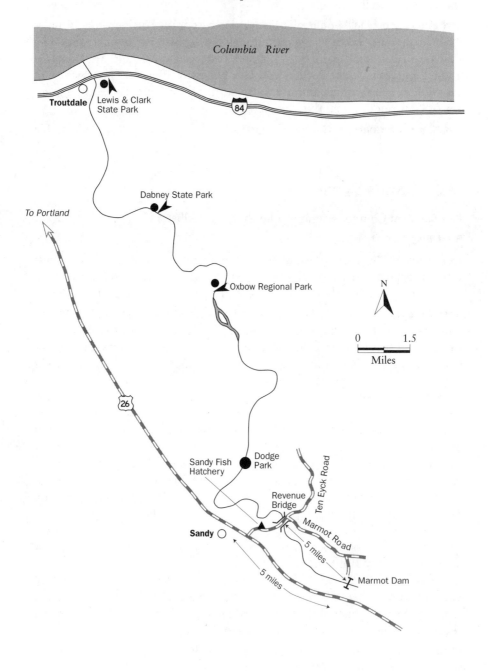

Columbia River

Troutdale

Lewis & Clark
State Park

To Portland

Dabney State Park

Oxbow Regional Park

N

0   1.5
Miles

Sandy Fish
Hatchery

Dodge
Park

Revenue
Bridge

Ten Eyck Road

Marmot Road

5 miles

Sandy

5 miles

Marmot Dam

under a bobber, and drifting jigs are typical bank angling techniques, while boaters add back-bouncing bait and plugs to the repertoire. Anglers will also fish by jet boat low on the river.

Fall Chinook angling is typically from Oxbow Regional Park downstream, using the same techniques as for spring Chinook. There are some nice fall Chinook salmon holes in the river at Dabney State Park. Fishing off the mouth of Trout Creek, by Oxbow Regional Park is another good spot. Coho are pursued much the same way on the same reach, although the water is very low in the fall when these fish are in, so drifting by boat in the upper river may not be feasible.

For winter steelhead, around the Revenue Bridge at Sandy and Marmot Dam are good bank fishing areas. Winter steelhead are usually at their peak in this area by late January or early February. Dodge Park, and the area just downstream, known as the "pipeline" is another spot worth checking out. Winter steelheaders will also float from Oxbow Regional Park on downstream, while anglers with jet boats fish downstream from Lewis and Clark State Park. Marmot Dam is a traditional bank fishing location for summer steelheaders. Fishing around the river's confluence with the Columbia can be productive as well, since steelhead bound for upper Columbia River destinations will spend time poking around here before continuing on their way. Typical Sandy River steelhead techniques include drifting eggs and Corkies or casting spinners.

Directions: Lewis and Clark and Dabney State Parks and Oxbow Regional Park can be reached by traveling south along the Sandy River off Interstate 84, Exit 18. To reach the Sandy Fish Hatchery from Sandy, turn left (north) off U.S. Highway 26 onto Ten Eyck Road at the last stoplight on the east end of town. Go 0.5 mile and make a sharp left-hand turn, then turn left onto S.E. Fish Hatchery Road and drive 1 mile to the hatchery. To reach Revenue Bridge, continue on Ten Eyck Road past the hatchery. The bridge is where the road crosses the river. To get to Marmot Dam, bear right at the fork on Ten Eyck Road after crossing Revenue Bridge (the other fork goes to Roslyn Lake) onto Marmot Road. Follow Marmot Road to milepost 4, at the top of the ridge. Take the unmarked gravel road to the right (it has a Portland General Electric Company sign and gates that are always open). Drive down this road a short distance to the dam.

For More Information: Oregon Department of Fish and Wildlife, Columbia Region and Sandy Fish Hatchery

34 Clackamas River

Key Species: Chinook salmon, coho salmon, steelhead

Best Way to Fish: boat, bank

Best Time to Fish: Chinook salmon, mid-April into July; coho salmon, September and October; steelhead, October through August

Description: Consistently one of Oregon's top salmon and steelhead rivers, the Clackamas offers fishing for spring Chinook salmon, coho salmon, and both summer and winter steelhead. The Clackamas River is a tributary of the Willamette, into which it flows at Clackamette Park in Oregon City, just south of Portland.

Spring Chinook are in the river beginning in mid-April, peaking in late May or early June, and continuing into July. Coho are available here for anglers in September and October. There are three separate stocks of winter steelhead in the Clackamas: Big Creek stock that enters the river beginning in late October or early November, Eagle Creek stock that shows up in mid-November or early December, and Clackamas stock that arrives in late December into January. The winter run lasts through April. The summer steelhead run gets going in May and lasts through August. Because the timing of the summer and winter steelhead runs butt against each other, steelheaders have an 11-month fishing window on the Clackamas.

Boat and bank access is very good along the lower approximately 20-mile reach from Milo McIver State Park down to the mouth. The river is closed to angling above North Fork Dam. There are a number of angling restrictions, including certain bait-fishing limitations, so be sure and study the most current angling regulations before heading out to the Clackamas.

Fishing Index: Anglers target Chinook salmon from either the bank or by drifting. The primary drifts on the Clackamas are from Feldheimer Ramp (a gravel, undeveloped boat launch) to Barton Park, Barton County Park to Carver boat ramp, Carver boat ramp to Riverside Park, and Riverside Park down to the mouth at Clackamette Park. A popular bank fishing area is High Rock Park in Gladstone, on the lower river. The best bank access is at Milo McIver State Park, an extensive stretch of public land along the west side of the river just west of Estacada. For drift boaters, back-bouncing eggs, shrimp, and Wiggle Warts are popular, effective salmon-getting strategies. Most bank fishers drift roe or sand shrimp under a bobber, or drift jigs.

The coho run is very weather dependent, requiring good rains to send them upriver, on their way to the hatchery on Eagle Creek. For this reason, Bonnie Lure State Recreation Area, where Eagle Creek flows into the Clackamas is a good bank fishing spot. Some people also drift fish for coho from Barton County Park on down. Drifting with roe is generally the most effective coho fishing technique here. While the bulk of the coho are hatchery fish, there are some wild ones as well, which must be released unharmed.

Clackamas River

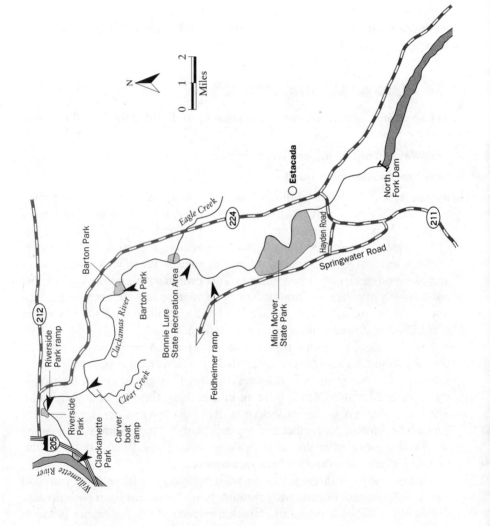

The most popular spot for summer steelhead fishing is from the bank at Milo McIver State Park, where drifting jigs, sand shrimp and roe, or casting spinners is very effective. By June the water is low enough that boating begins to get dicey, and you will mostly be fishing pocket water.

Winter steelheaders primarily drift fish—the same ones as for Chinook—or fish the lower river by jet boat using standard salmon methods. There is some bank fishing at Carver Bridge, where Clear Creek comes into the river.

Directions: The Clackamas River, along with its parks and boat launches, can be accessed via Oregon Highways 224 and 211, which parallel the river east from Interstate 205 at Clackamas. Milo McIver State Park is 4 miles west of Estacada, off Springwater Road.

For More Information: Oregon Department of Fish and Wildlife, Columbia Region Office and Milo McIver State Park

35 Lower Willamette River

Key Species: Chinook salmon, coho salmon, steelhead, American shad, sturgeon

Best Way to Fish: boat, bank

Best Time to Fish: year-round

Description: At 309 miles, the Willamette is Oregon's second longest river (after the Columbia) flowing from its headwaters in the Cascade Mountains to its confluence with the Columbia River at Portland. Although there are lots of angling and other recreational opportunities along this great Oregon waterway, the lower river is of special interest to anglers due to its varied fisheries and close proximity to urban centers. This proximity allows lots of anglers good fishing experiences without having to venture too far from home. The lower Willamette River is considered to be from Willamette Falls at Oregon City, 25 miles downstream to the river's mouth.

Spring Chinook salmon, the most sought-after fish here, average 10 to 15 pounds, although they often reach 20 to 25 pounds, and it is possible to occasionally catch one in the 40-plus-pound range. They generally begin entering the river in March or April, peaking in mid-April through mid-May. Coho salmon, which go up the Clackamas River to spawn, are around from September through November and typically weigh 4 to 6 pounds. Also, some steelhead are located in the lower Willamette, and since there are both summer and winter runs they are here year-round.

Another popular target for lower Willamette anglers is the American shad run, which happens in early May through June. These feisty gamefish average 1½ to 3½ pounds for males and females, respectively. Sturgeon are found in the river throughout the year and typically grow from 1½ to 6 feet long. There is also a "whatever is biting" fishery popular with more casual anglers who are not out to catch any particular species of fish. The variety of fish

The lower Willamette's proximity to urban areas make it a great option for anglers not wanting to travel far from home.

available in this category includes largemouth and smallmouth bass, bluegill, crappie, and walleye.

The spring Chinook fishery is tightly controlled by the Oregon Department of Fish and Wildlife through a catch quota system. The size of each year's runs are estimated by state fish biologists, and a maximum allowable catch for the year is established. When that quota is reached, fishing for spring Chinook on the river is closed. Make sure you are aware of the current quota situation before planning a Willamette River spring Chinook fishing outing.

There are lots of public boat launches along this section of the river, as well as a few areas of good bank access.

Fishing Index: Willamette River spring Chinook salmon are generally pursued by anchored boat or by trolling. Spinners, shrimp, eggs, and plugs such as Flatfish and Kwikfish—are all standard Chinook salmon techniques employed. Angling from an anchored boat is more common just below Willamette Falls, while in the lower reaches closer to Portland and in Multnomah Channel, trolling herring is the favored method. Some other areas to concentrate Chinook fishing include the mouth of the Clackamas River, in the Milwaukie area, and around the Sellwood Bridge in Portland. While Chinook fishing on this river is best from a boat, there is good public bank access in Oregon City at Clackamette Park and downstream about 0.5 mile to Meldrum Bar Park. Clackamette Park is at the confluence of the Clackamas and Willamette Rivers.

Lower Willamette River

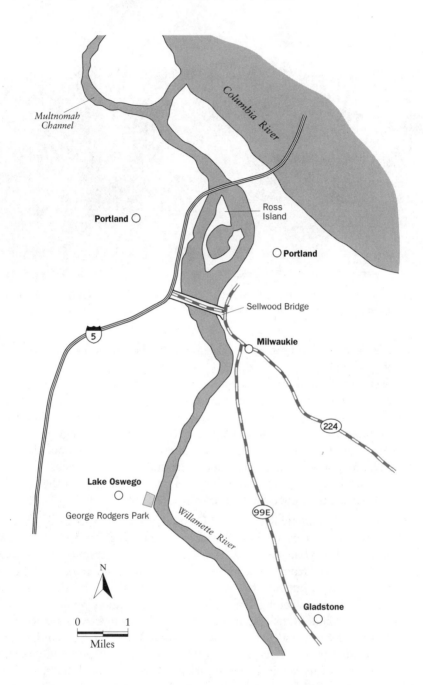

Lower Willamette River

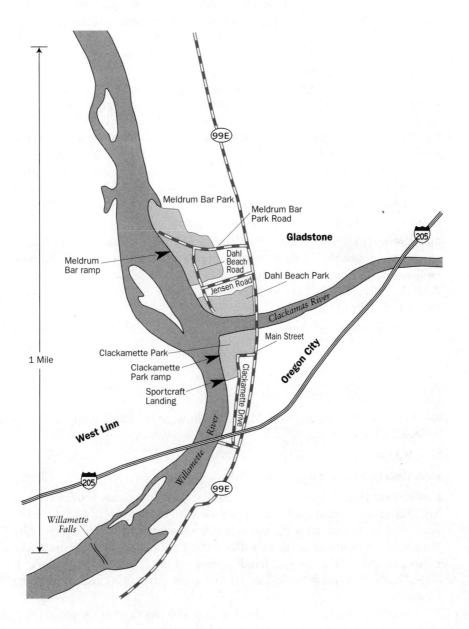

The park is also a good place to bank fish for steelhead, typically from October to December or January by drifting Corkies and Spin 'n Glos. Steelhead will fish well up to the deadline at Willamette Falls (by boat) through June, until the water begins to get too warm and the bite slacks off. Clackamette Park is also a good location to bank fish for coho salmon as the fish are migrating up the Clackamas River to spawn.

Use shad darts and small spinners with a light-to-medium weight spinning outfit for shad below Willamette Falls from an anchored boat, or off the bank by the sea wall near the falls on the east side of the river. The mouth of the Clackamas at Clackamette Park is also a good bank shad fishing location. For sturgeon, fish on the bottom with bait off the sea wall in Oregon City.

If you are interested in some of the miscellaneous warmwater species here, try a variety of bait and lures anywhere throughout the Multnomah Channel and where the outlet of Lake Oswego empties into the Willamette at George Rodgers Park in the city of Lake Oswego.

Directions: The lower Willamette River is accessible via a variety of local roads throughout the Portland metropolitan area. There are two public boat ramps around the mouth of the Clackamas River below Willamette Falls. Both the falls and Clackamette Park are accessible in Oregon City right off Oregon Highway 99E.

For More Information: Oregon Department of Fish and Wildlife, Columbia Region Office

36 Henry Hagg Lake

Key Species: smallmouth bass, bluegill, yellow perch, black crappie, brown bullhead, rainbow trout

Best Way to Fish: bank, boat

Best Time to Fish: spring, summer, fall

Description: Henry Hagg Lake is a 1,200-acre reservoir that provides excellent fishing opportunities for a variety of fish species. Constructed by the Bureau of Reclamation for irrigation and flood control, it is now operated by Washington County as Scoggins Valley Park. Park facilities include two boat ramps, several picnic areas, a handicapped fishing dock, and a network of hiking trails. A day use fee is charged to use the park. It is closed during the winter.

The lake averages 51 feet in depth and is 110 feet deep at its maximum.

The Oregon Department of Fish and Wildlife stocks the reservoir with rainbow trout along with excess steelhead fingerlings. The rainbows average about 12 inches, although they may reach as high as 6 or 7 pounds. Smallmouth bass average 4 to 6 pounds and are a prime quarry for anglers here. Brown bullhead average around 1 foot long.

Henry Hagg Lake is open to angling from April 22 through October 31.

Henry Hagg Lake

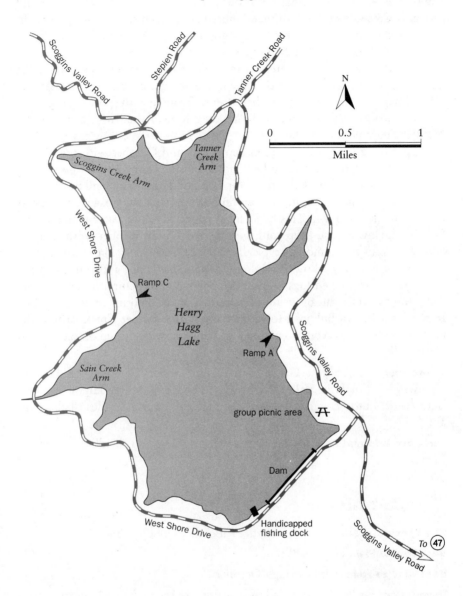

Fishing Index: April and May find the best angling for trout near the shoreline on the reservoir's northern portion, particularly in the Tanner Creek and Scoggins Creek arms. The southern shoreline between the handicapped fishing dock and the group picnic area is good as well. Effective baits for trout here include Power Bait, nightcrawlers, and salmon eggs.

As summer arrives, the water warms and the water level drops, forcing the trout into the deeper center of the lake and making a boat a necessity. At this time of year, you will need to fish bait deeper. Trolling with spoons, plugs, and bait also works well. Trolling with Wedding Rings baited with a worm and Needlefish are popular techniques.

Bass fishing tends to be best in September and October with the Tanner Creek and Sain Creek arms good locations to fish. Fishing by boat just off the dam on the south end of the reservoir is a good area for smallmouth bass. During the summer, though, you can find bass in shallow areas near shore as they get ready to spawn. This behavior is triggered when water temperatures fall into the low 60s, so keep your thermometer handy. Rubber worms, nightcrawlers, crankbaits, and jigs typically catch bass at Henry Hagg Lake.

Fish for bluegill, yellow perch, and crappie, using jigs and spinners, anywhere there are sunken logs and other underwater structure. It can be especially fun to catch bluegill using earthworms or mealworms under a bobber. If you want brown bullhead for dinner, check out Tanner Creek Arm at the north end of the reservoir. Power Bait and nightcrawlers fished on the bottom work well.

Directions: From Forest Grove, drive south about 2.5 miles on Oregon Highway 47 (Tualatin Valley Highway) to Scoggins Valley Highway. Turn right (west) onto Scoggins Valley Road and go about 3.8 miles to the park and lake.

For More Information: Oregon Department of Fish and Wildlife, Columbia Region Office

37 Detroit Lake

Key Species: rainbow trout, kokanee salmon, Chinook salmon

Best Way to Fish: boat, bank

Best Time to Fish: April through October

Description: Originally intended as a water storage and flood control reservoir when it went into operation in 1953, Detroit Lake has since became one of western Oregon's most popular recreational reservoirs. Formed by the damming of the North Fork Santiam River, Detroit Lake is 3,580 acres in size. Its average depth is 121 feet. The deepest section of the lake is nearly 450 feet.

Trout and salmon are the focus for anglers here as the lake harbors very good populations of rainbow trout, kokanee salmon, and Chinook salmon.

Detroit Lake

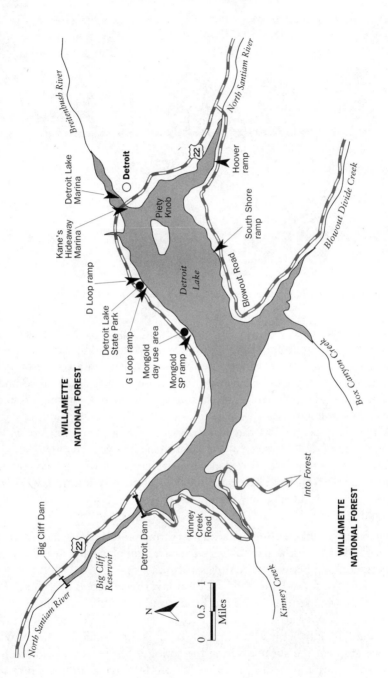

Kokanee salmon draw many anglers to Oregon's deep, coldwater lakes.

The state stocks both legal-sized (10 inches and larger) and fingerling trout. Average rainbow trout are in the 10- to 13-inch range, while carryovers—fish that survive through the season to the following year—run a couple of inches larger. Kokanee here typically run in the 10- to 14-inch range, as do the Chinook salmon. A few Chinook here top out at around 30 inches, although fish that size are not common.

While many people fish this reservoir from a boat, bank anglers will do just fine here as well. Detroit Lake is open to angling year-round.

Ample boat ramps are located along the reservoir as well as two commercial marinas (Detroit Lake Marina and Kane's Hideaway Marina), where you can purchase bait, tackle, and rent boats. There are also two state parks—Mongold Day Use Area and Detroit Lake State Park.

Fishing Index: Rainbow trout are scattered throughout the lake and fishing for them with bait from the bank is very effective. Popular baits here are nightcrawlers, corn, and Power Bait. You can also cast spinners and spoons as well. Krocodile spoons and Bang Tails are local favorites. A good overall rainbow trout trolling rig used here is a Ford Fender and a Kwikfish or Hot Shot.

There are lots of kokanee in the lake, but anglers don't catch as many as they should, mainly because most people often fail to fish deep enough. While kokanee are near the surface during the spring when the water is cooler, by summer you need to get your rig to the 80- or 100-foot depth to connect with them. Trolling Ford Fenders with a Wedding Ring or Needlefish is a good kokanee rig. You can also jig with Nordics or Crippled Herrings.

For Chinook salmon, cast or troll spinners and spoons just off the dam. Chinook fishing is usually best in April and May.

There are also some brown bullhead here. They tend to be in the northern end of the reservoir where it is shallower. Fish for them on the bottom with worms or shrimp.

Favorite locations for bank-bound anglers are around the reservoir's various inlets including near the Breitenbush River, North Santiam River, and Blowout Divide Creek. Anglers can also find shelter on windy days—a common occurrence here—by going up these arms. Even through the lake is open to angling all year, and fishing is generally pretty good during the winter months, most don't fish here from January through March because of typically harsh weather conditions.

Directions: To reach Detroit Lake from Salem, drive east on U.S. Highway 22 for about 50 miles.

For More Information: Oregon Department of Fish and Wildlife, Salem District Office and Detroit Lake State Park

38 North Santiam River

Key Species: Chinook salmon, steelhead

Best Way to Fish: boat, bank

Best Time to Fish: Chinook salmon, late April through early July; steelhead, February through August

Description: This picturesque stream plunges out of the central Cascade Mountains, through forest and farmland joining with the south fork to form the short mainstem Santiam River, which then flows into the Willamette River.

Runs of spring Chinook, along with winter and summer, steelhead are the attractions for anglers. Spring Chinook are in the river from late April through early July, peaking in May. Winter steelhead are here from February through May, peaking in March, while the summer run shows up in April, running through August. The summer fish peak is in May and June.

There are some bait restrictions as well as closed areas on this stream, so be sure and check the current angling regulations before beginning your trip.

Fishing Index: For both Chinook and steelhead, the river upstream from Stayton is best. Good drifts include from Mehama Bridge boat launch to Stayton Bridge boat launch, Fishermans Bend boat launch to Mehama Bridge, and the boat launch at Packsaddle Park to Mill City, or on to Fisherman's Bend. Bank anglers can find public access at parks and campgrounds upstream from Mehama as well as at turn-outs along the highway.

Typical salmon and steelhead angling techniques are employed here including drifting bait such as eggs and shrimp and, Corkies, back-bouncing

North Santiam River • South Santiam River

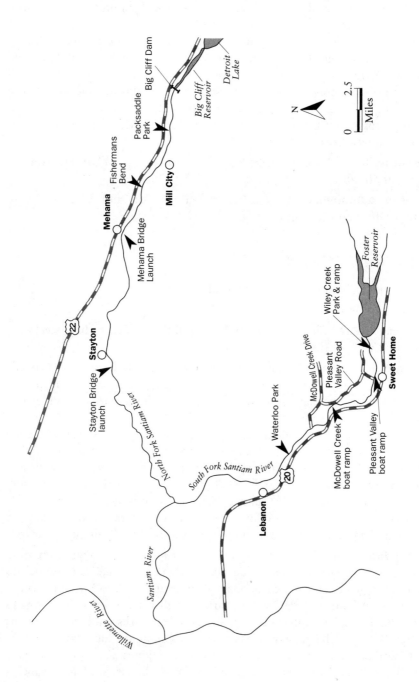

bait, and back-drifting Flatfish and Kwikfish. Bank anglers drift bait as well, or cast spinners. For Chinook, concentrate especially in deep pools.

There are also some rainbow and cutthroat trout in the river, but since they are catch-and-release-only angling, few people fish for them.

Directions: Bank access and boat launches along the North Fork Santiam River can be reached via U.S. Highway 22 east from Salem, which parallels the river for much of its length.

For More Information: Oregon Department of Fish and Wildlife, Salem District Office

39 South Santiam River

Key Species: Chinook salmon, steelhead

Best Way to Fish: boat, bank

Best Time to Fish: Chinook salmon, late April through early July; steelhead, April through summer

Description: Similar to the North Fork Santiam, this pretty mountain stream tumbles out of the Cascade Range, before joining the short Santiam River mainstem.

The South Fork has runs of Chinook salmon and summer steelhead, but unlike the North Fork, no winter steelhead runs. Spring Chinook are in the river from late April through early July, peaking in May. Steelhead are here from April through the summer, peaking in May and June. Chinook salmon tend to run in the 15- to 25-pound range on this stream, while steelhead average 8 to 14 pounds.

There are some bait restrictions on this fork, so be sure and check the current angling regulations before beginning your trip.

Fishing Index: There is good bank access for both Chinook and steelhead anglers around Sweet Home and Foster Dam. Waterloo Park is another good bank fishing location. For drift boaters, typical floats are from the boat launch at Foster Dam down to Pleasant Valley boat ramp, and from Pleasant Valley to McDowell Creek boat ramp or on to Waterloo Park.

For boaters, drifting bait such as eggs and shrimp and, Corkies, back-bouncing bait, and back-drifting Flatfish and Kwikfish are the typical techniques. If you are fishing from the bank, try drifting bait as well, or cast spinners.

Directions: Sweet Home and Foster Dam are located about 15 miles east of Lebanon off U.S. Highway 20. Waterloo Park is just north of US 20, about 5 miles east of Lebanon.

For More Information: Oregon Department of Fish and Wildlife, Salem District Office

40 McKenzie River

Key Species: rainbow trout, cutthroat trout, steelhead

Best Way to Fish: boat, bank

Best Time to Fish: rainbow trout, April through October; steelhead, late April through fall

Description: A beautiful, crystal-clear river, the McKenzie flows through a rugged forest canyon in its upper reaches, past small forest communities, then meanders along gentle pasture and farmlands before joining the Willamette River in Eugene.

The upper river is especially popular with trout anglers. There is, however, an excellent trout fishery on the lower river as well. Below Leaburg Dam, summer steelhead provide good angling from late April through the fall. The run typically peaks around the end of June and into July, with an additional peak later in the year when the first good fall rains send another spurt of fish upriver. Summer steelhead are not native to the McKenzie. The Oregon Department of Fish and Wildlife established this run in 1972 by stocking the river with hatchery-raised smolts. Since that time it has become an important and popular steelhead fishery.

Spring Chinook and bull trout are also present in the McKenzie River. However, angling for these species is not allowed.

There are nearly 20 public boat ramps along the river. That, combined with National Forest lands and a number of county and city parks makes angling access to the McKenzie pretty good.

The McKenzie has a variety of angling regulations and open seasons, depending on what sections of the river you are fishing, so be sure and check the current rules before heading out.

Fishing Index: There is a very large wild trout fishery in the lower river. From Leaburg Dam down to Bellinger Landing—a county boat ramp just west of Walterville—you will find mainly rainbow trout, along with a few cutthroats. From Bellinger Landing to the mouth, it is mostly cutthroats with some rainbows thrown in. The rainbows along this stretch average around 15 inches, with occasional fish up to 18 or 19 inches. The cutthroats run around 9 to 12 inches. The lower portion of this section is catch-and-release, artificial flies and lures only year-round, while the upper portion is catch-and-release artificial flies and lures only for part of the year. See the current regulations for details.

Anglers float this stretch by driftboat, or gain bank access on city parklands in the Springfield and Eugene areas. A good access point is off Deerhorn Road, across the bridge just west of Walterville.

The most heavily fished section of the McKenzie is above the town of Blue River for rainbow trout. Much of this upper section flows through Bureau of Land Management and USDA Forest Service lands, so there is

McKenzie River

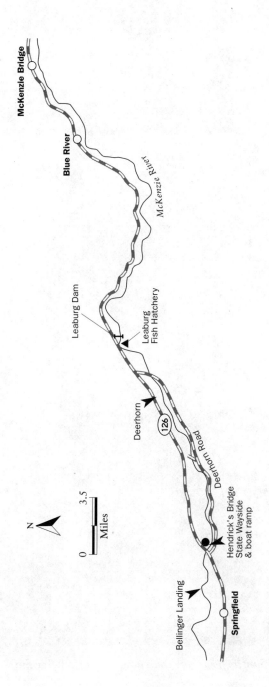

A McKenzie River fly fisherman concentrates on a drag-free drift.

excellent public access. This upper section is catch-and-release only for wild fish and restricted to artificial flies and lures.

The McKenzie River has outstanding fly fishing water, with lots of riffles, pools, tailouts, eddies, and seams to explore with a dry fly or nymph. Some good McKenzie River fly patterns include Humpys, Royal Wulffs, Adams, Elk-hair Caddis, and Pale Morning Duns. For nymphs, try Woolly Buggers, Pheasant Tails, and Hare's Ears. Although spinners, spoons and other, lures are allowed, you will find most trout anglers here fly fishing.

When the summer steelhead make their spawning migration up the McKenzie River beginning in late April, they are headed for the Leaburg Hatchery from which they were released. For this reason, most of the steelhead fishing here takes place along the few miles of river just below the hatchery, although they can also be caught farther downstream as they make their way upriver. There is good bank access along this stretch. Gear anglers drift Corkies, Spin 'n Glos, shrimp and eggs, and cast spinners. Fly anglers cover the water thoroughly with Babine Specials, Woolly Worms, Purple Perils, and other classic steelhead flies.

Directions: To reach the Deerhorn Road access area drive about 6 miles east from Springfield on Oregon Highway 126. Immediately before crossing the bridge, turn right onto Deerhorn Road. There is a boat ramp and bank access at Hendrick's Bridge State Wayside on the right, just east of the bridge. To reach the Leaburg Fish Hatchery dive east from Springfield on OR 126 for 17 miles. Turn right into the hatchery, at the sign for EWEB Water Board Park, immediately after crossing the bridge over the McKenzie River. To reach the Blue River area and the upper river, continue east on OR 126 past the hatchery for another 20 miles.

For More Information: Oregon Department of Fish and Wildlife, Springfield District Office and Willamette National Forest

41 Middle Fork of the Willamette River

Key Species: rainbow trout, cutthroat trout

Best Way to Fish: bank, wading, boat

Best Time to Fish: May through September

Description: This nice stretch of river between Lookout Point Reservoir and Hills Creek Reservoir is a great little wild rainbow and cutthroat trout stream. It flows through mostly National Forest Lands, and is paralleled by Oregon Highway 58, so public access is outstanding.

While most of the rainbows and cutthroats you will catch here will be in the 10-, 12-, or 14-inch range, some may approach 30 inches. This 12-mile reach of the Middle Fork Willamette is catch-and-release, artificial flies and lures only.

Middle Fork of the Willamette River

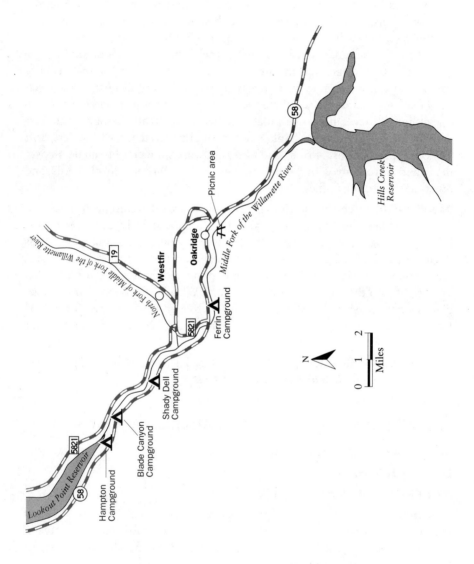

Fishing Index: You can fish here from the bank, wade, or drift in a boat or raft. With so much public access, the best bet is to drive along OR 58 and stop at various USDA Forest Service campgrounds and day use areas to check out the water, then fish whatever looks good to you.

There are very nice hatches of caddis here, along with mayflies and stoneflies. Fly fishing on this fork of the Willamette is especially good from May through early June.

Directions: From Springfield, drive about 25 miles east on Oregon Highway 58 to reach the lower end of this river segment. Continue another 6 miles, through the town of Oakridge, to reach Hills Creek Reservoir, and the upper limit of this reach. Along the way you will pass well-marked campgrounds and other public access points.

For More Information: Oregon Department of Fish and Wildlife, Springfield District Office and Willamette National Forest

Central Oregon

Sunny central Oregon attracts loads of vacationers each year, and more than a few of these people come specifically for the fishing. Trout are the featured fish here—giant rainbows, huge lake trout, monster brown trout in the high mountain lakes, and small, elegant beauties in crystal-clear flowing mountain streams. But there are warmwater fishing opportunities as well. Add to that selection the presence of the Deschutes River, among the best steelhead rivers in the state, and you have got a place that will keep the most demanding angler pretty busy.

In addition to the variety of fish and waters to be experienced here, there is also room enough for aficionados of different angling techniques. Lure and bait anglers often head for the reservoirs and lakes while fly anglers prowl local rivers (along with a few selected local lakes). Central Oregon also offers a unique fishing experience in the form of the landlocked Atlantic salmon available at Hosmer and East Lakes. Another signature central Oregon fish is the kokanee salmon, found in deep, cold lakes throughout the region.

Regulations for the waters listed in this section will be found in the Central Oregon Zone section of the *Oregon Sport Fishing Regulations* handbook.

42 Hood River

Key Species: steelhead

Best Way to Fish: bank

Best Time to Fish: February through July

Description: This steep-gradient glacial-fed river tumbles out of the Mount Hood National Forest, and flows into the Columbia River at the city of Hood River.

The Hood River has nice runs of both summer and winter steelhead. The summer run goes from April through early July and the winter run from February through April or May. Because of this overlap in run timing, the Hood River offers steelheaders a six-month unbroken stretch of angling opportunity.

A spring Chinook run has been introduced here and the first returns, in 1990, were excellent. Since then, the run size has been weak. Occasionally, during good run-sized years, a limited fishery for spring Chinook is allowed. Check current regulations. Spring Chinook return to the Hood River in May and June. You will also find some coho in the river during the fall. These fish are strays from other streams and are generally very late into their spawning cycle by the time they get here and completely beyond the point of being of any interest to angers.

The Hood River is open to steelhead fishing all year, but there are bait restrictions relating to hook size on the lower 4 miles of the river. Upstream, angling is restricted to flies and lures only.

An angler and his scrappy Hosmer Lake landlocked Atlantic salmon. This fish fell for a Woolly Bugger trolled behind the canoe.

Hood River

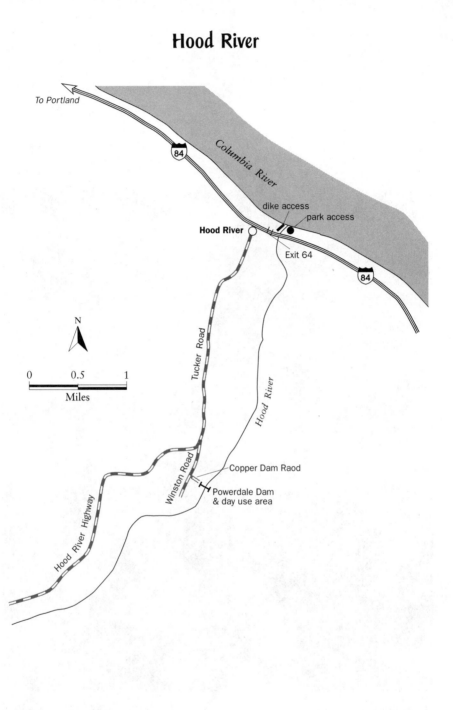

Fishing Index: Steelhead fishing takes place on the 4 lower miles of river from the Powerdale Dam to the mouth. Access is basically at the dam and at the river mouth. The dam's owners, Pacific Power, allow anglers to trespass on their property for fishing.

While there is a growing contingent of fly fishers here, most steelhead anglers drift shrimp and eggs from the bank.

Because two of the Hood River's three main tributaries send it glacial melt and debris, the river can muddy up and become unfishable very quickly anytime between mid-June and October, and even as early as April. It is a good idea to check out current river conditions before heading out.

Directions: Bank access at the mouth may be reached via the Hood River exit off Interstate 84 (exit 64, about 50 miles east of Portland). There is a county park on the east side of the river mouth and dike which parallels the river on the west side of the mouth. To reach Powerdale Dam and day use area, drive south from Hood River on Tucker Road about 1.5 miles, bearing right onto Winston Road. Go about 0.5 mile, then turn left onto Copper Dam Road. Follow this a short distance to the dam.

For More Information: Oregon Department of Fish and Wildlife, The Dalles District Office

43 Lower Deschutes River

Key Species: steelhead, rainbow trout

Best Way to Fish: bank, wading

Best Time to Fish: steelhead, August through December; rainbow trout, May through October

Description: For its lower 100 miles—from the lowermost dam of the Pelton-Round Butte hydroelectric project to where it flows into the Columbia River near Moody—the Deschutes River meanders through spectacular canyon and high desert country, making it one of the state's most striking waterways. Because the dam releases a steady flow of 50-degree-F water, the lower Deschutes is essentially one long tailwater fishery supporting an outstanding population of rainbow trout, known as Deschutes redsides, along with a fine run of summer steelhead.

Resident rainbow trout are, of course, in the river all year while the steelhead run generally begins in mid-July near the mouth, with fish still in the river in February. The peak is usually around the last two weeks of September.

A typical Deschutes River redside is 13 to 15 inches with large ones up to 18 inches. You'll find few trout here over 20 inches. There are two basic types of steelhead here—those that spend one year in the ocean before returning to the river, known as one salts, and those that spend two years called two salts. One salts average 5 to 6 pounds, while two salters run 7 to 10 pounds. Occasionally fish up to 20 pounds are caught. These are generally stray fish

Lower Deschutes River

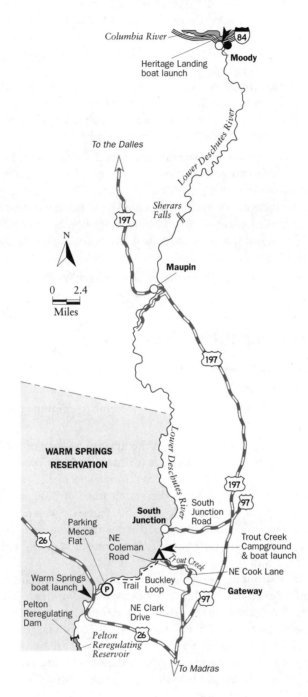

Columbia River

Heritage Landing
boat launch

Moody

84

Lower Deschutes River

To the Dalles

Sherars
Falls

197

N

0   2.4
Miles

Maupin

197

WARM SPRINGS
RESERVATION

197

97

Lower Deschutes River

South
Junction

South
Junction
Road

Parking
Mecca
Flat

NE
Coleman
Road

26

Trout Creek
Campground
& boat launch

Trout Creek

NE Cook Lane

Warm Springs
boat launch

P   Trail   Buckley
Loop

97   Gateway

Pelton
Reregulating
Dam

NE Clark
Drive

Pelton
Reregulating
Reservoir

26

To Madras

The Deschutes River is a nationally known stream, boasting over 2,000 eight-inch-plus rainbow trout per mile.

that should be returning to Idaho streams but have inadvertently wandered into the Deschutes River.

While the steelhead and rainbow trout fishery is the Deschutes' claim to fame, there are also small runs of fall and spring Chinook salmon here. During years with relatively strong runs, limited angling is permitted. These seasons are held irregularly.

With excellent bank and boat access, the Deschutes gets heavy use by both anglers and whitewater boaters and rafters. During the summer months, portions of the river can become quite crowded, particularly on weekends.

In general, the Deschutes River from the Pelton Reregulating Dam, at about river mile 101, to the northern edge of the Warm Springs Indian Reservation is open from late April to the end of October for trout, and through the end of the year for steelhead. It is open for steelhead and trout fishing all year from that point down to the mouth. About 31 miles of the river runs along the Reservation. Anglers are also restricted to the eastern side of the river on this segment—with some exceptions. Anglers may fish the reservation side of the river on the 6-mile section from Dry Creek to Trout Creek. A tribal fishing permit is required. They cost $6.25 and are available at local fishing shops.

With the exception of a 3-mile stretch below Sherars Falls where bait is permitted, the entire lower river is restricted to artificial flies and lures only. Also, no angling is allowed from a boat or other floating device. Be sure to consult the current angling regulations before fishing on the Deschutes River.

Fishing Index: Because the cold water released by the upstream dams is good for trout, the trout population is higher closer to the dam and drops as you move downstream. In its best sections—the Maupin and Warm Springs to Trout Creek—there are something on the order of 2,000 fish, 8 inches and over, per mile. Although lures are permitted here, the vast majority of trout anglers are fly fishers. The river has excellent hatches of mayflies and caddis. A major Deschutes River event is the salmonfly hatch, which usually begins around mid-May and slowly moves upriver, lasting roughly until mid-June. The best salmonfly hatches happen above Sherars Falls. Trout gorge on these big bugs voraciously, slurping up fly fishers imitations just as readily. In addition to salmonfly patterns (when this hatch is on) other good trout patterns for this river include Elk-hair Caddis, Pale Morning Duns, March Browns, Adams, and Knock-down Duns. Hopper and other terrestrial patterns work well in the fall. Good nymph patterns include Hare's Ears, Bead Head Pheasant Tails, and Zug Bugs.

Popular bank access areas to target trout include along the gravel road running upstream from Maupin, which provides about 7 miles of access to the east side of the river, and at Mecca Flat where a public trail follows the river downstream about 8 miles to Trout Creek. There is camping both at Mecca Flat and Trout Creek. Many anglers float from the put-in at Warm Springs down to the boat launch at Trout Creek Campground, or from Trout Creek to Maupin (a float requiring more river skills than the Warm Springs-to-Trout Creek trip).

The salmon fly hatch on the Deschutes draws many anglers. The natural insects are 2 to 4 inches in length and create a feeding frenzy among the river's trout.

This salmon fly imitation, the MacSalmon Fly, is one of many fly patterns that will trick a fish during this prolific hatch.

Steelheaders target the lower 10 or 15 miles of the river as early as mid-July as the run begins to enter the mouth. By the last two weeks of September, the run is peaking at Sherars Falls, about 40 miles upstream. By late October there are good numbers of fish in the South Junction-Trout Creek-Mecca Flat areas. Although the river section bordering the Indian Reservation closes at the end of December, there are still steelhead downstream through February. Access to the lower 25 miles of river is by boat or on foot. Anglers put in at Heritage Landing boat launch at the mouth and motor upstream. You can also hike, or mountain bike up the 19-mile access road along the east side of the river as well.

Casting Wiggle Warts, Hot Shots, and a variety of spinners from the bank or while wading are typical steelheading techniques here. Fly fishing for steelhead on the Deschutes is extremely popular with Green Butt Skunks, Purple Perils, Woolly Buggers, and other stand-bys. Because it is such a big river, covering as much water as quickly and efficiently as possible with your fly or lure will greatly increase your chances of a hook-up.

During years when Chinook salmon seasons are permitted, virtually all are caught using bait below Sherars Falls. This is the only section of the lower Deschutes where bait fishing is allowed.

Directions: The Deschutes River State Recreation Area (east bank) and Heritage Landing boat launch (west bank) are located at exit 97 off Interstate 84 about

90 miles east of Portland. To reach Maupin, drive south from The Dalles on U.S. Highway 197. The access road runs along the east side of the river. To reach Mecca Flat drive north on U.S. Highway 26 from Madras for 12 miles. Turn right onto the dirt road and continue about 1.5 miles to the parking area. To get to Trout Creek Campground and boat launch drive about 2.5 miles north from Madras on US 26. Turn left at the sign for Gateway (N.E. Clark Drive). Go about 4 miles, bearing left onto Buckley Lane. Go 2 miles through Gateway, then turn right after the railroad tracks, following the signs to the campground.

For More Information: Oregon Department of Fish and Wildlife, The Dalles District Office; Bureau of Land Management, Prineville Office; The Confederated Tribes of Warm Springs

44 Middle Deschutes River

Key Species: brown trout, rainbow trout

Best Way to Fish: wading

Best Time to Fish: spring and fall

Description: This 35-mile section of the Deschutes between the city of Bend and Lake Billy Chinook is generally regarded as the middle segment of the river. It flows through a mix of sagebrush, canyon country, grasslands, and agricultural fields. In recent years homes have sprouted along once empty reaches somewhat limiting fishing access in places.

You will find both rainbow trout and brown trout along this stretch. But because of decreased water quality due to the generally higher level of human development and agriculturel compared to the upper and lower river, brown trout, which are more tolerant of degraded water conditions, are more abundant here. A typical middle Deschutes brown trout is in the 14- to 16-inch range, with 18-inchers not rare. Although not often caught, some browns here will go in excess of 10 pounds.

The middle Deschutes River is open to fishing all year, but is restricted to flies and lures only from Lake Billy Chinook upstream to Benham Falls, about 12 miles above Bend.

Fishing Index: While there are a number of public angling access areas on this river segment—including at Tumalo State Park, Cline Falls State Park, and Tetherow Crossing—among the best action is at Lower Bridge just west of Terrebonne.

Because a substantial amount of water is withdrawn from this part of the river each year from mid-April though mid-October, early spring and late fall is typically the best time to fish Lower Bridge. Just after water is pulled from the river can be good as well, as the fish temporarily bunch up in pools before scattering. There can even be decent fishing during the summer low-water months, although you will do best fishing at dawn and dusk. At other times

Middle Deschutes River

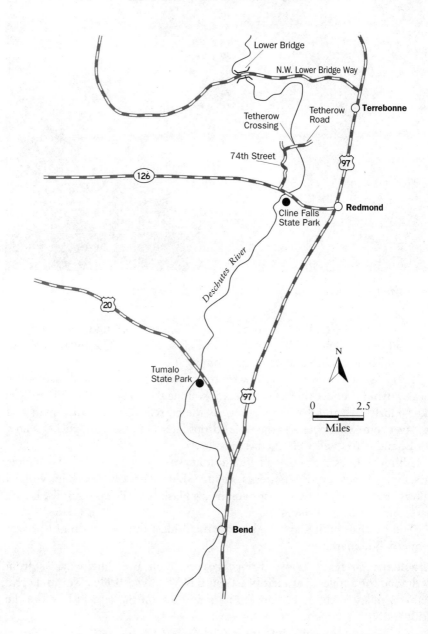

Lower Bridge
N.W. Lower Bridge Way
Terrebonne
Tetherow Crossing
Tetherow Road
74th Street
97
126
Cline Falls State Park
Redmond
Deschutes River
20
Tumalo State Park
97
N
0   2.5
Miles
Bend

An angler gently releases a Deschutes River redsides to fight again another day.

of the year the best fishing is from late morning through mid-afternoon. An especially good time to fly fish the Lower Bridge area is on warm days in March when good insect hatches are coming off.

Fish this section by wading toward the middle of the river and casting dry flies or nymphs under the dense vegetation along the banks, where big browns like to lurk. Be careful when wading, as the current can be rather swift and the river somewhat deep. As the water drops later in the season, pocket water, pools, and riffles will yield the best results.

Although lures are allowed here, most anglers opt for flies. Popular middle Deschutes River dry-fly patterns include Elk Hair Caddis, Blue-Winged Olives, and March Browns. For nymphs try Flash Back Pheasant Tails, Hare's Ears, and Beadhead Princes.

You can fish both above and below the bridge, but be mindful of private property boundaries.

Directions: To reach Lower Bridge go north on U.S. Highway 97 from Redmond for 5 miles. Turn left (west) onto N.W. Lower Bridge Way and drive about 6 miles to the river and the parking area on the left, just before the bridge.

For More Information: The Fly Fisher's Place

45 Upper Deschutes River

Key Species: rainbow trout, brown trout, brook trout

Best Way to Fish: wading, bank, boat

Best Time to Fish: spring, summer, and fall

Description: The 80 miles of river from Bend upstream to its headwaters at Lava Lake deep in the Cascade Mountains make up the upper Deschutes. From thundering waterfalls to narrow headwaters, the river here offers trout fishing in a mountain setting at its finest. And because the bulk of this section of the river flows through the Deschutes National Forest, public angling access is easy to come by.

While many of the big trout from Crane Prairie and Wickiup Reservoirs spawn here, the river has an excellent population of resident trout in its own right. Anglers will find rainbow trout and brook trout in the uppermost reaches above Crane Prairie Reservoir, and a mix of rainbows and browns below Wickiup. The river is dominated by brown trout from Wickiup Reservoir to Benham Falls, with the preponderance of trout switching to rainbows below the falls.

Brown trout grow up to several pounds on this stretch of river while rainbows average 10 or 11 inches, although larger fish are not uncommon. The brook trout in the upper reaches tend to be small, often only 4, 5 and 6 inches long.

Fishing with bait is allowed between Benham Falls and Wickiup Reservoir, but all wild rainbow trout must be released unharmed. This stretch is open from April 22 through September 30. The section above Crane Prairie Reservoir is open from June 1 through September 30 and is restricted to flies and lures only. All rainbow trout must be released.

Depending on the depth of the winter snowpack, some parts of the upper Deschutes may not be accessible until later in the spring or even early summer.

Fishing Index: Probably the most popular section of the upper Deschutes for anglers is from Wickiup Reservoir down to Benham Falls, with the first 16 or so miles providing the best public access. Private property becomes more predominant downstream, through the resort community of Sunriver. Although bank fishing has been the traditional approach on this stretch, anglers are increasingly fishing it by boat. Except for Pringle Falls and the Tetherow log jam—which present impassable barriers to the boater—the river is a nice, low gradient float. There are four boat launches on this stretch and a fifth just above La Pine State Park. One of the most common float trips is from the Tenino Boating Site just downstream from Wickiup Reservoir to the take-out at Wyeth Campground above Pringle Falls—about a 7-mile drift. Another popular float is from Tetherow log jam boat launch to the Big River Campground take-out, a distance of about 14 miles. You can also float down to the launch at Harper Bridge, where County Road 40 crosses the Deschutes by Sunriver.

Upper Deschutes River

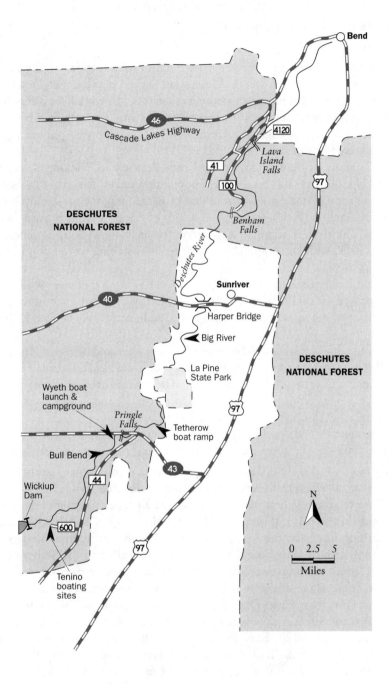

Upper Deschutes River

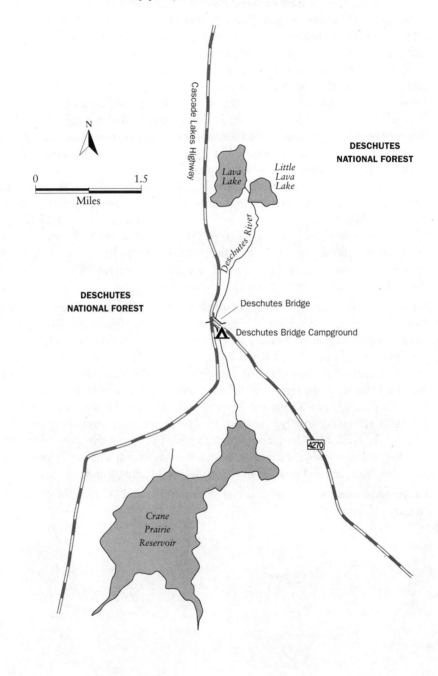

N

0   1.5

Miles

Cascade Lakes Highway

DESCHUTES
NATIONAL FOREST

Lava
Lake

Little
Lava
Lake

Deschutes River

DESCHUTES
NATIONAL FOREST

Deschutes Bridge

Deschutes Bridge Campground

4270

Crane
Prairie
Reservoir

The Deschutes also flows for about 7 miles through a section of the Deschutes National Forest between Benham Falls and Lava Island Falls, with good access via Forest Service Roads. Most of this stretch is made up waterfalls and rapids, but there is some good fishing to be had by walking the bank and picking and choosing good-looking pools and eddies.

Anglers use spinners such as Rooster Tails and Mepps with good success here, as well as the old standby—worms. Crawfish is another popular bait. Larger minnow-imitating lures offer the possibility of hooking into a big brown on the section above Benham Falls. For flies, just about any of the classics will work. Try Blue-winged Olives, Adams, Elk Hair Caddis, March Browns, and Pale Morning Duns. For nymph patterns go with Hare's Ears, Pheasant Tails, and Serendipities for starters.

If you like small-stream fishing for brook trout, the upper Deschutes can provide that, too. One of the best access points to the upper river is at Deschutes Bridge, located at the junction of the Cascade Lakes Highway (County Road 46) and Forest Road 4270. There is a USDA Forest Service campground along the river at this junction. From here you can walk upstream or downstream and cast small dry flies beneath the pines and firs for the swarms of small brook trout that thrive here.

Directions: To reach the Tenino Boating Site below Wickiup Dam go south from Bend on U.S. Highway 97 for about 24 miles. Turn right (west) onto County Road 43 and go 9 miles. Just before crossing the river at Pringle Falls, turn left (south) onto Forest Road 44 and drive about 6 miles. The turnoff to the boat ramp is on the right. You can also find bank access to the river along this road. To reach the river below Benham Falls drive west from Bend on the Cascade Lakes Highway for 6 miles and turn left onto FR 41. Bear left onto FR 4120, which eventually turns into FR 100. These roads run along the west bank of the river, affording many spots to park and access the water. To reach Deschutes Bridge go west from Bend on CR 46 (Cascade Lakes Highway) for 38 miles. Turn left at FR 4270 to the bridge and campground.

For More Information: Oregon Department of Fish and Wildlife, High Desert Region Office

46 Lake Billy Chinook

Key Species: rainbow trout, bull trout, brown trout, kokanee, smallmouth bass

Best Way to Fish: boat

Best Time to Fish: spring, summer, and fall

Description: Lake Billy Chinook is formed by Round Butte Dam on the Deschutes River, which backs up the Deschutes, Crooked, and Metolius Rivers. The resulting 4,000-acre reservoir has 60 miles of shoreline and is up to 400 feet deep in places. A portion of the reservoir is located within The Cove Palisades State Park, making it a very popular destination for anglers, water skiers, campers, and other outdoor recreationists.

Because the shoreline along much of the reservoir is steep and rugged, there are few places to fish from the bank. The best bet is a boat with a motor.

Lake Billy Chinook is open to fishing year-round, although few people visit the lake in the winter. The Metolius River Arm is open from March 1 to October 31. Since much of this arm is located on the Warm Springs Indian Reservation, a tribal fishing permit is required to fish on this stretch. They cost $6.25 and are available at sporting goods shops throughout the area.

With the presence of the state park, this area is well developed with many recreational amenities including campgrounds, day use areas, and boat ramps. Boats can be rented at the Cove Marina.

Fishing Index: Kokanee salmon, which run around 13 inches or so, are a prime draw for anglers. Spring and fall is the best time to pursue these land-locked sockeye salmon when they tend to be in shallower water. The upper end of the Metolius Arm holds the best numbers of kokanee year-round, with the Deschutes Arm taking second place. Trolling with Ford Fenders and Wedding Rings and white corn is the most used technique. Throughout the summer, kokanee tend to be at 40- to 100-foot depths as they pursue plankton, their food source. Jigging with Buzz Bombs and Nordics and white corn can be highly effective in the fall as the kokanee begin to gather in the upper Metolius Arm in anticipation of the spawning run.

Bull trout are scattered throughout the reservoir in March and April. At this time, you are more likely to hook into one in the lower part of the reservoir and around the dam. As the season progresses they begin to concentrate in the Metolius Arm. Large Rapalas are the lure of choice for trout that average 10 to 15 pounds but may go over 20 pounds. The state record bull trout, weighing in at 23 pounds, 2 ounces, was caught in Lake Billy Chinook in 1989.

For rainbow trout and brown trout, fish any of the arms. Trout are widely scattered throughout the reservoir. Nighcrawlers under a bobber, or casting or trolling Rooster Tails works well. The rainbow and brown trout in Lake Billy Chinook are typically about a foot long.

Fish the same areas for smallmouth bass, with an eye toward rocky locations or any other in-water structures. Although fishing for smallmouth is

Lake Billy Chinook

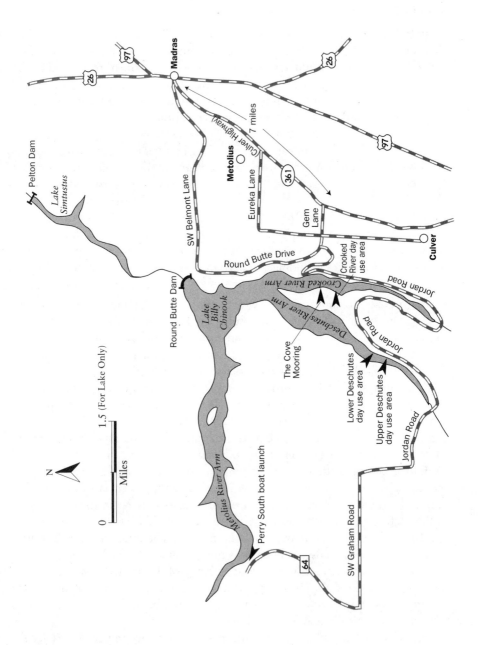

pretty good throughout the season, April and May seem to be the best months. A variety of lures and plugs will yield bass.

Smallmouth bass here tend to average around 10 or 11 inches, and most bass anglers practice catch-and-release. There are also some largemouth bass and crappie in Lake Billy Chinook, but there are so few of them they are not really a viable fishery.

Directions: From Madras go south on the Culver Highway (Oregon Highway 361) for about 7.5 miles to Gem Lane. Turn right (west) and follow Gem Lane past Feather Drive to Jordan Road, which leads to The Cove Palisades State Park and the lake.

For More Information: Oregon Department of Fish and Wildlife, Prineville District Office and The Cove Palisades State Park

47 Ochoco Reservoir

Key Species: rainbow trout, black crappie

Best Way to Fish: bank, boat

Best Time to Fish: year-round

Description: Ochoco Reservoir is an irrigation reservoir whose water level can vary greatly over the course of the year, depending on how much water is being diverted to local croplands. At its largest, it reaches up to 1,100 acres or so in surface area.

Rainbow trout are the attraction here. They average around 12 or 13 inches and they're stocked regularly by the state. There is also a growing population of black crappie.

Ochoco Lake Park, administered by Crook County, is located on the north shore of the reservoir and features camping. There are also two boat ramps on the reservoir.

Ochoco Reservoir is open to angling year-round and is a popular ice fishing location when winter temperatures freeze the reservoir's surface to a safe thickness.

Fishing Index: Bait and lures are the primary tactics to use at Ochoco Reservoir. For baits, anglers here (including ice fishers) have success with Velveeta, salmon eggs, Power Bait, and nightcrawlers fished off the bottom with a weight. The typical complement of trout spinners such as Panther Martins and Rooster Tails work here as well, either trolled from a boat or cast from shore. In the spring, good places to fish include the east end of the reservoir by the mouths of Mill and Ochoco Creeks. Throughout the rest of the year, bank fishing is good off U.S. Highway 26 at the Ochoco Lake County Park boat ramp and by the Lakeview Restaurant as well as in the deeper water on the west end of the reservoir by the dam.

Ochoco Reservoir does not reliably freeze to a safe thickness every winter, so ice anglers need to exercise extreme caution when venturing here.

Ochoco Reservoir

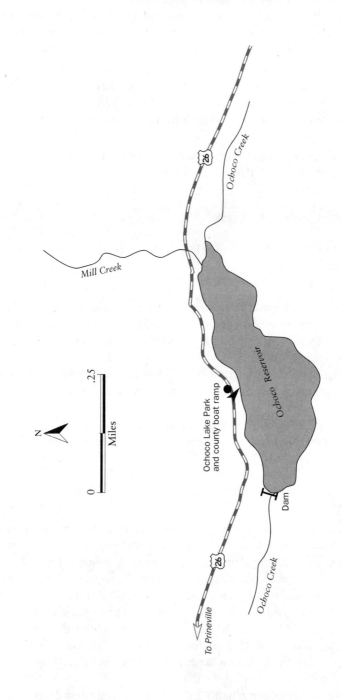

Directions: From Prineville, drive 7 miles east on U.S. Highway 26. The reservoir will be along the right (south) side of the road.

For More Information: Oregon Department of Fish and Wildlife, Prineville District Office

48 Prineville Reservoir

Key Species: rainbow trout, largemouth bass, smallmouth bass, black crappie, brown bullhead

Best Way to Fish: boat

Best Time to Fish: year-round

Description: Created by damming the Crooked River about 20 miles upstream from the city of Prineville, Prineville Reservoir inundates 18 miles of the river, and its sinuous shape caused by the narrow sagebrush and juniper dotted canyon it floods. A little over 3,000 acres in size, its primary purpose is to provide irrigation water for local farmers, so its water level may fluctuate. The reservoir is about 130 feet at its deepest; the lower section from Antelope Creek to the dam has the deepest water, and the upper section the shallowest.

Although it is possible to catch fish from the banks, to really be successful here you need a boat or float tube. Rainbow trout average around 10 inches, bass run 2 to 3 pounds, black crappie around 6 inches and brown bullheads, about 12 inches.

Prineville Reservoir State Park, located on the north shore, has camping. Boats can be rented at Prineville Resort at Jasper Point, 3 miles east of the park.

Prineville Reservoir is open year-round to angling.

Fishing Index: Bait is the technique of choice for Prineville Reservoir anglers after trout and brown bullhead. Nightcrawlers and Velveeta are the top contenders when trying to lure rainbows to the hook. Trout tend to be scattered throughout the reservoir, with the deeper water by the dam being one of the better areas to seek them out.

Nightcrawlers are the ticket for bullhead. Late May to early June is the best time to fish for these bottom-dwellers, especially around the upper east end of the reservoir.

You can catch largemouth and smallmouth bass with spinnerbaits, plugs, plastic worms, and spinners. Good bass locations include around the mouth of Sanford Creek, the Bear Creek Arm—just south of the Prineville Reservoir State Park boat ramp—and around the island.

Black crappie are abundant in the reservoir. They like to gather in large schools, so if you catch one, there are probably a lot more around. Some anglers report catching 50 or more in a single outing. Bait under bobbers and small spinners are good ways to entice these small gamefish. Crappie angling is often good just off the Prineville Reservoir Resort.

Prineville Reservoir

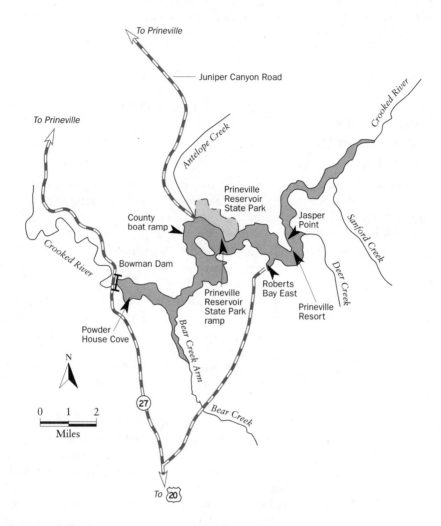

To Prineville

Juniper Canyon Road

Antelope Creek

Crooked River

To Prineville

Prineville
Reservoir
State Park

Jasper
Point

County
boat ramp

Sanford Creek

Crooked River

Bowman Dam

Deer Creek

Roberts
Bay East

Prineville
Reservoir
State Park
ramp

Prineville
Resort

Powder
House Cove

N

Bear Creek Arm

0   1   2

27

Bear Creek

Miles

To 20

Directions: From the east end of Prineville, take Oregon Highway 380 (Post–Paulina Highway) south for 2 miles. Bear right onto Juniper Canyon Road and follow it about 12 miles to Prineville Reservoir State Park.

For More Information: Oregon Department of Fish and Wildlife, Prineville District Office

49 Crooked River

Key Species: rainbow trout, whitefish

Best Way to Fish: wading

Best Time to Fish: September to March

Description: Flowing out of the Ochoco Mountains east of Prineville for more than 100 miles before joining Lake Billy Chinook near Madras, the Crooked River has risen to prominence in recent years as a prime Central Oregon fly fishing destination. The quarry here is rainbow trout, a distinct race known as "redsides." Crooked River trout only average 8 to 10 inches, but with a density of about 3,000 per mile, they can provide quite a bit of action.

The 6- or 7-mile stretch below Bowman Dam, which creates Prineville Reservoir, is the best section to fish, with great scenery in a desert canyon to boot.

Although it is open year-round, the best fishing is to be had in the fall and winter. No need to get up early to fish the Crooked River in the winter—late morning to mid-afternoon are the prime angling hours here. This section is catch-and-release, lures and flies only, from January 1 to April 23, and November 1 to December 31, but most anglers here practice catch-and-release fly fishing all the time.

Fishing Index: It is important to wade down the middle of the river when fishing here, as most of the trout will be found along the banks and in the weed beds. But don't entirely overlook the pocket water, riffles, and runs. While

An angler and his fishing "buddy" on the Crooked River below Bowman dam.

Crooked River

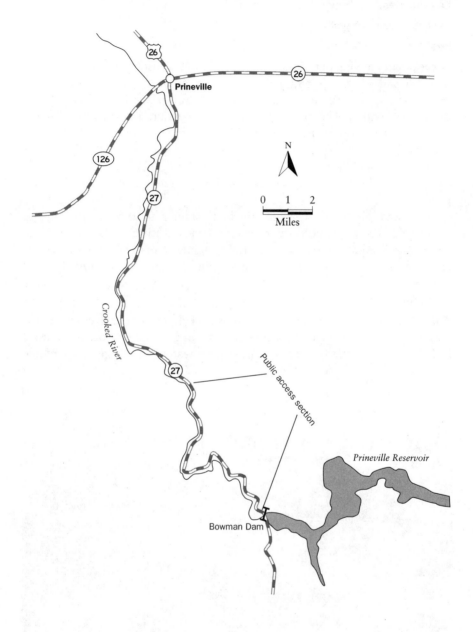

there can be good dry-fly action here, you will catch the most trout using nymphs. Since freshwater shrimp are the primary natural food of Crooked River trout, scuds are a favorite nymph. Beadhead Princes, Pheasant Tails, and Hare's Ears are other effective nymph patterns. For dries, Comparaduns, Blue-winged Olives, and Adams are good bets. During the fall, try hopper patterns. There is a good population of whitefish here, and, although rarely deliberately targeted, they are often caught incidentally by fly fishers.

The Crooked River often runs rather murky and cloudy, but that doesn't seem to affect the fishing.

A word of caution: although the Crooked River is relatively shallow, its bottom is strewn with boulders that may be difficult to see. Felt-soled wading boots are helpful, and even a wading staff is not a bad idea.

Directions: From Prineville drive south about 12 miles on Oregon Highway 27 to the beginning of the best water. The road parallels the river for the next 7 miles to Bowman Dam (there is no fishing for the first 150 feet below the dam).

For More Information: The Fly Fisher's Place

50 Metolius River

Key Species: rainbow trout, bull trout

Best Way to Fish: bank, wading

Best Time to Fish: year-round

Description: Rising fully formed from underground springs originating in the Cascade Mountains, the Metolius River flows through a beautiful forest of ponderosa pine, cedar, and firs, making fishing here one of the most aesthetically pleasing spots in the state.

The Metolius is open year-round to catch-and-release fly fishing only with barbless hooks downstream to Bridge 99 (also called Lower Bridge), and catch-and-release with flies and lures only below that. The most popular stretch is the length of river between Camp Sherman and Bridge 99.

The primary quarry here is wild rainbow trout and to a lesser degree, bull trout. The state of Oregon ceased stocking rainbows in the Metolius in 1996 in order to protect the wild rainbow population, which averages 10 to 13 inches in size, although larger fish into the 15-inch range are also caught.

The Metolius basin is also one of the few remaining strongholds in the western U.S. for bull trout, which were listed as threatened by the federal government in 1998. Even so, catch-and-release angling is still permitted for bull trout on the river under a provision of the Endangered Species Act, which permits carefully managed fisheries for listed fish species.

The Metolius has a reputation for being difficult to fish, and knowing the river's hatches can be a crucial factor for success. One of the top draws for fly fishers is the green drake hatch which comes off in late spring, early summer,

Metolius River • Suttle Lake

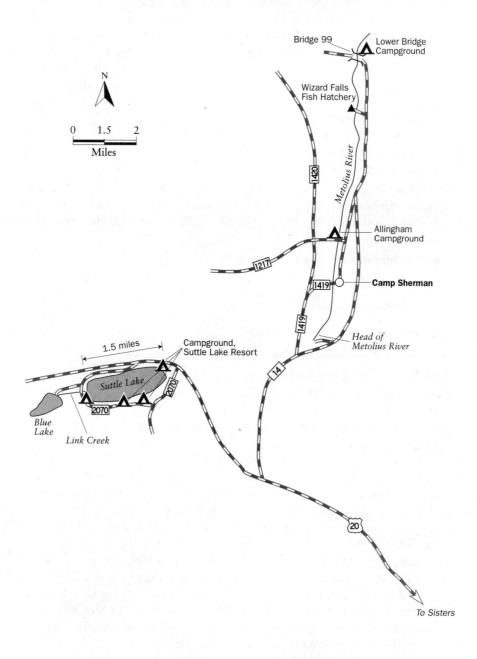

Despite being difficult to fish, the Metolius River is a beautiful place to spend the day casting a fly.

and early fall. The golden stone hatch on the Metolius, which occurs from about the Fourth of July to mid-October, is unique in that it usually only lasts a few weeks in most Western rivers. Blue wing olives hatch from November to April.

The Metolius River runs through the Deschutes National Forest, and there are ten USDA Forest Service campgrounds between Camp Sherman and Bridge 99. The general store in Camp Sherman has fishing supplies.

Fishing Index: Most anglers fish the fly fishing-only portion of the river between Camp Sherman and Bridge 99, parking at one of the riverside campgrounds. The parking area at Allingham Bridge, Wizard Falls Fish Hatchery, and directly across from Lower Bridge Campground are popular staging areas. Fishing usually doesn't pick up on the Metolius until 9:30 or 10:00 A.M. Because there is little instream structure in the middle of the river for fish to take shelter in, thoroughly fishing along the banks, beneath overhanging brush, and by submerged streamside logs is important. In fact, you can often fish good water close to the bank without wading. Deep pools and seams between fast and slow water can also be productive. Because the character of the river ranges between shallow and slow to deep and swift, along with heavy whitewater in places, care is essential when wading.

Some good fly patterns to use here include Green Drakes, Golden Stones, and Pale Evening Duns. Patterns that resemble crippled insects such as Captive Duns, Knock-down Duns, and Sparkle Duns are also effective. Anglers after bull trout usually swing nymphs and streamers through the deeper pools.

Because the water is clear and the fish wary, long leaders up to 15 feet are recommended. More experienced anglers adept at "matching the hatch" will do best on the Metolius River.

Directions: From Sisters drive west on U.S. Highway 20 for about 8 miles. Turn right (north) at the Camp Sherman turnoff onto Forest Road 14 (going straight at the Y onto FR 1419) and go 6 miles to the small community of Camp Sherman and the river. This road parallels the east side of the river to Bridge 99.

For More Information: The Fly Fisher's Place

51 Suttle Lake

Key Species: kokanee, brown trout

Best Way to Fish: boat, bank

Best Time to Fish: May, June, and September

Description: Tucked amidst the heavily forested slopes along U.S. Highway 20, a major route over the Cascade Mountains between the Willamette Valley and eastern Oregon, Suttle Lake is a destination for kokanee anglers. There is good fishing for respectable-sized brown trout here as well. Resting at an elevation of just under 3,500 feet, glacier-formed Suttle Lake averages 44 feet deep, going down to 72 feet at its deepest.

Good populations of kokanee ply the lake's blue waters; they average 9 to 12 inches. Brown trout can reach 4 or 5 pounds and measure over 20 inches.

Although it is possible to fish from the bank, and many people do, the best success will be had from a boat. If you don't own one, they can be rented at Suttle Lake Resort. There are also three USDA Forest Service campgrounds located along the lake. There is also camping at the resort.

Suttle Lake is open to angling year-round, but is typically iced-in and covered by heavy snowpack during the winter months, as are most of the Cascade Mountain lakes.

Fishing Index: Fish movements, and therefore fishing strategies, follow the general pattern of most lakes—the fish are in the shallow water near the shore during the early part of the season, then move into deeper central portions of the lake as the summer weather warms the surface water. For this reason, May and June tend to be the best times to fish here since the browns and kokanee are more readily accessible then.

Still-fishing with bait is the technique of choice for kokanee anglers here. While long-time standbys such as salmon eggs, corn, and nightcrawlers work, caddis fly larvae and periwinkles are favored. Kokanee may gang up off Cinder Beach, on the northeast corner of the lake, so check that area out. But it will also be necessary as the season progresses to explore waters throughout the lake, moving out into deeper water and away from the shoreline. If the kokanee bite drops off in the summer, it often picks up again by September as they prepare to spawn. At this time of year, try near the outlet of Link Creek, at the lake's west end.

Brown trout trolled throughout the lake will take Rapalas and other lures that mimic minnows and other small baitfish. Fish progressively deeper as the warmer weather arrives. Fly fishers take them with such nymph patterns as Princes and Hare's Ears. Streamer patterns, which are intended to look like small fish, are effective for browns as well. Try for brown trout with flies in the shallow, rocky areas near the resort. Typically, evenings are the best time to go after brown trout, as they feel more secure and less wary under cover of the fading light.

Suttle Lake

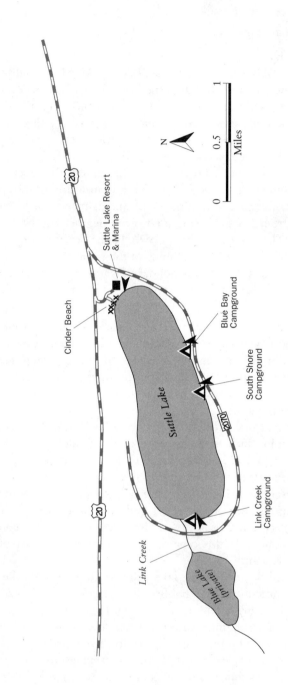

Directions: From Sisters, drive about 14 miles west on U.S. Highway 20. Turn left at the sign for Suttle Lake Resort and go about 1 mile on Forest Road 2070 to the fork. The right fork will take you to the northeast shore; the left fork runs along the south shore to the resort.

For More Information: Suttle Lake Resort

52 Sparks Lake

Key Species: brook trout, cutthroat trout

Best Way to Fish: canoe, float tube

Best Time to Fish: late May and June

Description: A good brook trout fishery, clear, shallow Sparks Lake, with its wary fish population, makes for a challenging outing for any fly fisher. Nestled in the Deschutes National Forest against a spectacular mountain backdrop, Sparks Lake is a mere 12 feet at its deepest and it averages only a foot. This shallowness, combined with glass-clear water, makes trout hard to approach.

Trout here average in the 12-inch range. Although the lake is open year-round for fly fishing with barbless hooks only, its 5,400-foot elevation means that it is usually not accessible to anglers until well into May.

Fishing Index: As this lake's already marginal water level drops over the course of the summer, fishing here is usually best as soon as the ice melts—generally by late May and into June. The deeper areas in the south arm are

Sparks Lake is known for spunky brook trout.

Sparks Lake • Elk Lake • Hosmer Lake • Cultus Lake

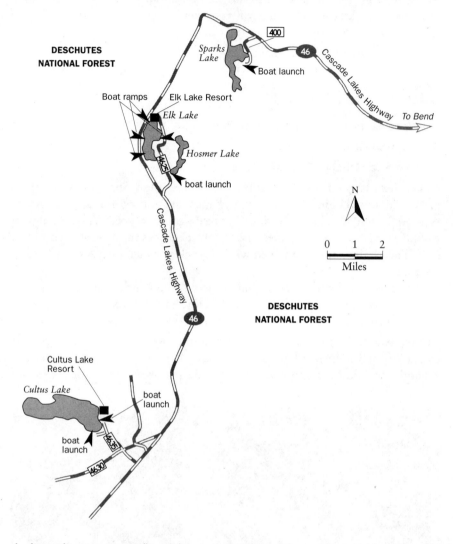

the best places to cast a fly, and so are portions of the northern end where tributary streams flow into the lake. Good fly patterns to try here include leeches and Woolly Buggers.

Most anglers use a canoe to get around here. A float tube works too, until water levels get too low. Long leaders, up to 15 feet, are a good idea, as the resident trout can be difficult to approach.

Directions: From Bend, take the Cascade Lakes Highway (Oregon Highway 46) west for about 25 miles. Turn left (south) onto Forest Road 400 and go 2 miles to the lake and a ramp where you can launch a canoe.

For More Information: The Fly Fisher's Place

53 Elk Lake

See map on page 164

Key Species: kokanee, brook trout

Best Way to Fish: boat, bank

Best Time to Fish: June, September, October

Description: Elk Lake is 405 acres in size and only 62 feet deep at its deepest point. It averages about 12 feet deep. Although more popular with sailors than anglers, it has a good population of kokanee as well as some decent-sized brook trout in the 10- to 13-inch range, and sometimes larger.

Located in the Deschutes National Forest, there are several campgrounds along the lake and many others in the surrounding forest. Boats may be rented at Elk Lake Resort.

Elk Lake is open year-round, but, as with most lakes in this area, access is often blocked by snow until late May.

Fishing Index: Trolling lures, bait fishing, and even fly fishing are effective techniques at Elk Lake. Fishing for brook trout by boat or from shore with spinners or worms is the most common approach.

Kokanee concentrate in the deepest southwest portion of the lake, known as the "Kokanee Hole." Jigging with Buzz Bombs and Nordics is a good approach. A piece of white corn added to the hook helps.

Good fly patterns to use on brook trout here include leeches and Woolly Buggers.

Elk Lake has both kokanee salmon and brook trout. With a backdrop of rugged peaks, this mountain lake is a splendid getaway.

Directions: From Bend, drive about 30 miles west on the Cascade Lakes Highway (Oregon Highway 46) to Elk Lake, located along the east side of the road.

For More Information: Elk Lake Resort

54 Hosmer Lake

See map on page 164

Key Species: landlocked Atlantic salmon, brook trout

Best Way to Fish: Boat, canoe, float tube

Best Time to Fish: June through October

Description: This unique Oregon fishery offers anglers an opportunity to catch Atlantic salmon, which are stocked here by the Oregon Department of Fish and Wildlife. When they turn on, these salmon can provide nearly non-stop action. They can reach 15 to 20 inches in length. Lunker-sized brook trout can be found here too, but most anglers come for the Atlantics.

Hosmer Lake is located about 35 miles west of Bend, off the Cascades Lakes Highway in the Deschutes National Forest, with fine views of Mount Bachelor and the surrounding Cascade Mountains. The lake is roughly hour-glass-shaped, consisting of two water bodies separated by a narrow channel. Its southern pool is deeper and generally provides the best fishing. There is a boat launch and two USDA Forest Service campgrounds located here.

Only fly fishing with barbless hooks is allowed on the lake, and all Atlantic salmon must be released unharmed. Motorized boats are permitted, but you cannot fish from a boat when its motor is running. Although Hosmer Lake is open all year, access is generally blocked by snow until early June.

Fishing Index: Fly fishing is the name of the game here, and the techniques and fly patterns that work for trout generally work for Atlantic salmon. You will definitely need a boat, canoe, or float tube to have any success, since most of the fish seem to hold farther offshore, and much of the lake's banks are choked with reeds and rushes. Fly rods in the 4- to 7-weight range are appropriate.

You can cast at rising salmon much as you would when fishing for trout, using such dry-fly patterns as Caddis, Adams, Callibaetis, and Comparaduns. But many Hosmer Lake anglers find making long casts with leeches and nymphs, then stripping the line back in at a moderate rate, to be highly effective, particularly when there is not a great deal of surface feeding activity going on. Trolling nymph patterns such as a Gold-ribbed Hare's Ear behind a paddle-powered canoe also works well. The south and east shores of the lake's southern pool tend to yield the best fishing.

Brook trout may reach 3 and 4 pounds and can be seen cruising along the lake bottom. They're wary and hard to catch. Most anglers don't accept the challenge, but if you want to give it a try, use leech and nymph patterns with a sinking line. Brook trout may be taken home for dinner.

Directions: From Bend, drive 33 miles east on Cascade Lakes Highway, then west for 2 miles on Forest Road 4625.

For More Information: Oregon Department of Fish and Wildlife, High Desert Region Office

55 Cultus Lake

See map on page 164

Key Species: lake trout (mackinaw), rainbow trout

Best Way to Fish: boat

Best Time to Fish: late May to October

Description: Big lake trout are the primary draw for anglers at this 790-acre lake nestled at 4,668 feet in the central Cascade Mountains. Cultus Lake averages about 80 feet deep, dropping to 211 feet at its deepest section in the lake's east end. The western portion of the lake is shallowest—80 feet at the most.

Lake trout caught here are commonly in the 8- to 10-pound range, and specimens over 20 pounds are not unheard of. Rainbows average 8 to 12 inches. There is a small brook trout population here that provides a negligible fishery and are not particularly sought after by anglers. They are typically in the 6- to 8-inch range.

There are campgrounds, cabins, a store, a restaurant, and boat rentals available at Cultus Lake Resort.

Cultus Lake is open to angling year-round, although access is usually blocked by snow from late fall to as late as the middle of May.

Fishing Index: You may find lake trout in the shallower sections of the lake early in the season, just after the ice has melted off, but as summer arrives they go deep—into the 150- or 200-foot range. At this time it is important to troll deep with downriggers. Popular and effective lures used here include Rapalas, Flatfish, Rebel spoons, and J-Plugs. During the summer and fall, trolling the middle of the lake is the best bet.

The many rocky areas along the lake are worth checking out for rainbows. Casting or trolling spinners, or fishing over worms and Power Bait will take these species.

Directions: From Bend, go south for about 12 miles to the Sunriver turnoff. Go right (west) and follow Forest Road 40 for about 25 miles to the junction of the Cascade Lakes Highway (Oregon Highway 46). Cross the highway and continue on FR 4630 about 2 miles and turn right (north) onto FR 4635 and drive about 3 miles to the lake.

For More Information: Cultus Lake Resort

56 Crane Prairie Reservoir

Key Species: rainbow trout, brook trout, kokanee, largemouth bass

Best Way to Fish: boat, float tube

Best Time to Fish: late April through October

Description: One of the famed lakes along the Cascade Lakes Highway, Crane Prairie Reservoir is nearly 5 square miles in size and formed by a dam on the upper Deschutes River. A trophy trout fishery, rainbows average 12 to 13 inches, and specimens in the 5-pound range are not unusual. Brook trout as large as 6 pounds have been caught here. Kokanee average 14 to 16 inches.

In the late 1970s, someone illegally introduced largemouth bass to the reservoir. This planting took, and now anglers target these gamefish as well. Crappie and bluegill were also illegally planted here some time ago and Oregon Department of Fish and Wildlife fishery managers encourage anglers to take home as many as they catch, since their presence potentially threatens the reservoir's trout fishery. Bass run 12 to 14 inches and weigh in at 2 to 5 pounds.

The reservoir is relatively shallow, averaging about 11 feet deep and dropping off to a maximum of 20 feet in the channels. It is open to fishing from April 24 through October. Although located in the mountains, the ice is usually out by early April.

Because margins of the reservoir are littered with snags and downed trees and the bottom is muddy, wading and bank fishing is not really an option. To fish Crane Prairie Reservoir you will need a boat or float tube. Boats can be rented at Crane Prairie Resort. There are also a number of campgrounds in the immediate area.

Fishing Index: Early in the season, fish tend to be scattered throughout the reservoir, making them sometimes difficult to find. One tried-and-true approach is to start fishing in likely spots, and if you haven't caught anything in a half-hour or so, move on.

Trout anglers here use just about anything to catch trout. Popular baits include dragonfly larvae, Power Bait, and nightcrawlers fished on the bottom or under a bobber. Panther Martins, Mepps, and Rooster Tails are favorites with spinner fishermen. Since the reservoir's ample sunken logs provide good cover for trout and bass, these are good areas to explore.

As the water level drops and temperatures rise during the summer and fall, the trout seek cooler water in the deeper channels and some of the bays that are cooled by inflowing springs. Throughout the summer and fall, concentrate your fishing in the Quinn, Cultus, and Deschutes channels.

Try bait and spinners in the middle of the reservoir for kokanee in the channels where they are mainly found. Early season is the best time to pursue these landlocked salmon.

Crane Prairie Reservoir • Wickiup Reservoir

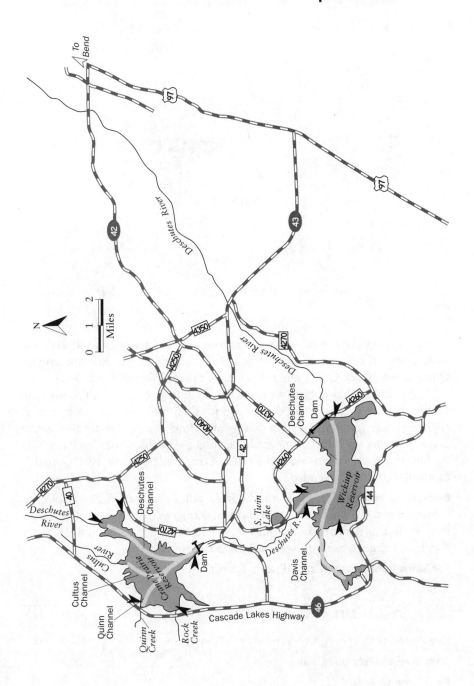

The Adams is a fly pattern that will catch fish on many of Oregon's lakes, rivers, and small streams.

Bass anglers like plastic worms, crankbaits, and nightcrawlers, and so do the bass. Good areas to check out for bass include the western shoreline around Quinn Creek, Rock Creek, and the center of the reservoir in weedy areas.

Crane Prairie has a variety of hatches including midges, Callibaetis, and caddis, making it an excellent destination for fly fishing. Trolling with streamers is an effective technique as is casting and slowly retrieving dry flies. Some good patterns include Comparaduns, Light Cahills, Adams, Parachute Callibaetis, Woolly Buggers, and leeches. Long leaders in the 12-foot to 15-foot range are recommended.

Directions: From Bend, go south about 25 miles and turn right (west) onto County Road 43. Drive about 13 miles and turn left (west) onto CR42. Go 6 miles and turn right (south) onto Forest Road 4720. Follow FR 4720 for 4 miles to Crane Prairie Resort and the boat launch.

For More Information: Crane Prairie Resort

57 Wickiup Reservoir

See map on page 169

Key Species: kokanee, brown trout, rainbow trout

Best Way to Fish: boat, bank

Best Time to Fish: May through July

Description: At over 10,300 acres when full, Wickiup Reservoir is the largest lake in the Cascade Mountains and the second largest reservoir in Oregon.

Like nearby Crane Prairie Reservoir, Wickiup was created by damming the upper Deschutes River. The water in the reservoir is used to irrigate croplands in the Deschutes River basin. It got its name from the abandoned Native American lodges early ranchers found in the area, before the reservoir was created.

A shallow reservoir, its maximum depth is 70 feet but it averages only 20 feet. Its deepest sections are in the Davis and Deschutes River channels which run from their respective inlets on the south and northwest ends of the reservoir through the middle of the lake to the dam on the northeast shoreline.

Although there are a number of fish species inhabiting the reservoir, anglers generally come here in search of kokanee, and to a lesser extent brown trout. At one time there was a coho salmon fishery here made up of surplus hatchery fish. Currently, there are just remnant coho in the reservoir, occasionally caught by kokanee anglers. Rainbows, along with whitefish, are usually caught incidentally as well. Kokanee may run anywhere from 8 to 16 inches, depending on population levels—the larger, more crowded the population, the smaller the fish. Browns are typically in the 5- to 10-pound range, while rainbows run 2 to 5 pounds, although they can get much larger. Browns can reach over 20 pounds.

Wickiup Reservoir is open to fishing from April 22 to October 31, although, as with all mountain lakes, the ice may not be melted by opening day. The area around the reservoir is crisscrossed with roads that allow anglers to reach just about every portion by vehicle. But it is good idea to have a map with you when you visit.

Fishing Index: Most anglers target Wickiup Reservoir during the first couple of months of the season, when fishing is best. Early on, kokanee are usually scattered throughout the lake, but by June they'll begin gravitating to the cooler, deeper water of the Davis and Deschutes channels.

Spinners and bait will take kokanee. Flashers can help attract these fish to your offerings.

Jigging with Buzz Bombs and white corn is a good technique when fishing the channels. June and early July are the best times for kokanee angling, as these fish spawn early and begin turning inedible by August.

For browns, troll with Rapalas or other minnow-mimicking lures. Early in the season, troll near the surface, going deeper into the channels as the season progresses. You can cast for browns from shore. As with kokanee, browns tend to be scattered early in the season, but can be found fairly consistently in the deep channels during the day, moving to shallower areas to feed in late afternoon and evening. For rainbows, go with spinners and bait. Davis Arm is a likely spot to search for them.

Although not a popular fly fishing destination, fly anglers can get to some good-sized browns around the dam and off Gull Point using Woolly Buggers, streamers, and leeches.

Directions: From Bend, drive south about 25 miles on U.S. Highway 97. Turn right (west) onto County Road 43 and go about 10 miles, turning left (southwest) onto Forest Road 4380. Follow FR 4380 for 3.5 miles to the reservoir.

For More Information: Oregon Department of Fish and Wildlife, High Desert Region Office

58 Davis Lake

Key Species: rainbow trout, largemouth bass

Best Way to Fish: float tube

Best Time to Fish: spring, summer, fall

Description: Three thousand-acre Davis Lake was formed when a lava flow blocked Odell Creek several thousand years ago. It's a large but shallow body of water deep in the central Cascade Mountains, 25 feet deep at the most. A designated fly fishing-only lake for most of the past 60 years, it holds a population of rainbow trout averaging 2 to 5 pounds. Largemouth bass were illegally introduced here some years back and now provides good fly fishing sport as well, in spite of the fact that the bass' predatory nature endangers the lake's first class trout fishery. Largemouth bass here average 3 to 4 pounds.

A series of droughts in the early 1990s seriously affected the Davis Lake fishery, but it is making a comeback, with higher rain and snowfall in recent years.

Wading or bank fishing is difficult here due to the lake's muddy bottom and weedy shoreline. A boat or float tube is the best approach. There is a paved boat ramp at Lava Flow Campground, but it is only open from September 1 to the end of the year to protect bald eagles, which nest nearby. You'll find an undeveloped boat launch at West Davis Campground.

Although Davis Lake is open to fly fishing with barbless hooks year-round, snow blocks access during the winter.

Fishing Index: Because the basalt lava dam that formed the lake is porous, water seeps through, causing the lake's water level to fluctuate. In good water years, fish tend to be scattered throughout the lake, moving into cooler, deeper areas during the warm summer months and on into the fall.

Try your luck offshore from the lava dam on the northeast section of the lake, and also along the west shoreline. As the season and the water warms, fish will move into deeper areas, such as the Odell Channel on the east portion of the lake. The deepest area of the lake is off the lava dam.

Good patterns for trout include Woolly Buggers, green leeches, dragonfly nymphs, and damsel fly patterns. The lake also has good mayfly and midge hatches. For largemouth bass, leech patterns and poppers produce good results.

Directions: From Bend, drive south on U.S. Highway 97 for about 43 miles to Crescent. Turn right (west) onto County Road 61 and go 8 miles. Turn right

172

Davis Lake

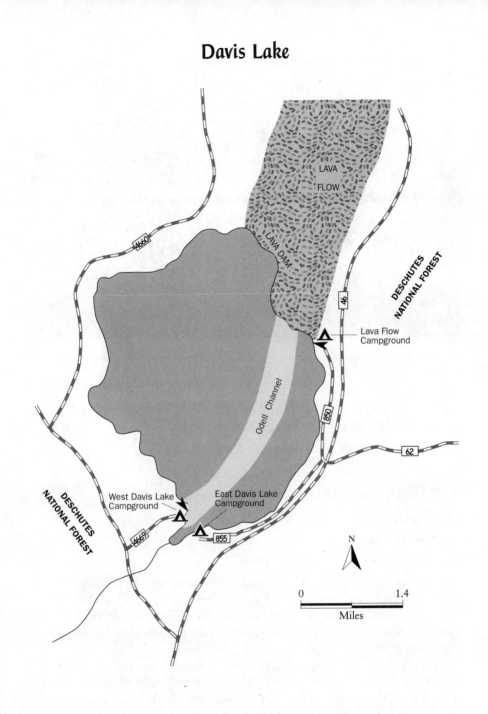

LAVA
FLOW

LAVA DAM

4660

46

DESCHUTES
NATIONAL FOREST

Lava Flow
Campground

Odell Channel

850

62

West Davis Lake
Campground

East Davis Lake
Campground

DESCHUTES
NATIONAL FOREST

4669

855

N

0   1.4
Miles

In the heart of the central Cascades, Davis Lake beckons fly fishers searching for trout or largemouth bass.

(north) onto Forest Road 46 and drive 7 miles to the turnoff (on the left) for Davis Lake and Lava Flow Campground.

For More Information: The Fly Fisher's Place

59 Odell Lake

Key Species: kokanee, lake trout, rainbow trout

Best Way to Fish: boat

Best Time to Fish: May through October

Description: At over 3,500 acres in size, Odell Lake is among the largest lakes in the Cascade Mountains. Sitting at an elevation of 4,787 feet, it is surrounded by dense stands of conifers within the Willamette National Forest. The lake's average depth is about 130 feet, and it's just over 280 feet in its deepest sections.

Although it has a good population of rainbow trout, anglers come here specifically for the kokanee and lake trout—locally called mackinaw. The state record lake trout, a 40-pound, 8-ounce behemoth, was caught here in 1984. Since then, other anglers have, from time to time, come close to beating that record. Typical lake trout in Odell Lake average about 8 pounds. Kokanee average around 10 to 13 inches while rainbows are typically in the 14-inch range, although they can reach up to 20 inches. There are some bull

Odell Lake

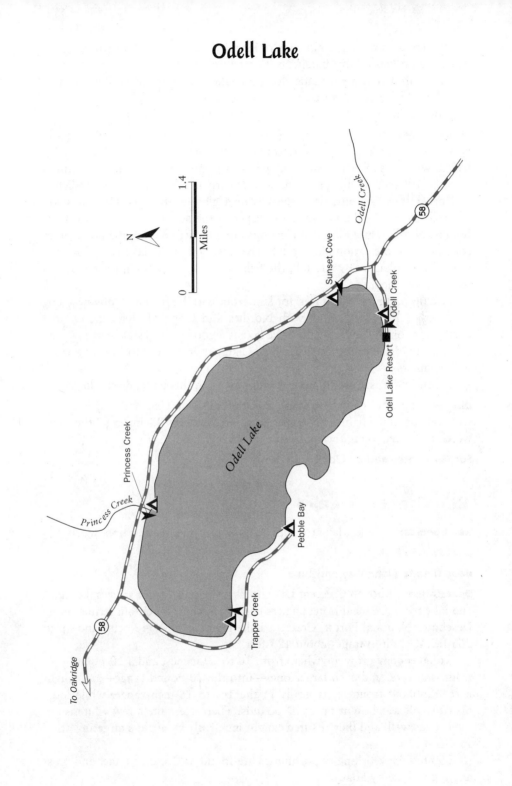

trout present in the lake, but they're illegal to catch. Any bull trout caught inadvertently must immediately be released unharmed.

There are five campgrounds along the lake and boat access. Boats can be rented at Odell Lake Resort.

Odell Lake is open to fishing from April 22 to October 31.

Fishing Index: Trolling and jigging are the primary methods used here. Early in the season the kokanee tend to stay near the surface, generally less than 20 feet down. As summer wears on, they move into deeper water, sometimes down to 100 feet. Trolling near the surface early in the season with Needlefish and other small spoons, or flashers with a glow-in-the-dark lure are good methods to try. As the kokanee go deeper in the summer, jigging with Buzz Bombs, Nordics, and Crippled Herrings are effective. Baiting the hooks with corn can help the action along a bit. The west end of the lake is a good area to troll for kokanee. By late fall, the fish darken as they begin to spawn and they become inedible.

Fish deep, down to 150 feet, for lake trout with Flatfish with downriggers, troll with a Kwikfish, or jig with Nordics and Crippled Herrings. Off the north shore on the eastern half of the lake is a good area to start with. Off the mouths of Odell and Princess Creeks are likely spots to troll for rainbow trout with spinners.

A fish finder is a useful piece of equipment on this large, deep lake.

Directions: From Bend, drive south about 60 miles on U.S. Highway 97. Turn west on Oregon Highway 58 and go approximately 23 miles to the lake, which is located along the south side of the highway.

For More Information: Odell Lake Resort

60 Crescent Lake

Key Species: kokanee, lake trout (mackinaw), brown trout, rainbow trout

Best Way to Fish: boat

Best Time to Fish: May and June

Description: Although Crescent Lake holds a variety of trout species, kokanee and lake trout are what bring anglers here. In a scenic mountain setting in the Deschutes National Forest, Crescent Lake is just over 4,540 acres and up to 265 feet deep; it averages about 125 feet.

Kokanee may grow anywhere from 10 to 20 inches, and a 10-pound lake trout isn't rare, and even larger ones—into the 20-pound range—are caught here. Rainbow trout are typically in the 14- to 16-inch range, while large browns will weigh in at up to 12 pounds. There are quite a few whitefish in the lake as well, and they're often caught incidently by anglers targeting other species.

Limited bank fishing opportunities are found at Crescent Lake, and most angling is done by boat.

Crescent Lake

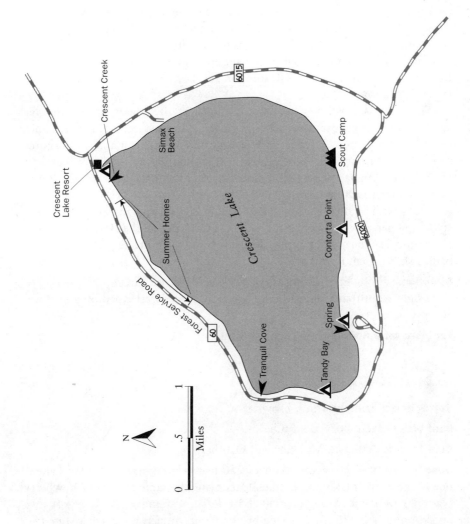

There is a resort with boat rentals, several campgrounds, and day use areas. The lake is open to angling year-round, although it is frozen over during the winter.

Fishing Index: The best kokanee fishing is typically had in the beginning of the season, usually by trolling flasher set-ups with Wedding Rings baited with white corn or by trolling with spinners. Jigging with Nordics and Buzz Bombs is also effective if you find a school. As with many kokanee lakes, a fish finder can be very helpful. By June and July, the kokanee have gone deep, and fishing for them drops off. Downriggers will help you get to the 50- to 100-foot depths where they roam. As the water and weather cools in September and October, the kokanee become more active again as they begin to gang up near Crescent Creek at the northeast corner of the lake, in preparation for spawning. A good area to troll for kokanee is just offshore between Contorta Point and Simax Beach and in front of the summer homes on the north shoreline. Just out from Crescent Lake Resort, on the northeast shoreline, is another favorite location.

The lake trout will be in shallower water just after the ice melts. Popular areas for anglers in search of these big guys include just out from the summer homes, and off Simax Beach and the scout camp, on the east and south shores respectively. The area off Contorta Point can also hold promise. Trolling with Flatfish and Rapalas work well. Remember that the mackinaw will go deeper as hot summer weather arrives.

Along with nightcrawlers and Power Bait, anglers take rainbows on a variety of spinners. For browns, troll with Rapalas or any other lure that mimics a minnow. Try the area off Simax Beach for brown trout. It is also possible to bank fish for them in this area.

Directions: From Eugene, go about 70 miles east on Oregon Highway 58. Turn right (south) at Crescent Lake Junction onto Forest Road 60 and travel about 4 miles to the lake.

For More Information: Crescent Lake Resort

61 Paulina Lake

Key Species: rainbow trout, brown trout, kokanee

Best Way to Fish: Boat, float tube

Best Time to Fish: late May through October

Description: At 1,530 acres and over 250 feet deep in places, Paulina Lake is one of the deepest lakes in the state. Occupying the same caldera in Newberry National Volcanic Monument as East Lake, Paulina Lake is a kokanee hotspot and home to trophy-sized brown trout. In fact, the current state trophy brown trout—27 pounds, 12 ounces—was caught here in 1993.

Historically, there were no fish in Paulina Lake until the state began stocking trout here in the late 1800s. The average Paulina Lake brown trout runs

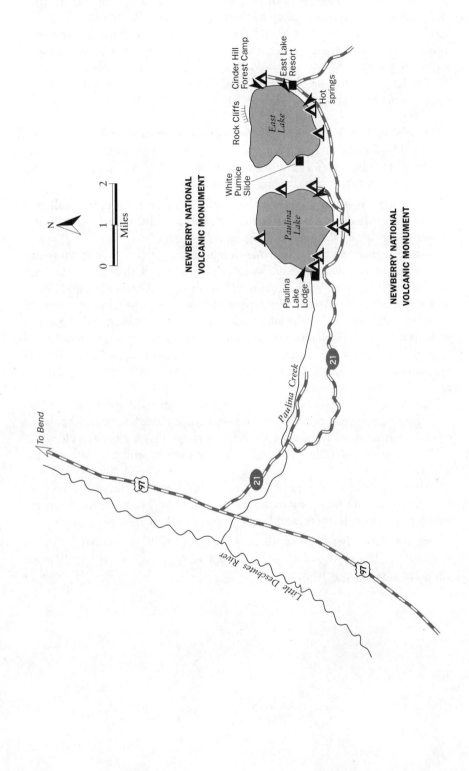

between 12 and 18 inches and 10-pounders are not especially unusual. Rainbow trout are typically in the 9- to 14-inch range while kokanee are generally 14 to 18 inches and go up to 20 inches or so.

Deeper and colder than East Lake, Paulina Lake averages a little over 160 feet deep. Less than 3 percent is under 3 feet deep, so wading opportunities are limited and you will do best with a boat or float tube.

The lake is open to angling from April 22 to October 31, but, as with East Lake, its high elevation of 6,331 feet often means that it is not ice-free until late May.

Newberry National Volcanic Monument was established in 1990 and is managed by the USDA Forest Service. There are campgrounds along the lake and boats may be rented at Paulina Lake Resort. There is a two-day entrance fee of $5 per car. You can also buy a season pass for $25.

Fishing Index: As is typical of most lakes, the fish tend to be in the shallower water near shore during the spring and summer months, retreating to deeper, colder water during the heat of the summer.

In the spring, when the kokanee frequent waters just off the shoreline, trolling with a Wedding Ring and white corn or jigging with Nordics and Buzz Bombs will take them. Still-fishing with bait such as nightcrawlers and Power Bait is also effective. As summer arrives, the kokanee will move out into the deeper middle portions of the lake, and still-fishing or trolling the whole lake is the best strategy. Kokanee are typically at depths of anywhere between 25 to 100 feet, and a fish finder can be useful for locating schools. By late September and into October, they begin spawning and become too dark to eat.

Spinners, such as Rooster Tails, along with bait, are good for rainbow trout as well as brown trout. If you are after trophy-sized browns, Rapalas or other lures that mimic minnows are the way to go. Fish for browns along the shallower, weedy sections of shoreline in the early morning or late evening hours.

Although not a particularly favorite lake for fly fishers, there are Callibaetis hatches here as well as scuds. Your best bet for trout is casting streamers, Woolly Buggers, and leeches from a boat or float tube.

Directions: From Bend, go south on U.S. Highway 97 for about 20 miles. Turn east on County Road 21 and go about 12 miles to Paulina Lake Resort.

For More Information: Paulina Lake Resort

See map on page 179

Key Species: brown trout, rainbow trout, Atlantic salmon, kokanee

Best Way to Fish: boat, float tube, wading

Best Time to Fish: late May through October

Description: Located in the Newberry National Volcanic Monument south of Bend, East Lake, along with nearby Paulina Lake, has been extremely popular with anglers for decades. Occupying part of the Newberry Caldera, the lake is 1,044 acres in size and up to 180 feet deep. It is particularly known for its trophy-sized brown trout. The current record is a 22.5-pound monster caught in 1981. Typical brown trout average 14 to 25 inches. Rainbow trout average 10 to 19 inches and Atlantic salmon average up to 17 inches. Kokanee are usually in the 14- to 16-inch range.

Although the season runs from April 22 to October, its high elevation (nearly 6,400 feet) generally keeps it locked in ice until late May. Although most fishing here is done by boat, float tubes are also used. There is also some opportunity for wading in shallow, weedy areas, a method most commonly employed by fly fishers.

One note of caution: Because of mercury contamination, the State of Oregon recommends limitations on the amount of fish eaten from East Lake. See the Oregon fishing regulations handbook for details.

Newberry National Volcanic Monument was established in 1990 and is managed by the USDA Forest Service. There are three campgrounds along the lake and boats may be rented at East Lake Resort. There is a two-day entrance fee of $5 per car. You can also buy a season pass for $30.

Fishing Index: Early-season fishing is concentrated around the southeast section of the lake where the ice melts first due to the presence of underwater hot springs. At this time of year, most fish concentrate in this area, moving off into other parts of the lake as the ice clears and the water warms. This is a good time to try using baits such as salmon eggs, worms, Power Bait, and Velveeta cheese under a bobber. There are good bait-fishing areas near the shoreline just north of the White Pumice Slide and off the rock cliffs west of Cinder Hill Forest Camp. Trolling with spinners and spoons and other lures is also effective.

As warm summer weather arrives, the fish tend to go deeper, which means trolling at greater depths with bait-and-flasher set-ups or Flatfish. A good trolling area can be found offshore of East Lake Resort. If you are after brown trout, try trolling Rapalas along the shoreline. Atlantic salmon tend to be found in the open water in the middle of the lake. Scrappy fighters, they are taken with flies and spinners. By October, the most productive fishing tends to be in shallower water around the shoreline.

The lake's shallow, weedy areas provide good habitat for insects, making it an excellent fishery for fly fishers. Parachute Adams, Elk Hair Caddis, Woolly Buggers, scuds, and Gold-ribbed Hare's Ears are all good bets. For browns, troll or strip streamers such as Zonkers, Marabou Muddlers, and Matukas. There is some good wading in the shallows at the southwest corner of the lake just south of White Pumice Slide, although overall you'll have more versatility fly fishing East Lake from a float tube or boat.

Directions: From Bend, go south on U.S. Highway 97 for about 20 miles. Turn east on County Road 21 and go about 17 miles to East Lake Resort.

For More Information: East Lake Resort, Deschutes National Forest

63 Fall River

Key Species: rainbow trout, brown trout, brook trout

Best Way to Fish: wading

Best Time to Fish: late June through August

Description: Much like the Metolius River, albeit on a smaller scale, the Fall River emerges fully formed from underground springs, and it meanders through a pine forest for about 8 miles before flowing into the Deschutes River near La Pine State Park.

There is a state fish hatchery (Fall River Hatchery) below the river's headwaters. About 4 miles below the hatchery is a falls. Hatchery rainbow trout dominate the river above the falls, while wild rainbows, along with some wild brown and brook trout, prowl the waters below. Trout in the Fall River typically run in the 8- to 12-inch range.

The Little Yellow Stone fly pattern is a must for every angler's fly box. It works well in the summer months on many trout streams.

Fall River

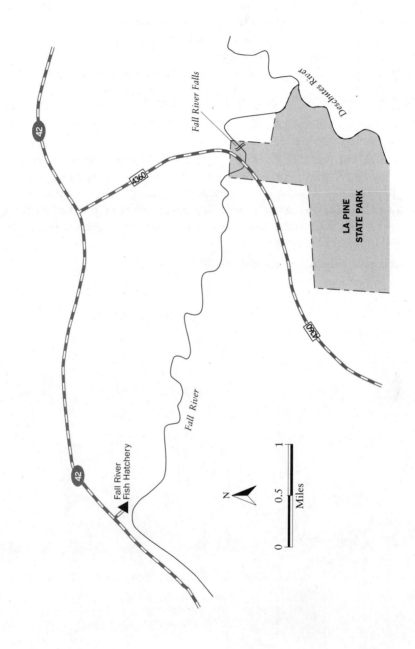

The river is fly fishing, barbless hooks only. Wild fish caught below the falls must be released.

Fishing Index: The summer months typically offer the best fishing on the Fall River, especially during the afternoon and evenings. Fishing trips beginning at the hatchery are most popular with Fall River anglers Those looking for wild fish and more species to catch usually fish below the falls. The lower 4 miles of the Fall River crosses private property.

Typical flies used here include Light Cahills, Yellow Sallys, and Elk Hair Caddis. Blue-winged Olives and Pale Morning Duns are good all-purpose flies that work well here throughout the summer. Fall River is a particularly nice stream for aficionados of light fly tackle—a great place to give your 2-weight outfit a try.

Location: To reach the Fall River Hatchery, drive 12 miles south from Bend on U.S. Highway 97. Turn right at the Sunriver turnoff, turning right onto County Road 42 just before crossing the Deschutes River, and go about 12 miles to the Fall River Hatchery, on the left (south). You can get to the falls, in La Pine State Park, by turning left (south) onto Forest Road 4360 about 3 miles before the hatchery and going about one mile.

For More Information: The Fly Fisher's Place

Southeast Oregon

Trophy fly fishing waters, lakes and reservoirs big and small, along with remote desert country where you would never suspect to find good fishing all characterize this vast region, which occupies the southeastern quadrant of Oregon from the Cascade Mountains to the California and Nevada borders, then east to Idaho.

Expect a plethora of angling opportunities to choose from. Although this is largely trout country, the warmwater angler won't be left out altogether. Fishing experiences range from fly angling for big browns in streams meandering through forest and pastureland to exploring reservoirs, lakes, and streams in a vast expanse of open desert country.

When ranging this wild and woolly part of the state, make sure you've got plenty of maps, a good reliable vehicle, and are prepared for "going it on your own."

Regulations for the waters listed in this section will be found in the Southeast Zone section of the *Oregon Sport Fishing Regulations* handbook.

64 Williamson River

Key Species: rainbow trout

Best Way to Fish: boat, wading, limited bank

Best Time to Fish: June to October

Description: One of Oregon's top trophy fly fishing waters, the Williamson River heads from springs in the Winema National Forest east of the Klamath Marsh National Wildlife Refuge and flows around 75 miles into Upper Klamath Lake, 7 miles southwest of Chiloquin.

The river's claim to fame is its large rainbow trout, which migrate upstream from Upper Klamath Lake in late summer and fall. They average 17 or 18 inches and can reach up to 20 inches. There are also a few brown trout in the lower river.

With a combination of clear water and big, wary trout, the Williamson has a well-deserved reputation as a difficult place to fish, requiring casting skill and stealth. That aside, the river's primary drawback is the fact that much of it flows through private lands, so there is not a great deal of bank access. The best approach to fishing the Williamson is by floating it in a boat or canoe. Once on the river, anglers will find a variety of likely trout-holding water to fish.

The easiest, and most popular bank access is at Collier Memorial State Park, although, many anglers float the 4-mile stretch from the county boat access (Chiloquin Access) at the town of Chiloquin to the fee take-out at Waterwheel RV Park where U.S. Highway 97 crosses the river. Williamson River anglers will handle the shuttle for you on this stretch. You can also

The Blitzen River in southeast Oregon offers remote, uncrowded fishing and subtle scenic beauty.

Williamson River

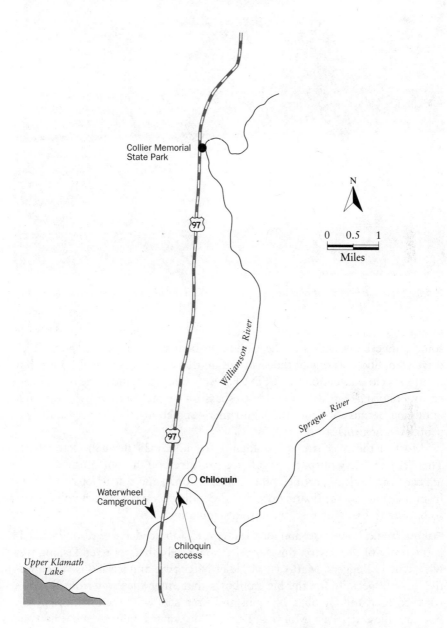

Collier Memorial
State Park

97

N

0 0.5 1
Miles

Williamson River

Sprague River

97

○ **Chiloquin**

Waterwheel
Campground

Chiloquin
access

Upper Klamath
Lake

Collier State Park is a popular access point for Williamson River anglers.

motor into the river from boat launches on Upper Klamath Lake. There is some public bank access at the Chiloquin boat ramp. It is also possible to drive to public portions of the river within the Winema National Forest, but it requires close attention to a USDA Forest Service map and some time devoted to exploring. Be careful not to trespass on private property without first obtaining permission from the landowner—something that is occasionally a problem along this river.

Most of the river is open to angling from May 27 through October 31. There are a variety of special regulations enforced on the Williamson, including catch-and-release, artificial flies and lures only, and restrictions on fishing from boats and other floating devices, depending on what stretch you are on, so be sure to carefully read the current regulations.

Fishing Index: Long casts and long leaders (15-foot leaders are recommended) is the order of the day on this crystal clear, largely shallow river. Fishing wet with Woolly Buggers, Matukas, Muddler Minnows, and leeches is very effective here, especially for the big rainbows that enter the river from the lake between June and October. Nymphs and streamers will take browns as well. For dry flies, try Pale Morning Duns, Blue-winged Olives, and Elk Hair Caddis. In late summer and fall, grasshoppers, ants, and beetles do well.

The best dry-fly action happens from early July through early August, when the Hexagenia hatch comes off. These big yellow mayflies hatch in the late evening, as the light is fading, and provides some unforgettable action as the rainbows feed on them voraciously. You'll want to have a good selection of Hex patterns in your fly box at this time of year.

Because of the challenging nature of the fishing here, experienced Williamson hands often recommend that first-timers hire a guide to show them the ropes before venturing off on their own.

Directions: To reach Collier Memorial State Park, drive 30 miles north from Klamath Falls on U.S. Highway 97. The park is on the east side of the highway along the river. The boat access is at Chiloquin, off US 97, 5 miles south of Collier Memorial State Park, on the west side of the river.

For More Information: Oregon Department of Fish and Wildlife, Klamath Falls District Office and Williamson River Anglers

65 Wood River

Key Species: rainbow trout, brown trout

Best Way to Fish: canoe, pontoon boat, other small craft

Best Time to Fish: May to October

Description: This small, spring-born river winds its way through pasture lands in the Klamath Basin before it emptys into Agency Lake, approximately 30 miles from its source at Jackson F. Kimball State Park.

Trophy-sized rainbow and brown trout in the 4- to 5-pound range and larger prowl its cut-banks and log jams waiting for an angler's fly. The only catch is that Wood River flows virtually entirely through private lands, necessitating a small boat, such as a canoe or pontoon boat, to fish it.

A bucolic setting and the potential for big trout are the main attractions on the Wood River.

Wood River

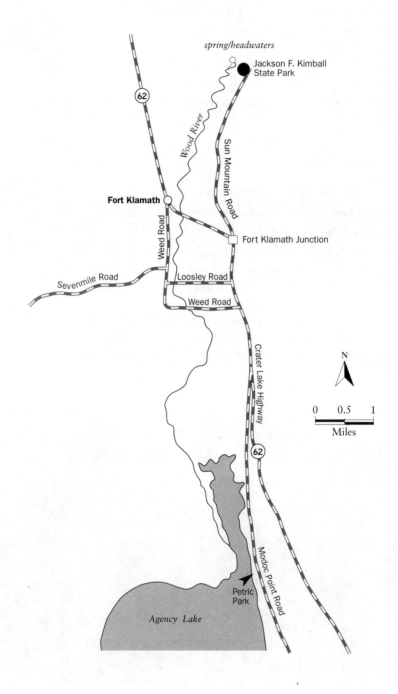

spring/headwaters

Jackson F. Kimball
State Park

62

Wood River

Sun Mountain Road

Fort Klamath

Weed Road

Fort Klamath Junction

Sevenmile Road

Loosley Road

Weed Road

Crater Lake Highway

N

0   0.5   1
Miles

62

Modoc Point Road

Petric
Park

Agency Lake

There are several places to put in and take out. You can launch at the springs at Jackson F. Kimball State Park and float down from there, taking out where Loosely Road crosses the river at Fort Klamath, 12 miles downriver; at Weed Road another 3 miles downstream; or at Petric Park at the north end of Agency Lake, an additional 15 miles downstream. You can, of course, put in at either of the road crossings as well. It is also possible to launch at Petric Park and boat about a mile up Agency Lake's northern arm and into the Wood River at its mouth. Land along the first 2 miles of the river is public, managed by the Bureau of Land Management.

In addition to the promise of big trout, a Wood River float trip is enjoyable in its own right as it meanders lazily through lush farmlands. You'll need to be alert though, for it is easy to wander up an irrigation diversion, thinking you are still on the main river. You are also likely to have to portage around irrigation dams, log jams, and, perhaps, low-clearance bridges. The larger fish tend to be in the lower river. You must remain in your boat when floating the Wood River through private property unless you have permission from the landowner to fish from the banks. Trespassing by anglers is occasionally a problem along this river.

The Wood River is open April 22 to October 31, and it's catch-and-release with artificial flies and lures only.

Fishing Index: You will encounter a mix of open and brushy banks as well as lots of logs and other in-water structure on the Wood. Muddler Minnows, Hare's Ears, and leech patterns cast along the cut-banks and

While fishing the Wood, stealth, presentation, and a willing fish must all come together for success to be had.

instream structures will entice both rainbows and browns. Streamers are also a good choice for predatory browns. Effective dry-fly patterns include Elk Hair Caddis and Parachute Adams.

The best surface action happens in August and September as grasshoppers make their appearance, and the trout slurp down any of the creatures unfortunate enough to fall into the water. At this time of year, cast hopper patterns and other terrestrials near the banks and under overhanging vegetation.

Lure anglers typically go with spinners such as Panther Martins, Mepps, and Rooster Tails.

If you access the river via Agency Lake, take the time to cast some flies and spinners, since this is where the Wood River's big rainbows originate.

Directions: To reach the put-in at Jackson F. Kimball State Park, go 21 miles north on U.S. Highway 97 from Klamath Falls. Bear left onto Oregon Highway 62 (Crater Lake Highway) and go 11 miles to Fort Klamath Junction, then north onto Sun Mountain Road for 2.5 miles to the park on the left (west) side of the road. To get to Fort Klamath, stay on the Crater Lake Highway past the Fort Klamath Junction for 1.5 miles. Weed and Loosley Roads can be accessed from OR 62. Petric Park is located off Modoc Point Road on the northeast corner of Agency Lake.

For More Information: Oregon Department of Fish and Wildlife, Klamath Falls District Office

66 Sprague River

Key Species: rainbow trout, brown trout, brown bullhead, largemouth bass

Best Way to Fish: bank, wading

Best Time to Fish: May to October

Description: This lovely tributary of the Williamson River rises in the Gearhart Mountain Wilderness, located in the Fremont National Forest. Its two major tributaries, the North and South Forks of the Sprague, also offer good fishing opportunities in a forested setting. It flows a total of about 100 miles from its source until merging with the Williamson River just below the city of Chiloquin.

Large rainbow trout—3 pounds and more—migrate from August through October into the river's lower reach, below the dam at Chiloquin. The upper river also has trout as well, albeit in smaller sizes. Brown trout may be found throughout the mainstem. The upper forks hold brook and rainbow trout, as well as some bull trout. The Sprague's middle reach, upstream from Beatty, is slower moving and has largemouth bass and brown bullhead.

As with the nearby Williamson and Wood Rivers, much of the Sprague flows through private property. There are some stretches that flow through the Winema and Fremont National Forests, and some that parallel the Sprague River Highway, which offer public access to trout fishing. The bridge

Sprague River

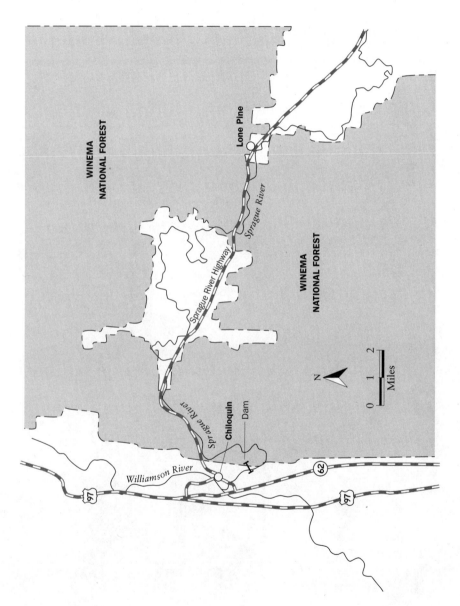

Sprague River

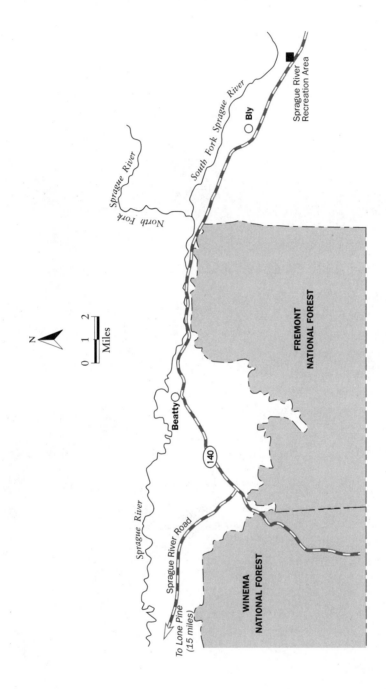

Sprague River
North Fork
Sprague River
South Fork Sprague River
○ Bly
Sprague River
Recreation Area
FREMONT
NATIONAL FOREST
Beatty ○
140
Sprague River Road
WINEMA
NATIONAL FOREST
To Lone Pine
(15 miles)
N
0   1   2
Miles

off Oregon Highway 140 between Beatty and Bly is another favorite angling spot, as is the Sprague River Recreation Site, which is managed by the USDA Forest Service. There is also some access to the lower river below the dam at Chiloquin. Be careful not to trespass on private property without first obtaining permission from the landowner, which is occasionally a problem along this river.

The upper Sprague and its tributaries are not heavily fished, which gives you an opportunity to get away from the crowds—if you're willing to explore Forest Service access roads. You will need national forest maps to find your way around.

The Sprague River below the dam is open to angling from May 27 through October 31 for artificial flies and lures only. The remainder of the river, including its north and south forks, is open from April 22 through October 31 for bait, lure, and fly angling.

Fishing Index: Lures, bait, and flies all work here. Good dry flies include such standbys as Elk Hair Caddis, Adams, and Blue-winged Olives. Grasshopper and other terrestrial patterns are good choices from midsummer through fall. Go with Muddler Minnows, leeches, Woolly Buggers, and Matukas for the larger rainbows and browns. Mouse patterns and other poppers can be effective for brown trout as well.

For the non-flyfisher, nightcrawlers and spinners, including Mepps and Rooster Tails, are good bets. In the slower middle reaches, nightcrawlers fished off the bottom will take bullheads and bass.

Fishing in this river is heavily influenced by water flows, and sudden snowmelt or downpours in the mountains can easily blow out the fishing, at least temporarily. It's not a bad idea to call the Oregon Department of Fish and Wildlife to see what river conditions are like before making a trip here.

Fishing for trout is best after June, when the initial snowmelt runoff from the mountains has subsided. For bass and bullheads, from July on is best. Later in the season, fishing for trout in the higher elevation tributaries is often better than in the mainstem. Here, you may run into bull trout. When fishing in this area, it is important to be able to distinguish bull trout from brook trout, since both species are here. Angling for bull trout is closed on this river system, and any accidently caught must be immediately released unharmed.

Directions: From Chiloquin (which is 25 miles north of Klamath Falls off U.S. Highway 97), go east on the Sprague River Highway (County Road 858) paralleling the river. This first 5-mile stretch is located within the Winema National Forest. After passing through about 6 miles of private lands, the road, and river, pass through another stretch of national forest. To reach the upper river and the north and south forks, continue on to the junction of Oregon Highway 140 and follow that highway east to Bly. From just east of Bly, various Forest Service roads lead to the river's forks in the Fremont National Forest. The Sprague River Recreation Site is located 4 miles east of Bly, off OR 140.

For More Information: Oregon Department of Fish and Wildlife, Klamath Falls District Office

67 Upper Klamath Lake

Key Species: rainbow trout

Best Way to Fish: boat, float tube

Best Time to Fish: late fall, winter, and spring

Description: Upper Klamath Lake is often regarded as essentially the same body of water as Agency Lake, to which it is attached on the north by a relatively wide channel.

Upper Klamath Lake is over 61,000 acres in size, but it only averages 14 feet in depth and is just 50 feet at its deepest. If you include Agency Lake, its size increases to 70,000 acres. Upper Klamath Lake is the largest natural freshwater lake in Oregon and is among the largest lakes in the country.

Upper Klamath Lake rainbow trout are predators, feeding on tui chub, blue chub, and fathead minnows. This high-protein diet results in trout up to 10 or 15 pounds and more. An average fish might run 4 or 5 pounds.

A boat (or float tube) is necessary here. Access for boaters is excellent, with 11 launches along Upper Klamath Lake and another six along Agency Lake. U.S. Highway 97 parallels the east side of the lake, while Oregon Highway 140 runs along its west side. There is a popular resort at Rocky Point on Upper Klamath Lake's west shore with cabins, camping, a store, and a variety of other amenities.

Rocky Point is a popular access point during the summer, while Moore Park Marina is more popular in the spring. Other good access areas include Hagelstein Park on the lake's east side, Pelican Marina off Lakeshore Drive, and Petric Park on Agency Lake.

Predatory Upper Klamath Lake rainbow trout may push the 10-pound barrier.

Upper Klamath Lake

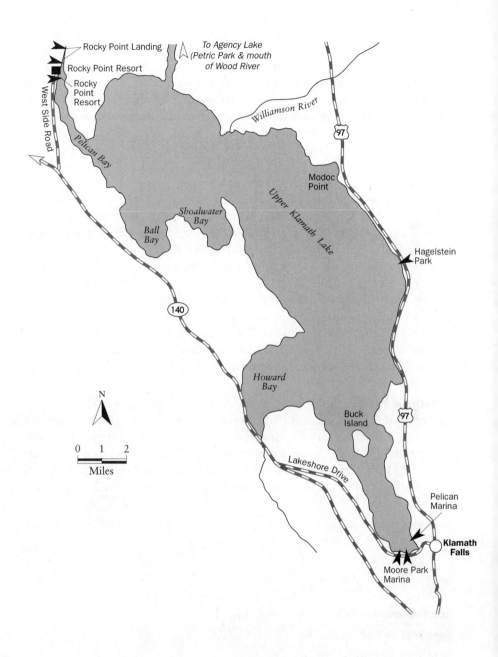

Rocky Point Landing

Rocky Point Resort

Rocky Point Resort

To Agency Lake
(Petric Park & mouth
of Wood River

Williamson River

97

West Side Road

Pelican Bay

Modoc
Point

Shoalwater
Bay

Ball
Bay

Upper Klamath Lake

Hagelstein
Park

140

Howard
Bay

Buck
Island

97

N

0   1   2
Miles

Lakeshore Drive

Pelican
Marina

Klamath
Falls

Moore Park
Marina

Fishing Index: To a great extent, the quality of fishing in Upper Klamath Lake is determined by prevailing water conditions. This lake is very eutrophic, and its loads of nutrients contribute to the trout's large size. But it also results in considerable algae blooms during the summer, which can put a serious damper on fishing. For this reason, the best angling here is during late fall, winter, and spring, when water quality is at its best. At these times, the trout are scattered throughout the reservoir in search of the baitfish on which they prey. As the water quality decreases with the warmer weather, the fish will seek out areas that still have colder, clear water. You will find the most fish where springs and other cold water sources flow into the lake. Good areas to search out trout during the summer months include along the west side of the lake, around Rocky Point, and the mouths of the Wood and Williamson rivers, where the fish begin to gather in July and August in preparation for their upstream spawning run.

A variety of standard techniques for catching trout work well here including bait, spinners, and flies. A basic rig such as a nightcrawler under a bobber is always effective, as is casting or trolling just about any spinner and spoon that will fool a big rainbow into thinking it's about to chomp on a tasty minnow. If you are looking to entice a whopper, you might want to try trolling a Rapala or Flatfish.

This is also a popular lake for fly anglers, who concentrate on its northern end. Pelican Bay is a favored location, as the water here tends to stay consistently clearer throughout the year. Good patterns for Upper Klamath Lake's lunkers include Woolly Buggers, Zonkers, leeches, and, a local favorite, Denny Rickards' Seal Bugger. When fishing in clear water, a long leader—up to 15 feet—is a good idea.

Directions: From Klamath Falls, go north on U.S. Highway 97. This highway runs along the lake's east side. To access the west side, go south from Klamath Falls on US 97 for about 2 miles. Turn right (west) onto Oregon Highway 140, which runs along the west side of the lake. To reach Rocky Point Resort, go about 25 miles north on OR 140 from its junction with US 97 in Klamath Falls. Turn right (north) onto West Side Road and drive about 3 miles to the resort.

For More Information: Oregon Department of Fish and Wildlife, Klamath Falls District Office and Rocky Point Resort

68 Klamath River

Key Species: rainbow trout

Best Way to Fish: bank, wading

Best Time to Fish: spring and fall

Description: About 40 miles of the Klamath River flows through southern Oregon between the California border and Klamath Lake.

Klamath River

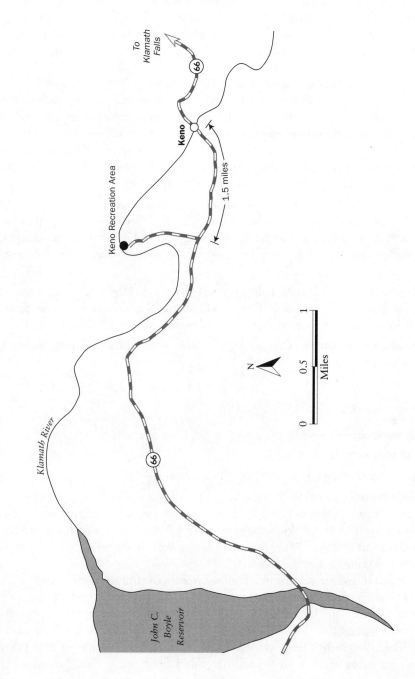

Perhaps the best, and most productive, stretch to fish is the 4.5-mile section from the town of Keno to J.C. Boyle Dam. This section of the river is significantly influenced by dams, and it's difficult to fish because of its irregular bottom and sudden drop-offs and holes. Anglers need to be sure-footed and alert. Restricted to artificial flies and lures only, it is a popular area for fly and spin fishers.

Rainbow trout here range around 18 inches on average, although it is possible to catch considerably larger ones. Because of high summer water temperatures, this section is closed to angling from mid-June to the end of December to minimize stress on the fish.

Easiest access to the upper end of this stretch is at the Keno Recreation Area. You can also park along Oregon Highway 66 west of Keno (watch for turnouts) and hike down the steep canyon to the river.

Fishing Index: There are lots of hatches along this piece of river, but nymphs and streamers tend to give better results than dry flies. Let your wet patterns go deep around boulders and in fast-moving waters. For spinners, cast Mepps, Panther Martins, and Rooster Tails, fishing the water thoroughly before moving on.

Directions: From Klamath Falls drive south on U.S. Highway 97 for about 2 miles. Turn right (west) onto Oregon Highway 66 for about 9 miles to Keno. The Keno Recreation Area turnoff is just west of Keno off OR 66.

For More Information: Oregon Department of Fish and Wildlife, Klamath Falls District Office

69 Lake of the Woods

Key Species: rainbow trout, brown trout, kokanee salmon

Best Way to Fish: boat, bank

Best Time to Fish: late April through October

Description: Lake of the Woods, located within the Winema National Forest in the southern Oregon Cascades, is a magnet for water recreationists ranging from anglers to water skiers. At just under 1,200 acres in size and located at an elevation of about 5,000 feet, Lake of the Woods averages 27 feet in depth with a maximum depth of 55 feet.

Open to fishing year-round, the lake freezes over in the winter, although it is typically melted out by the season opener in late April. The lake is usually frozen over by late December. It is a popular ice-fishing destination during the winter months.

The lake's brown trout average 14 to 19 inches while rainbows tend to fall into two categories—10-inch legal-size, and trophy fish in the 2-pound range. Kokanee average around 12 inches. In recent years, someone illegally stocked yellow perch in the lake, and state fishery managers encourage people to catch

Lake of the Woods

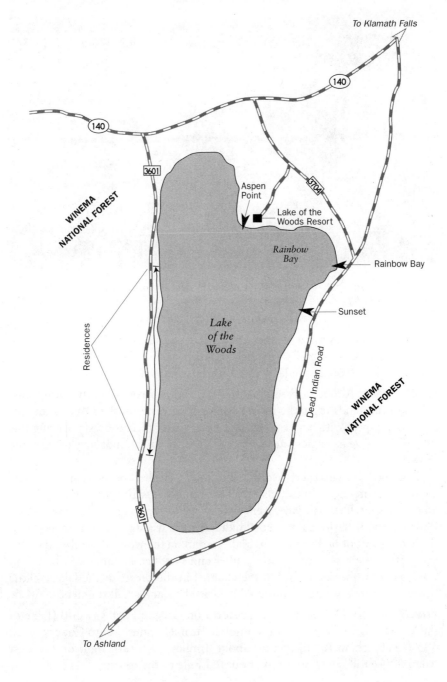

Nestled in the forests of the southern Cascades, Lake of the Woods fishes best just after ice-out in late April.

(and take home) as many as they can. There are also a few largemouth bass although they do not make up much of a fishery.

There is a resort at the lake and a fee boat launch.

Fishing Index: Although fishing is pretty good year-round, early spring, just after ice-out, tends to be the most popular time. Later in the summer anglers have to compete with water skiers and other water recreationists. During this busy time of year, anglers need to get out early in the morning to beat the crowds.

The lake's brown trout are difficult to catch. The best bet is trolling Rapalas along the shoreline. You can also troll for rainbows with spoons and spinners along the shoreline. Bait is very effective as well—especially nightcrawlers and Power Baits in flashy colors. For kokanee, troll Wedding Ring spinners with flasher set-ups, or jig Buzz Bombs and Nordics on the west side of the lake, off-shore from the residences. In September and October, kokanee will be found offshore from the resort and in the channel in the center of the lake. Yellow perch can be taken throughout the lake with bait and small spinners.

Directions: From Klamath Falls, go north on Oregon Highway 140 (Lake of the Woods Highway) for about 65 miles. Turn left (south) onto County Road 533 (Dead Indian Road) and go about 3 miles, then turn right onto Forest Road 3704, following the signs about 0.5 mile to the resort.

For More Information: Oregon Department of Fish and Wildlife, Klamath Falls District Office and Lake of the Woods Resort and Winema National Forest

70 Chewaucan River

Key Species: rainbow trout

Best Way to Fish: bank, wading

Best Time to Fish: spring, summer, fall

Description: A lesser-known, and off-the-beaten-path Oregon trout stream, the Chewaucan River nevertheless offers fine trout angling in a forested and open meadow setting. A visit here is an aesthetically pleasing experience.

The rainbows found in the Chewaucan range from 8 to 10 inches on average, although they can reach up to 16 inches. The state stopped stocking the river with hatchery fish in 1999, so it is beginning to revert back to a wild fishery.

Because much of it flows through the Fremont National Forest, there is good fishing access to the river. There is, however, a good deal of private land along the stream as well, especially in the meadow areas. Most landowners allow anglers to trespass, although some require written permission to do so. Some private property signs in the area have the landowner's phone number on them, so you can give them a call to seek permission. If you see someone working in an adjacent field, you can also try walking over to ask permission on the spot, which is often granted. Some good fishing can be had on these upper sections, so it is worth the effort to get permission to trespass from local landowners.

Fishing Index: The best bet for anglers is the first 10 miles above the small town of Paisley. Most of this section is either in national forest or owned by the Bureau of Land Management, making access excellent. Forest Road 33

The Elk Hair Caddis: an important staple and reliable stand-by for every fly fisher.

Chewaucan River

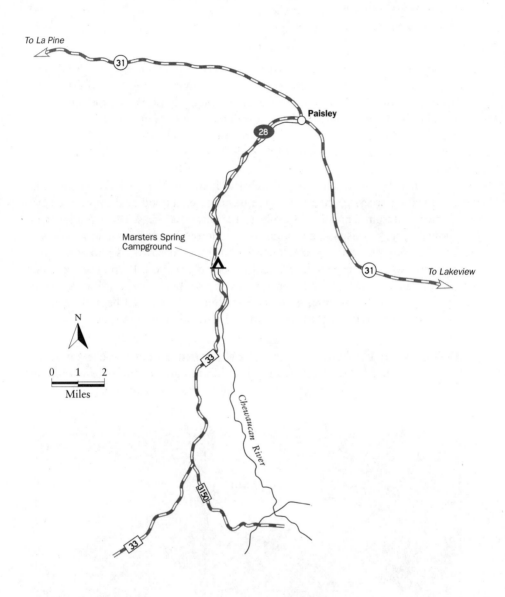

To La Pine

31

Paisley

28

31   To Lakeview

Marsters Spring
Campground

N

0   1   2
Miles

33

Chewaucan River

3150

33

parallels this river segment. Marsters Spring Campground, about 6 miles upriver from town, makes a good starting point. Above the 10-mile section, more private land becomes interspersed with public land, and you will need to be careful about where you are fishing, or secure permission. It is a good idea to have a Fremont National Forest map along with you to help you determine where the private lands are.

The river fishes well throughout the season, but it can temporarily blow out from high water, especially during the spring. Although some water is pulled out of the Chewaucan for irrigation, this happens downstream from Paisley, so it does not affect fishing on the upper reaches.

While lots of people fish spinners here, it is becoming more frequented by fly fishers. From mid-July on is a favorite time for fly anglers; the grasshoppers come out in full force, and anglers fish hopper patterns to full effect. At other times the basic standby fly patterns such as Adams, Elk Hair Caddis, and Royal Wulffs work quite nicely here.

Directions: From La Pine, drive south on Oregon Highway 51 for 97 miles to Paisley. From Paisley, take County Road 28 west, which eventually becomes Forest Road 33. It is about 6 miles to Marsters Spring Campground.

For More Information: Oregon Department of Fish and Wildlife, Lakeview District Office; Fremont National Forest

71 Ana River and Ana Reservoir

Key Species: rainbow trout, white-striped bass

Best Way to Fish: bank, boat (on reservoir)

Best Time to Fish: May, June, September, and October

Description: Flowing clear and cold from Ana Reservoir to Summer Lake in the Summer Lake Wildlife Area, the Ana River offers some nice angling in a desert environment for stocked rainbow trout in the 12- to 14-inch range. Although there are a small number of rainbows in the 58-acre reservoir, most of the fishing action here centers around the white-striped bass hybrids which the state stocks. The state record 18-pound, 8-ounce white-striped bass was taken at Ana Reservoir in 1996.

Ana Reservoir is open to angling year-round. The Ana River is open from April 22 through October 31. Only one bass—minimum 16 inches long—may be taken over a 24-hour period. There is primitive camping along the reservoir and at the nearby Summer Lake Wildlife Area. There is a boat ramp at the reservoir. Groceries and gas are available at the town of Summer Lake.

Fishing Index: Although rather small and out of the way, the Ana River is a nice fly fishing stream. Its clear water provides a challenge for dry-fly anglers who walk the banks looking for rising fish to gingerly cast to. The river is shallow, but wading is seldom necessary to fish it. Use such dry flies as Adams,

Ana River and Ana Reservoir

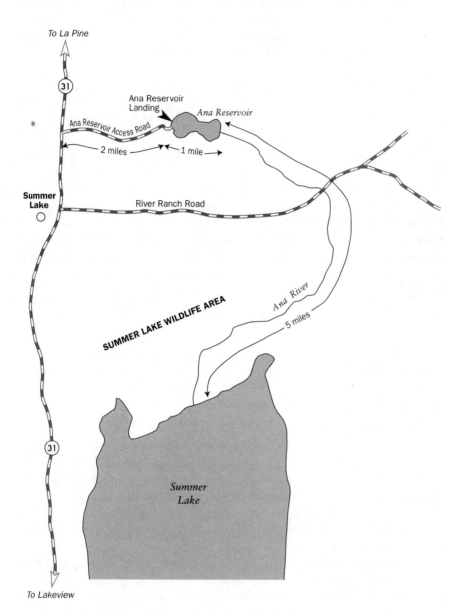

Comparaduns, Blue-winged Olives, midges, and Pale Morning Duns. For nymphs, go with scuds, Hare's Ears, and Pheasant Tails. Fishing tends to be better upriver; it drops off below, where the river crosses River Ranch Road and nears the wildlife area it: becomes slow moving and thick with chubs. There are some deep pools in this area, however, which hold a few nice rainbows that run to 3, 6, and 8 pounds.

Although trout in the reservoir are few and far between, you may catch some using a variety of bait and spinners. Nightcrawlers, prawns, plastic worms, and lures that mimic minnows work well for the bass hybrids. Although Ana Reservoir is easily fished from its banks, a boat and fish finder is far more effective since the bass tend to travel throughout the reservoir in schools. The bass are difficult to catch, requiring quite a bit of time and effort.

As with most desert fishing areas, the best angling will be had in the spring and fall, rather than during the hot and dry summer months.

Directions: From La Pine, drive south on U.S. Highway 97 for about 3 miles. Turn left (south) onto Oregon Highway 31 for 65 miles. Turn left (east) at a paved road with a sign for Ana Reservoir. Follow this road, which eventually turns to gravel, for about 2 miles to the reservoir and river.

For More Information: Oregon Department of Fish and Wildlife, Lakeview District Office

72 Chickahominy Reservoir

Key Species: rainbow trout

Best Way to Fish: wading, float tube, boat

Best Time to Fish: April and May, September and October

Description: This 500-acre irrigation reservoir smack in the middle of the sagebrush flats of eastern Oregon has one redeeming factor for anglers—big rainbow trout, or at least the distinct possibility. Chickahominy Reservoir is stocked with fingerling rainbow trout each year, and if they survive three years or so (there is no natural reproduction here) they may reach 3 to 4 pounds and be in excess of 20 inches. Average fish are in the 16- to 18-inch range.
There is primitive camping available here, and a fish cleaning station and boat ramp are on the south end of the lake. Chickahominy Reservoir is open to angling year-round with bait, lures, and flies.

A word of caution: The dirt roads leading to and around the reservoir become extremely muddy after rains, especially in the early spring, and they're notorious for swallowing up vehicles—even the rugged four-wheel-drive kind—so be cautious when traveling here under wet conditions.

In addition, the reservoir has dried up in years past, so it is a good idea to check with the Oregon Department of Fish and Wildlife on current conditions before traveling all the way out there.

Chickahominy Reservoir

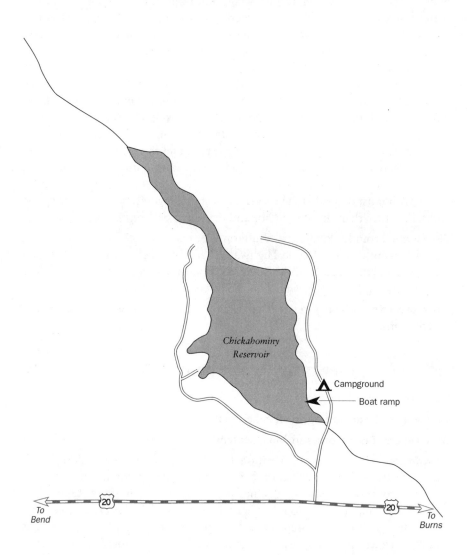

Chickahominy Reservoir

Campground

Boat ramp

To
Bend

To
Burns

Fishing Index: Anglers start showing up here in earnest as soon as the ice melts in March or April. As with all the desert lakes, fishing tends to be best early in the season, then again in the fall when cooler air and water temperatures prevail. Hot desert summers raise water temperatures and encourage algae growth, which puts a damper on fishing.

In early spring, fish tend to be in shallower water along the reservoir shoreline, and you can cast to them with flies or spinners. The west side of the lake is a good area to fish, especially in the coves. Concentrate on the edges of the reservoir in the fall as well. During the summer, as the water warms, the deep areas near the dam are best.

Typical flies to use here include black leech patterns, Woolly Buggers in dark colors, Pheasant Tail Nymphs, Zug Bugs, Princes, and Hare's Ears. These patterns are attractive to the reservoir's larger fish, especially when retrieved in jerky motions. Bait anglers favor nightcrawlers and Power Baits.

Along with potentially vehicle-trapping roads, another thing Chickahominy is famous for is its wind, which often comes up with a vengeance during the afternoons. There is little to be done but get in your best fishing early in the day.

Chickahominy is also a popular ice-fishing destination when it freezes solidly enough, which is not until January or February, and not every winter. Ice fishers typically use Power Bait, worms, Velveeta cheese, or jig.

Directions: From Bend drive about 100 miles east on U.S. Highway 20. Turn left (north) on the signed dirt entrance road to the lake, which is just off the highway.

For More Information: Oregon Department of Fish and Wildlife, Hines District Office

73 Delintment Lake/Yellowjacket Lake

Key Species: rainbow trout

Best Way to Fish: bank, boat, float tube

Best Time to Fish: May and June, September and October

Description: These two small lakes (50 and 35 acres, respectively) are popular destinations for anglers from the high-desert city of Burns. But they also attract fly fishers from other parts of the state, as they offer the opportunity for some pleasant fishing in a mountain environment. Delintment Lake is in the Ochoco National Forest. Yellowjacket Lake is in the Malheur National Forest.

Rainbow trout in both waters may reach up to 20 inches, although fish in the 12- to 14-inch range are more common. Although bank fishing is entirely possible here, many anglers launch small boats. Float tubes are an excellent option for fly fishers.

Delintment Lake/Yellowjacket Lake

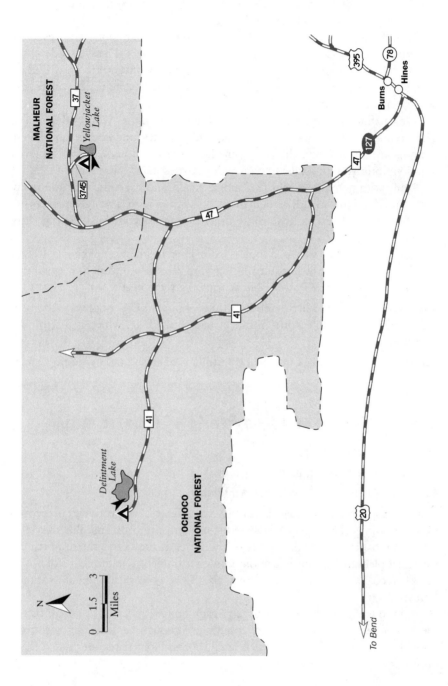

The stealth and mobility of a float tube increase an angler's versatility.

Both lakes are open to angling year-round, although, as is typical for most stillwaters in the high-desert country, spring and fall are best since low water and algal blooms often make midsummer fishing problematic.

Access into both lakes can be difficult early in the season when roads are muddy from snowmelt. Before venturing out, it is a good idea to call ahead for road conditions.

There are USDA Forest Service campgrounds at both lakes.

Fishing Index: Most people fish bait, such as Power Bait and nightcrawlers, at Yellowjacket Lake. Bait works just as well at Delintment.

Fly anglers will do best with such patterns as black leeches, Woolly Buggers in dark colors, Pheasant Tail Nymphs, Zug Bugs, Princes, and Hare's Ears. As is typical of desert lakes, the trout will be nearer the surface and shorelines during the spring, going deeper as the water warms throughout the season.

Both lakes have good ice fishing when winter weather turns cold enough to make the ice thick enough to walk on, although, when snow accumulates on access roads, snowmobiles are the only way in. Ice fishers use bait and jig.

Directions: To reach Delintment Lake from Hines (immediately south of Burns), go northwest on Forest Road 47 about 14 miles. Turn left (west) onto FR 41 and go about 35 miles to the lake. To reach Yellowjacket Lake, follow FR 47 off U.S. Highway 20 at Hines, for about 30 miles. Turn right (east) onto FR 37 and go about 4 miles to the lake.

For More Information: Ochoco National Forest, Malheur National Forest

74 Krumbo Reservoir

Key Species: rainbow trout, largemouth bass, white crappie

Best Way to Fish: bank, boat, float tube

Best Time to Fish: April, May and September, October

Description: One of a number of small desert lakes with excellent fishing, 150-acre Krumbo Reservoir is located within the Malheur National Wildlife Refuge south of Burns. It holds rainbow trout that average in the 16-inch range, along with largemouth bass and some white crappie.

As is typical of desert lakes, fishing is best in the spring and fall when the weather and water is cooler. Fishing in summer, under the blazing desert sun, can be quite uncomfortable and the bite tends to be off when the water warms up.

Krumbo Reservoir is open to angling from April 22 through October 31.

Fishing Index: Although many anglers still-fish with nightcrawlers and Power Bait, it is also a popular location for fly fishers. Pheasant Tail nymphs, leeches, and Woolly Buggers are good all around choices.

While bank fishing is possible early in the season, a small boat or float tube is necessary later in the year when the water level drops.

Directions: From Burns, go east on Oregon Highway 78 for 2 miles, then south for 45 miles on Oregon Highway 205. Turn left (east) at the sign for Krumbo Reservoir and drive about 4 miles to the reservoir.

For More Information: Oregon Department of Fish and Wildlife, Hines District Office

75 Blitzen River

Key Species: rainbow trout

Best Way to Fish: wading

Best Time to Fish: September and October

Description: Although commonly referred to as the Blitzen, its true name is the Donner und Blitzen River, German for thunder and lightning. It was awarded that moniker by U.S. Army troops who crossed the river during a ferocious electrical storm in the 1860s while in pursuit of Snake Indians.

A small stream flowing through a narrow canyon laced with ponderosa pines and junipers, the Blitzen's headwaters are on Steens Mountain, one of the great geologic features of Oregon's Great Basin Desert and a wondrous and wild area in its own right.

In addition to its remoteness and grand open spaces, what attracts anglers to the Blitzen River is its population of redband trout, a type of rainbow trout that has evolved to survive in the harsh environment of this high-desert country. The native redbands here average around 12 inches, although it is possible to catch fish up to 20 inches or so.

Krumbo Reservoir • Blitzen River

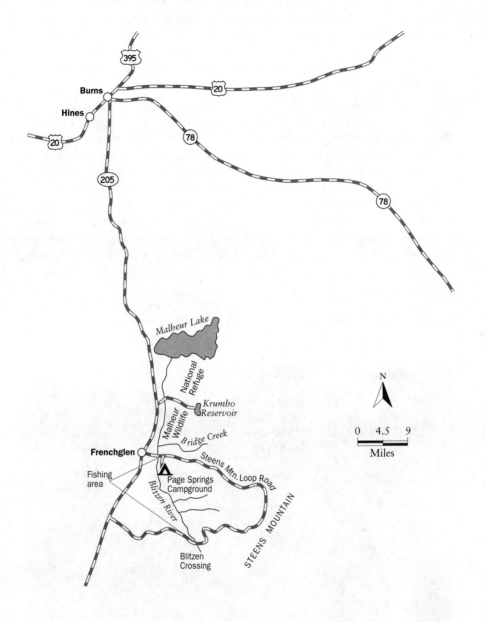

The Blitzen is open to fishing year-round, with artificial flies and lures only. Only the upper river, above Bridge Creek on the Malheur National Wildlife Refuge is open to fishing. Most anglers start at Page Springs Campground, just south of the refuge boundary and fish upstream from there. The upper 35 miles of the river, located mostly on public lands, has been designated a Wild and Scenic River and is managed by the Bureau of Land Management.

Fishing Index: Because the Blitzen is fed by snowmelt from Steens Mountain in the spring, the water is high, murky, and not very fishable until July. But hot summer temperatures sometimes make fishing during this time of year uncomfortable, and many who fish here regard September and October as the prime time to visit. Fishing can be good in the winter as well but it sometimes freezes over, so watch local temperatures before you make the drive.

The best fishing is along the 15-mile stretch between Page Springs Campground and where the river crosses the Steens Mountain Loop Road at Blitzen Crossing. Since most anglers start at Page Springs and only go upstream a mile or two, the farther you are willing to walk, the better fishing you will have, although, the fish tend to become smaller the closer you get to the headwaters.

Approach the Blitzen as you would any other trout stream, concentrating on riffles, pocket water, eddies, and pools. Deeper water under cut-banks tend

The Blitzen River is home to a popular strain of rainbow trout, the redband. The redband trout have evolved and adapted to southeastern Oregon's desert climate.

For small-stream angling, fly fishing is often a better recipe for success than spin fishing.

to hold some of the larger fish. Generally, the river is shallow and easily waded throughout its length.

Most anglers on the Blitzen fly fish using such classic patterns as Elk Hair Caddis, Adams, Royal Wulffs, Prince Nymphs, and Hare's Ears. Grasshoppers and other terrestrials are especially good patterns to use in the fall. If you decide to brave the cold weather for some winter fishing, you will want to stick with nymphs. Lure anglers generally go with spinners year-round.

Directions: From Burns, drive east on Oregon Highway 78 for 2 miles. Turn right (south) on Oregon Highway 205 and go 60 miles to Frenchglen. Turn left (east) onto the dirt road at the south end of town toward Page Springs Campground and drive 3.5 miles to the campground turnoff, which is on the right.

For More Information: Oregon Department of Fish and Wildlife, Hines District Office

Key Species: rainbow trout

Best Way to Fish: bank, wading

Best Time to Fish: mid- to late October

Description: A major river system in the high and dry desert country of south-eastern Oregon, the Malheur also has a nice trout fishery, at least in certain spots at certain times of the year. Generally accessible from adjacent roads, the mainstem and North Fork are the primary destinations for anglers. The South Fork flows through mostly private property and has lesser water quality than the other two, making it considerably less desirable to fish.

Rainbow trout here typically average in the 8- to 12-inch range. The Malheur is open all year to angling with flies, lures, and bait. Only flies and lures are allowed on the North Fork, upstream from Beulah Reservoir to its headwaters.

Because of the hot summer desert temperatures and water withdrawals from the river for irrigation, fall is the best time to visit the Malheur. There are lots of places for primitive, undeveloped camping throughout the area.

Fishing Index: Most anglers fish the 15-mile section of the Malheur from Riverside, below Warm Springs Reservoir to Juntura. Water levels fluctuate seasonally because the river flow is controlled for irrigation at the Warm Springs Reservoir. During the summer months, it runs at a fairly constant level of about 150 cubic feet per second, providing even flows. While it is possible to catch fish then, few anglers visit during the summer because of the very hot and dry weather conditions. By mid-October, the river flow below the dam is shut way down to around 15 cubic feet per second, creating a nice assortment of pools and riffles to fish. This is the time when most anglers fish the Malheur. Bait, spinners, and flies are all commonly and successfully used here. This section of river is owned by the state of Oregon and is within the Riverside Wildlife Area. It is open to public access.

Fewer anglers fish the 8- or 10-mile stretch of river below Juntura, even though there can be some pretty good fishing here. It is accessible via U.S. Highway 20. Look for turnouts to park your vehicle, then walk down to the river.

The North Fork headwaters area, within the Malheur National Forest, also offers good fishing for rainbow trout. There are bull trout in this fork, but fishing for them is not allowed.

Directions: From Burns, drive east on Oregon Highway 78 for about 30 miles to the small hamlet of Crane. At Crane, follow the dirt road east for 34 miles to Riverside (a small collection of buildings). At Riverside, turn right onto the dirt track and follow it a short distance to the Riverside Wildlife Area, where you can park near the river. To reach the stretch of river below Juntura, drive east from Burns on OR 20 for about 55 miles. To reach the upper North Fork

Malheur River

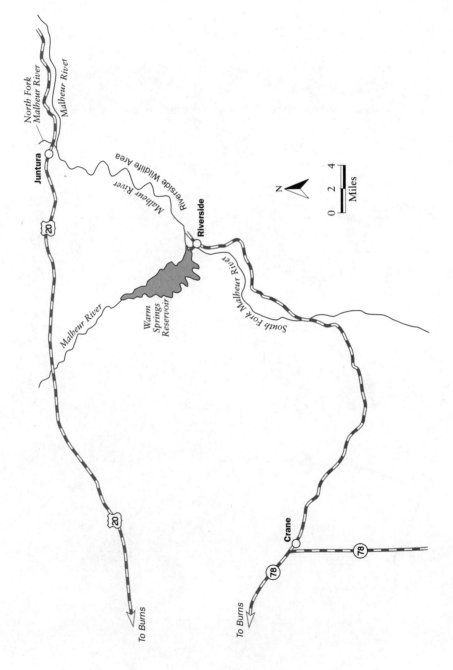

Malheur River

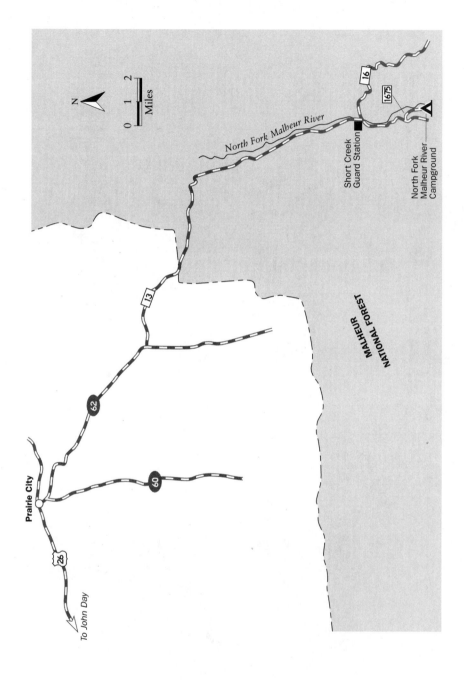

Malheur drive east from John Day on US 26 for 12 miles. At Prairie City, go south on County Road 62 for about 6 miles to Forest Road 13. Turn left (east) on FR 13 and drive for about 17 miles, passing the Short Creek Guard Station. Turn left onto FR 1675 and drive 3 miles to the North Fork Malheur Campground, a good starting point to fish.

For More Information: Oregon Department of Fish and Wildlife, Hines District Office

77 Mann Lake

Key Species: cutthroat trout

Best Way to Fish: wading, float tube

Best Time to Fish: April and May, September and October

Description: This 270-acre lake in the middle of the desert features a type of hatchery-raised Lahontan cutthroat trout stocked here by the Oregon Department of Fish and Wildlife. They average about 14 inches, but fish up to 20 inches are not particularly rare.

Although Mann Lake is open year-round, spring and fall are the best times to fish here. Hot summer temperatures combined with increased aquatic plant growth slows fishing down considerably. During the winter the lake freezes over, but not many brave the remote location and bitter winter temperatures to take advantage of the ice-fishing opportunities here.

There are two gravel boat ramps along the lake, although most anglers here wade or use float tubes, which may be easily launched from anywhere along the lake shore. There are also primitive, undeveloped camping areas along the lake.

Mann Lake is limited to angling with flies and lures only.

Fishing Index: Most anglers come to Mann Lake in March and April, just after the ice melts out and the fish are hungrily cruising the weed beds for insects. As the water temperatures drop in September and October, in the wake of the intense heat of a desert summer, fishing gets good once again.

Most of the cutthroats tend to be along the shoreline, so fishing from the banks is fairly easily accomplished. You can also wade—which most anglers do—and cast toward shore. Some anglers use float tubes or boats to increase their mobility.

Mann Lake has good Callibaetis hatches along with damselflies and midges, but nymphs and streamers tend to be most effective. Try such patterns as leeches, Woolly Buggers, and Zug Bugs. For lures, spinners are popular, including Mepps and Panther Martins.

Directions: From Burns, drive southeast on Oregon Highway 78 for about 64 miles. Turn south on Fields-Denio Road (a good gravel road) and go about 35 miles to the sign marking the access turn-off to the lake on the west side of the road.

Mann Lake

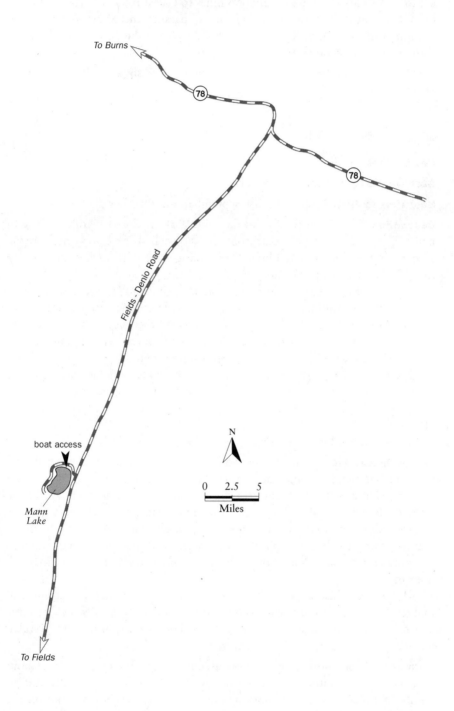

To Burns

78

78

Fields - Denio Road

boat access

Mann
Lake

To Fields

N

0   2.5   5
Miles

For More Information: Oregon Department of Fish and Wildlife, Hines District Office

78 Owyhee River

Key Species: rainbow trout, brown trout

Best Way to Fish: bank, wading

Best Time to Fish: April through October

Description: This 10-mile stretch of the Owyhee River below Owyhee Dam is a classic tailwater trout fishery, created by regular cold water releases from the Owyhee reservoir. Once considered a remote location fished primarily by locals, it has become popular with fly fishers. But because of its proximity to the Idaho border and distance from Oregon population areas, anglers you meet here are more likely to be from Boise than Portland.

Hatchery rainbow and brown trout make up the quarry on this desert river. They grow big, averaging around 18 inches, with fish up to 30 inches not unheard of.

Because the water held back by the dam is used for irrigation, the flow to the lower river is shut off around mid- to late October, then turned on again in April, after a winter's worth of water has been stored in the reservoir. This makes for roughly a six-month window of good fishing. Winter flows are

During summer, riffles, like this one, hold more oxygen and thus more trout. Drifting a nymph or large dry fly through the broken current will produce.

Owyhee River • Lake Owyhee

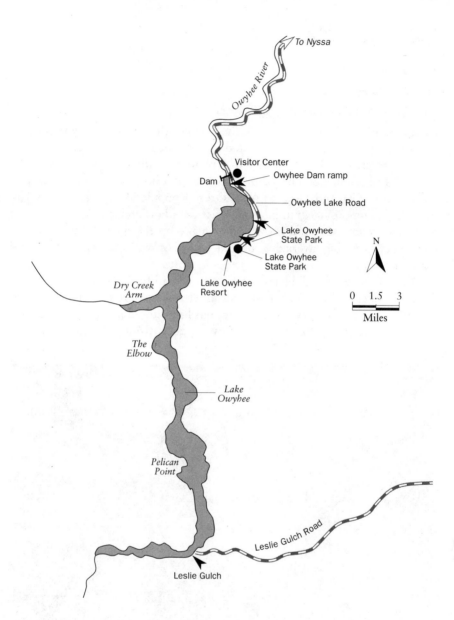

To Nyssa

Owyhee River

Visitor Center

Owyhee Dam ramp

Dam

Owyhee Lake Road

Lake Owyhee
State Park

Lake Owyhee
State Park

Lake Owyhee
Resort

Dry Creek
Arm

The
Elbow

Lake
Owyhee

Pelican
Point

N

0   1.5   3
Miles

Leslie Gulch Road

Leslie Gulch

generally around 10 to 20 cubic feet per second, while summer flows average around 200.

Access to the river is good, with a paved road running along the river, through mostly public lands managed by the Bureau of Land Management and the Bureau of Reclamation.

The Owyhee is open to angling year-round. Angling for brown trout is catch-and-release only.

Fishing Index: Most anglers concentrate along the upper part of the river, closer to the dam, accessing it via the day use area at the end of the road right after you cross over the dam.

Bait anglers find the best time is April, just before the water is turned on for the summer, and in late October, just after the water is turned off. At these times the water level is low, which concentrates the trout into pools and makes them easier to locate. When fishing at this time of year, concentrate in these isolated, deeper areas. A variety of typical baits do just fine here, including nightcrawlers, eggs, cheese, and Power Bait.

Fly anglers find the fishing better during the summer months when flows are steady, creating a long series of pools and riffles. Any small fly imitation works here—try Adams and Elk-hair Caddis. On the Owyhee, you are often casting to individual, rising fish, rather than simply floating your offering to see what might take it. Watch for feeding activity as you go. Dredging deep water with a nymph can hold promise for hooking into a big one. Matukas and Woolly Buggers are also good patterns with which to probe deep areas.

Spinners are also effective here. Try using Rooster Tails and Panther Martins. There is a bit of algae throughout the river, which can hang-up your lures—but this biological productivity is why the fish here get so big.

Directions: From Nyssa, follow Oregon Highway 201 south about 12 miles (following the signs to Lake Owyhee). As you drive south on Owyhee Lake Road, you will pass Snively Hot Springs. The road parallels the river from here upstream to Owyhee Dam where you can gain river access. Most of the river along this stretch flows through public lands.

For More Information: Oregon Department of Fish and Wildlife, Ontario District Office

79 Lake Owyhee

Key Species: black crappie, largemouth bass, smallmouth bass, channel catfish

Best Way to Fish: boat, some bank

Best Time to Fish: May through September

Description: At 139,000 acres, Lake Owyhee is Oregon's largest reservoir. Used both to provide irrigation water for surrounding farmlands and for water-based recreation, the lake was formed by damming the Owyhee River, which flows out of the high-desert country and into the Snake River near Nyssa, on the Oregon-Idaho border. Lake Owyhee is located in a rugged desert canyon and has about 150 miles of shoreline. Average depth of the reservoir is about 80 feet. Maximum depth is 117 feet.

An excellent warmwater fishery, it is especially known for its black crappie, although it also contains excellent populations of largemouth and smallmouth bass and channel catfish. Crappie here average around 7 or 8 inches. Largemouth bass are typically in the 14- to 16-inch range, while smallmouth grow to 12 to 14 inches. Channel catfish are typically about 2 pounds, although fish up to 8 pounds prowl the lake's depths.

One note of caution: Because of mercury contamination, the State of Oregon recommends limitations on the amount of fish eaten from Lake Owyhee. See the Oregon fishing regulations handbook for details.

There are five boat ramps along the reservoir, but most anglers use the ramp by the dam. Lake Owyhee is open to angling year-round.

Fishing Index: Lake Owyhee has an outstanding black crappie fishery. Jigs and small spinners prove the most effective technique for catching them. Most of the crappie concentrate in the lower reservoir, making the area around the dam a good place to focus your efforts. There is a boat ramp at the dam for convenient access. It is also possible to fish for crappie from shore along the 4-mile stretch of road that parallels the reservoir upstream from the dam. Just pull over, park, and try casting spinners, or fish with worms under a bobber. Largemouth bass are more likely found in the backs of coves in the upper reservoir, while smallmouth hang out in colder, clearer water, preferring the lower reservoir near the dam. Typical bass lures—plastics, plugs, spinnerbaits, and poppers—all work well here.

Channel catfish are caught by fishing bait, mainly nighcrawlers, on the bottom in deeper holes. They are more common in the upper reservoir.

Directions: From Nyssa, follow Oregon Highway 201 south about 25 miles, following the signs to Lake Owyhee and the dam.

For More Information: Oregon Department of Fish and Wildlife, Ontario District Office and Lake Owyhee State Park

80 Powder River

Key Species: rainbow trout, smallmouth bass

Best Way to Fish: bank, wading

Best Time to Fish: spring, summer, fall

Description: Draining a big piece of some of Oregon's wildest country, the Powder River system encompasses numerous high lakes, small wild trout-bearing tributary streams, and four good-sized reservoirs as well as the mainstem itself. The Powder River eventually flows into Brownlee Reservoir at Richland.

Powder River

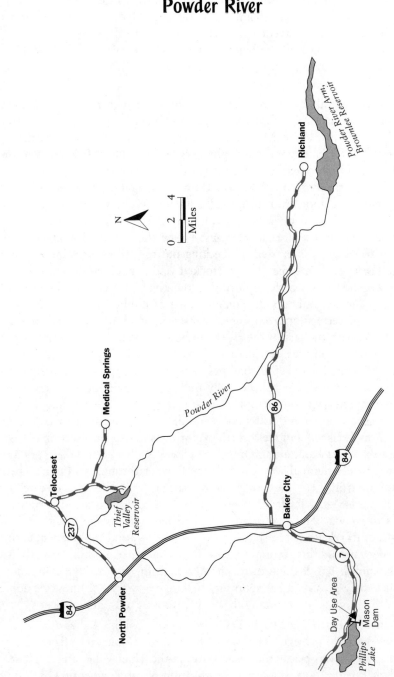

N

0 2 4
Miles

Richland

Powder River Arm,
Brownlee Reservoir

Medical Springs

Powder River

86

84

Telocaset

Thief
Valley
Reservoir

237

Baker City

84

7

North Powder

Day Use Area

Mason
Dam

Phillips
Lake

Primarily a rainbow trout stream, there is also a nice, accessible small-mouth bass fishery just upstream from Richland. Trout in the Powder are mostly stocked fish and average 8 to 10 inches, although larger ones are possible. Smallmouth bass generally grow to a maximum of around 12 inches.

The Powder River is open to angling from April 22 through the end of October.

Fishing Index: While much of the Powder flows through private land, there are several good stretches of interest to anglers. One of these is the mile stretch of public access just below Mason Dam at Phillips Lake. The rainbow fishery here attracts everyone from worm plunkers to fly anglers. It is good in the spring when season opens, and because of the constant stream of cool water released from the bottom of Mason Dam for irrigation downstream, this stretch remains a good trout fishery all summer. As the water level drops in the fall, fishing slows but can still provide some decent sport. There is a USDA Forest Service day use area located just below the dam and boat launches above it, for anglers interested in checking out the stillwater rainbow trout fishery. There are also some illegally stocked yellow perch in the reservoir.

The second area worth exploring is the river just below Thief Valley Reservoir. There is only about a quarter mile of public lands here, but it is possible to get permission from some downstream landowners to fish on their property. As with the rest of the river, rainbows average in the 8- to 10-inch range, although you may catch some up to 14 inches. Access is right at the dam, by walking down a spur road past the gate. Late spring and early summer are the best times to fish here. By mid-June algae appears in the river, slowing fishing down considerably. There is also some decent fishing here in the fall, as the weather and water cools and the summer algae growth dies off.

Not heavily fished, but well worth exploring is the 15-mile section of public accessible river bank along Oregon Highway 86 between Baker City and Richland, where the highway parallels the Powder through a canyon. There are rainbow trout here, best sought in the spring when the odds of catching some of the larger, wild fish are greater as they gather to ascend tributary streams to spawn. (Since there are plenty of hatchery fish in this river, it is always best to release wild fish, even when the regulations do not require it.)

As the water on this section warms—from June through mid-September—the smallmouth bass fishing turns on. Although the fish are typically under 12 inches, they provide great sport and will take a variety of lures, including plastics that imitate worms and other baits, Rooster tails, and poppers.

Directions: To reach the Mason Dam area below Phillips Lake, drive south from Baker City on Oregon Highway 7 for about 14 miles. The day use area is on the left (south) below the dam. To reach the Thief Valley Reservoir section of the Powder, go about 8 miles north from North Powder on OR 237 to Telocaset. Take the road from Telocaset southeast toward Medical Springs for about 15 miles to the dam. To reach the smallmouth bass stretch, take the

OR 86 exit of Interstate 84 just north of Baker City. Go east on OR 86 for about 15 miles to where it intersects with and begins paralleling the river.

For More Information: Oregon Department of Fish and Wildlife, Northeast Region Office

81 Brownlee Reservoir

Key Species: black crappie, white crappie, channel catfish, smallmouth bass

Best Way to Fish: boat

Best Time to Fish: spring and fall

Description: This reservoir on the Snake River is operated by Idaho Power, of Boise, and is eastern Oregon's top warmwater fishery. In recent years, however, water withdrawals for flood control and salmon conservation sometimes have caused the reservoir to become low enough to affect fishing and the ability to launch a boat—a necessity for effectively fishing this water.

In addition, Brownlee's signature fishery of crappie, has dropped off in recent years, most likely due to a normal cyclic fluctuation in the population combined with a series of good water years, which has suppressed the high nutrient concentrations that benefit these fish. Nevertheless, Brownlee Reservoir continues to be an excellent fishery that's well worth a visit if water levels are right.

Before making a fishing trip to Brownlee, it is prudent to check reservoir levels to determine where boats may be launched. When the reservoir level is at it slowest, the only place to launch a boat may be at Idaho Power's Woodhead Park on the Idaho side. Call Idaho Power's reservoir level information line (1-800-422-3143) for current conditions. If the conditions at Brownlee are less than ideal, consider a trip to Lake Owyhee to the south rather than giving up on your outing all together.

One note of caution: Because of mercury contamination, the State of Oregon recommends limitations on the amount of fish eaten from Brownlee Reservoir. See the Oregon fishing regulations handbook for details.

Brownlee is open to angling year-round. Not all of the reservoir is considered Oregon waters. Brownlee Reservoir angling regulations will be found in the Snake River Zone section of the *Oregon Sport Fishing Regulations* handbook. There are six boat launches on the Oregon side of the reservoir.

Fishing Index: Spring and fall are best for both white and black crappie. Summer is fine too, but you will have to fish a bit deeper. Black crappie fishing is best in the upper reservoir, while white crappie are more abundant in the lower section. Fish off points, around structure, and in back bays where tributaries come in. Crappie here average 8 to 10 inches. Crappie jigs and small spoons are effective lures.

Smallmouth bass fishing is also best in the spring and fall. Brownlee Reservoir has lots of straight, even-sloped sides, so anywhere there's a break

Brownlee Reservoir

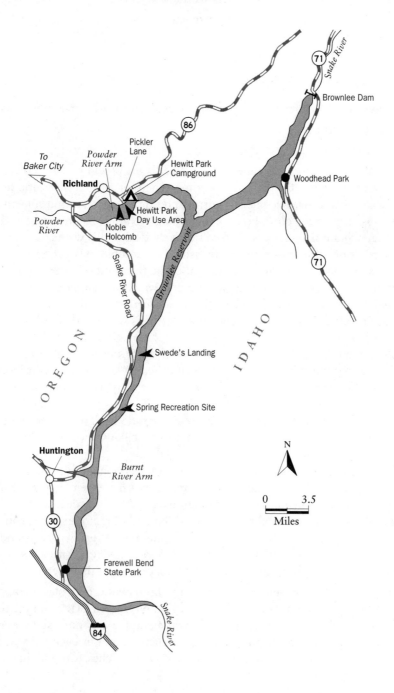

in the topography, such as points, is a good bet. There are over 200,000 small-mouth bass in the lake. The bass here tend to top out at 12 inches, largely because that is the minimum legal size, so anglers usually take them home for dinner rather than releasing them to grow larger. Poppers, crankbaits, spinnerbaits, and plastics are all good approaches.

There is also a large population of channel catfish (and some flathead catfish) that averages around 16 inches—and there are some in the 20-pound range. Fish the bottom with bait for these fish. Good spots for catfish include the Powder River arm, off the mouth at the Burnt River, and upstream from Farewell Bend (if the water is high enough to get there).

There are rainbow trout here also, but this fishery is insignificant.

Directions: Drive east from Baker City on Oregon Highway 86 for about 38 miles to Richland to reach the Powder River arm of Brownlee Reservoir. The Farewell Bend State Park access point is about 25 miles north of Ontario, off Interstate 84.

For More Information: Oregon Department of Fish and Wildlife, Northeast Region office

Northeast Oregon

The mountainous landscape of this part of Oregon has more in common geologically with the Rocky Mountains than with the Cascades. While the images of fishing for wild trout in rugged mountain settings is true, there are steelhead and salmon streams out here as well.

Unless you live here, fishing this country will probably require a bit of a drive, so advance planning will be in order. Although boats are useful for some rivers and on lakes and reservoirs, much of the angling here is classic bank and wading. For this reason your excursion is likely to take you onto back roads and forest trails. Having a good complement of topographic and Forest Service maps is a good idea for expeditions to this area.

Unless otherwise noted, regulations for the waters listed in this section will be found in the Northeast Zone section of the *Oregon Sport Fishing Regulations* handbook.

82 John Day River

Key Species: steelhead, smallmouth bass

Best Way to Fish: boat, some bank

Best Time to Fish: steelhead, September through March; smallmouth bass, May through early July

The John Day River offers an excellent smallmouth bass fishery along with steelhead amidst a striking desert canyon.

John Day River

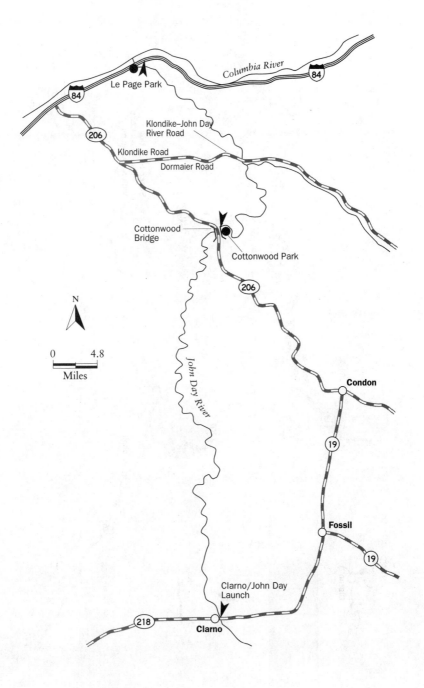

John Day River

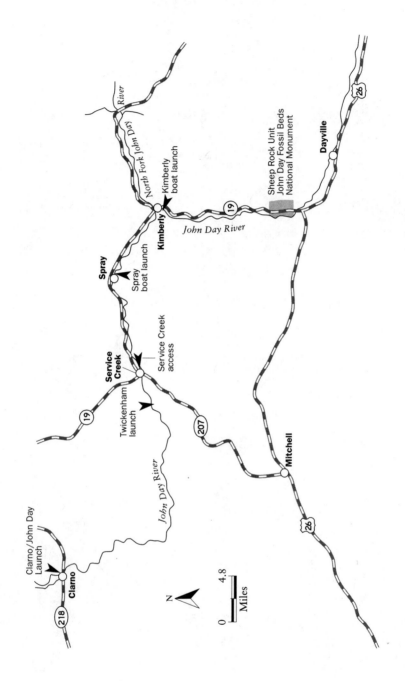

Description: The John Day River meanders from its headwaters in the Blue Mountains of northeastern Oregon through ranch lands and desert canyons and empties into the Columbia River just upstream from the John Day Dam. A long-time favorite for steelhead anglers, a highly popular smallmouth bass fishery has also developed in recent years.

While the river passes through public lands, much of it flows through private ranch and rangeland, making angling access a mixed bag. In many cases, boaters have an advantage over bank anglers, since they can float through sections where those on foot are not allowed.

Steelhead are in the John Day system from September into April and beyond, although exactly where and when to fish for them depends, since they are in different river reaches at different times as they make their way upstream for their annual spawning run.

John Day steelhead average around 4 to 6 pounds. The river's smallmouth are typically in the 8- to 10-inch range, but can get as large as 20 inches.

A variety of angling regulations apply on this river, depending on what segment you are on and whether you are fishing for steelhead or bass. Be sure and study the latest fishing rules before setting out.

Fishing Index: Steelhead are in the river from its mouth to Cottonwood Bridge from September to December. At this time of year, at least into early November when the water is not yet too cold and the fish fairly active, fly fishing is the most popular technique. Fly fishers rely on such standby steelhead flies as Woolly Worms, Purple Perils, and Babine Specials. This segment, from Cottonwood Bridge downstream, is the most popular on the river. Boaters can put in at Cottonwood Park and float downstream from there. There is also some bank access around Cottonwood Bridge and at the mouth of Rock Creek, as well as on some scattered patches of Bureau of Land Management land. You will need to pick up one of the BLM's maps of the lower John Day River area to help find your way around. Contact BLM if you plan to float the river, as there are a variety of regulations in force on some sections.

As the water cools off from November on and the fish need a bit more motivation to strike, anglers switch from flies to standard steelhead drift techniques. Drifting a Corky and nightcrawler is a favorite on the John Day.

By December and January, the fish are on the river reach between Cottonwood Bridge and Kimberly. There is little public access between Cottonwood and Service Creek. By February and into March, the fish move upriver. Anglers can get good bank access where the river passes through the Sheep Rock Unit of the John Day Fossil Beds National Monument. From March and into mid-April when the season finally closes, the steelhead move up into the North Fork John Day.

The smallmouth fishery is mostly confined from Service Creek downstream to the mouth. Because of the limited bank access on this reach, it is mainly a boat fishery. There are seven boat launches where anglers can put in and take out between Service Creek and the Columbia River.

The John Day is large and wide, but don't be intimidated because fish in the John Day hold in the same places as they do in smaller rivers.

In April and May, when water temperatures are still low, smallmouth are best taken with crankbaits. Bass action really gets into full swing in late May and goes through early July. During this warmer time of year, many anglers target smallmouth on the surface with poppers. Cast for them over gravel runs and around boulders and other in-stream structure.

Directions: To reach Cottonwood Bridge, go south from Biggs (on the Columbia River) on U.S. Highway 97 for about 10 miles, then follow Oregon Highway 206 south for about 15 miles. To reach bank access around the John Day Fossil Beds National Monument, drive 77 miles east from Prineville on US 26. Turn left (north) onto OR 19. This road passes the park headquarters and parallels much of the river, with many turn-outs where you can park and fish.

For More Information: Oregon Department of Fish and Wildlife, John Day District Office and Bureau of Land Management, Prineville Office

83 Umatilla River

Key Species: Chinook salmon, coho salmon, steelhead, rainbow trout

Best Way to Fish: bank

Best Time to Fish: Chinook salmon, September through December and May through June; coho salmon, September through December; steelhead, September through mid-April; rainbow trout, June through October

Umatilla River

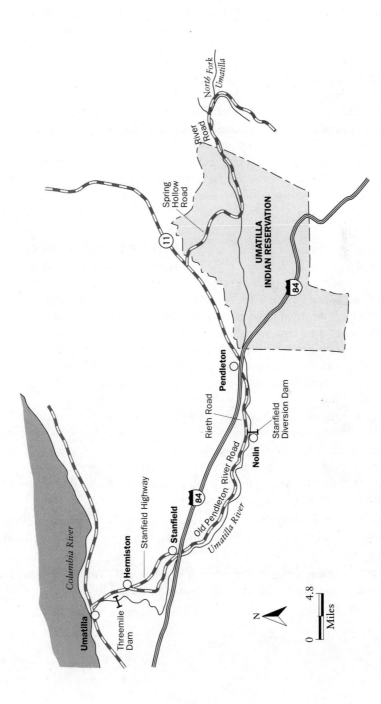

Description: The Umatilla River flows out of the Umatilla National Forest and joins the Columbia River at Umatilla, north of Hermiston. In its lower reaches, it offers steelhead and coho and fall Chinook salmon angling. The season on spring Chinook varies from year to year, depending on run projections made by state fishery mangers. The upper river has a nice population of rainbow trout, as well as lots of whitefish and some bull trout.

Fall Chinook salmon and coho salmon are in the river from August through December, peaking in October and November. Spring Chinook typically make their spawning run here between mid-April and early July. Steelhead are in the river from September and into May, although the season closes for them in mid-April. They peak from October through December.

A variety of angling regulations are in effect for the Umatilla River, depending on which stretch you are fishing and what species you are after. Check the current regulations for the latest details. A tribal fishing permit is needed for angling on sections of the river within the Umatilla Indian Reservation.

Fishing Index: The Umatilla is mainly a bank fishery. Fishing for steelhead and Chinook and coho salmon takes place between Pendleton and the river's mouth. There are rainbow trout in this reach as well.

A lot of the access to this river is around bridges. Access is good around Pendleton, but downstream the river flows through mostly private lands. Fortunately, many area landowners are pretty good about giving permission to fish on their properties. The area around the Stanfield Diversion Dam at river mile 35 near Nolin is another good access area. Between Threemile Dam (at river mile 3) downstream to the mouth is also a good stretch. This section is all on public lands administered by the Bureau of Reclamation.

Angling techniques for salmon are a mix of casting spinners and drifting eggs, shrimp, and Corkies from the bank. The same techniques are used as well for steelhead, although many anglers fly fish.

Very nice rainbow trout fishing can be had in the upper river, with excellent access, particularly within the Umatilla National Forest. Trout angling here is artificial flies and lures, catch-and-release only.

Directions: The lower Umatilla River is accessible via U.S. Highway 730 at Umatilla. To reach Nolin, go west from Pendleton for about 15 miles on Rieth Road, which parallels the river.

For More Information: Oregon Department of Fish and Wildlife, Pendleton District Office; Umatilla National Forest; Umatilla Indian Reservation

84 Grande Ronde River

Key Species: steelhead, rainbow trout

Best Way to Fish: boat, bank, wading

Best Time to Fish: steelhead, September through mid-April; rainbow trout, summer

Description: Flowing out of the Blue Mountains, then across the state line into Washington to its confluence with the Snake River, the Grande Ronde offers outstanding summer steelhead fishing as well as an excellent summer rainbow trout fishery.

Steelhead begin entering the river in September into May, although the season closes in mid-April. The best time to fish for them is from October through February. When the steelhead are not available, a nice rainbow trout fishery—with specimens up to 18 inches—keeps anglers occupied throughout the summer months.

There are also bull trout and Chinook salmon in the Grande Ronde. However, angling for these species is not allowed.

Most fishing on this river happens on its lower reaches. There is road access between Wildcat Creek and the Washington-Oregon state line. Fishing other sections of the river requires a boat or raft.

Fishing Index: When the steelhead show up in the fall, fly fishing takes center stage, with traditional steelhead wet flies. As the season moves on and the water cools, making the fish less active, drifting worms or casting spinners become the techniques of choice for bank anglers. Floating bait under a bobber, drifting Corkies with eggs or shrimp, and back-bouncing bait and back-trolling plugs are all typical approaches later in the season for anglers floating the lower river. Anglers with boats or rafts put in along the road which parallels the river and float to the state line. Some put in on the Minam or Wallowa Rivers and float down to Wildcat Creek, Mud Creek, or the small community of Troy. These longer floats take several days if you are going to do any serious fishing and require good planning. Most people fish this river from the bank.

During the summer, trout anglers fish the same stretch of river—from Wildcat Creek to the state line with bait, spinners, and flies. Only adipose fin-clipped trout may be kept. The Oregon Department of Fish and Wildlife no longer stocks the Grande Ronde with trout, so most of the hatchery fish caught here are steelhead that did not migrate to the sea.

Directions: From Enterprise, go north on Oregon Highway 3 for about 35 miles. Turn left (east) at the Flora turnoff and drive about 18 miles to Troy. At Troy, you can access the gravel road running along the river's west bank.

For More Information: Oregon Department of Fish and Wildlife, Enterprise District Office

Grande Ronde River

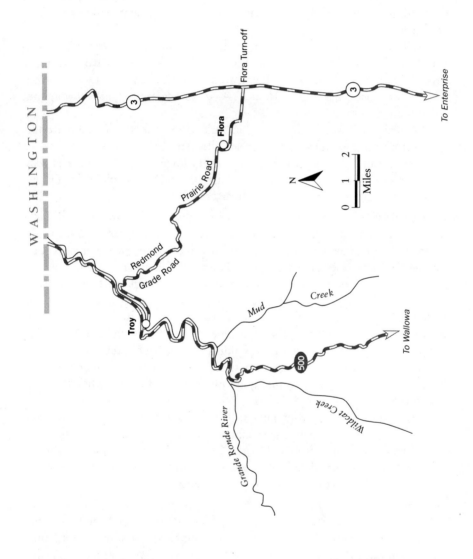

85 Wallowa River

Key Species: rainbow trout, steelhead

Best Way to Fish: bank

Best Time to Fish: February through October

Description: Meandering some 50 miles from its outlet on the north end of Wallowa Lake to its confluence with the Grande Ronde River, the Wallowa is an excellent rainbow trout fishery with a good steelhead run to boot.

While the resident rainbow population is in the river year-round, steelhead begin showing up in mid-February, peaking between mid-March and mid-April, when the season for them closes. Steelhead here run from 4 to 10 pounds, with 4- to 6-pounders being typical.

The Wallowa River has a mix of angling regulations, depending on what section of the river you are on and whether you are fishing for trout or steelhead. See the latest regulations for details.

Fishing Index: A popular river with fly anglers, the reach between Rock Creek and Minam State Recreation Area is where most anglers congregate.

The Wallowa is also a favorite of river runners during the summer months, although most of them don't fish during their trips.

Even though the season opens here in late May, trout anglers usually need to wait until the spring runoff from the mountains is spent and the river clears off, typically by mid-July. The best trout fishing runs from then through October, when the trout season closes.

Steelheaders fish the same stretch with a mix of techniques including casting flies and spinners and drifting shrimp, nightcrawlers, eggs, Corkies, and Spin 'n Glos. As with the rainbow trout fishing, the steelhead fishery here is from the bank.

The river upstream from this reach flows through private land, where you will have to secure permission to trespass if you want to give it a try.

Directions: The confluence of Rock Creek and the Wallowa River is about 6 miles north of the town of Wallowa off Oregon Highway 82. There is a large turn-out here where you can park. Minam State Recreation Area is about 1 mile north of Minam.

For More Information: Oregon Department of Fish and Wildlife, Enterprise District Office

Wallowa River

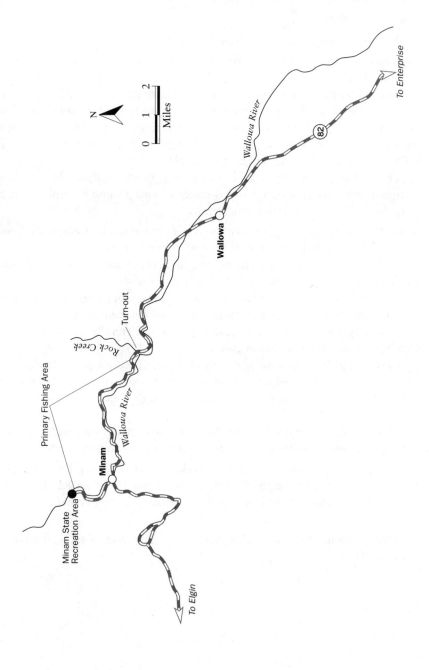

86 Minam River

Key Species: rainbow trout, brook trout

Best Way to Fish: bank, wading

Best Time to Fish: Summer

Description: This river, designated as part of the Wild and Scenic River System, flows some 50 miles through remote and beautiful country from its headwaters deep in the Wallowa-Whitman National Forest's Eagle Cap Wilderness to its confluence with the Wallowa River at the town of Minam.

In addition to rainbow and brook trout, bull trout, steelhead, and spring Chinook are found here as well. There is, however, no fishing for the latter three species.

Fishing Index: An excellent wilderness fishery, the Minam River is a perfect choice for anglers looking to combine a wilderness experience with fishing. The river is open to all types of angling—bait or flies and lures—from May 27 through the end of October. However, state fishery managers strongly encourage anglers to practice catch-and-release-only fishing here.

While rainbow trout are found throughout the river, brook trout are concentrated in the upper reaches. If you are going to go after brook trout for the frying pan, though, you will need to be sure you can tell the difference between those and bull trout, since bull trout here are protected by federal law. Brook trout and bull trout can be difficult to differentiate, especially smaller, immature fish (see Fish Identification at the beginning of this book).

Directions: A trail runs along the river. To access the lower river, drive west from Minam on Oregon Highway 82 for about 5 miles, then turn left onto an unimproved access road. It is about 6 miles to the national forest boundary. Much of this road is washed out and is suitable for foot or horse travel only. Another good access point further upriver, is via Moss Springs Campground, which is reached by driving east from the town of Cove on Moss Springs Road (which becomes Forest Road 6220) for about 6 miles. The trail to the river is about 8 miles, which will take you Minam Lodge, a wilderness lodge on the river's west bank.

For More Information: Oregon Department of Fish and Wildlife, Enterprise District Office and Wallowa-Whitman National Forest

Minam River

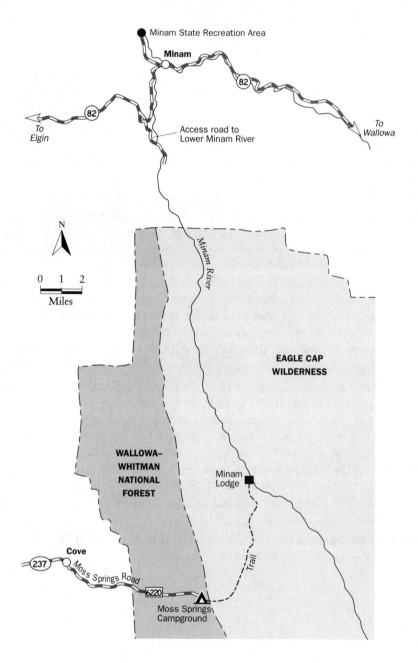

Minam State Recreation Area

Minam

82

To
Elgin

82

Access road to
Lower Minam River

To
Wallowa

N

0 1 2
Miles

Minam River

EAGLE CAP
WILDERNESS

WALLOWA–
WHITMAN
NATIONAL
FOREST

Minam
Lodge

Trail

Cove

237

Moss Springs Road

6220

Moss Springs
Campground

87 Wallowa Lake

Key Species: rainbow trout, kokanee salmon

Best Way to Fish: boat and bank

Best Time to Fish: May through October

Description: Located in a spectacular alpine setting, Wallowa Lake is deep and cold. Sitting at an altitude of nearly 4,383 feet, with Chief Joseph Mountain jutting into the sky behind it, this glacier-created lake is about 1,500 acres in size, averages 160 feet deep, and is nearly 300 feet at its deepest.

You will find good kokanee salmon populations here, averaging 9 to 10 inches and rainbow trout running 9 to 12 inches. There is also a small population of lake trout, including some up to 30 pounds, but they are seldom caught.

Although more than half of the lake shore is privately owned, there is a state park (Wallowa State Park) here with camping and a marina. There is also a county boat ramp on the lake as well as a collection of small rustic commercial resorts.

Wallowa Lake is open to angling year-round.

Fishing Index: Kokanee fishing is best in May and June when the fish move closer to the surface. As summer arrives, they go deeper, requiring anglers to get their lures down deeper as well. Trolling Wedding Rings or Hot Shots on a flasher set-up is a popular and effective kokanee technique, as is jigging with Nordics, Buzz Bombs, and Crippled Herrings. Although these fish are widely scattered, the northwest section of the lake is a favorite area for kokanee anglers to concentrate.

Trolling or casting spinners for rainbows is very effective, as is fishing with bait. If you want to take a stab at hooking into one of the rare monster lake trout, troll deep with Flatfish and Rapalas.

There is bank angling off the Joseph–Wallowa Lake Highway, which runs along the east side of the lake, and at the boat launches where you can cast lures or still fish with bait.

Fishing on Wallowa Lake tends to be better in the spring before the water-skiers and other water-sports enthusiasts come out in full force for the summer. Wallowa Lake has good ice fishing for rainbow trout during winters when the lake freezes over.

Directions: Wallowa Lake is located immediately south of Joseph off the Joseph–Wallowa Lake Highway. The county boat ramp is on the north end of the lake. Wallowa Lake State Park is on the south end.

For More Information: Oregon Department of Fish and Wildlife, Enterprise District Office and Wallowa Lake State Park

Wallowa Lake

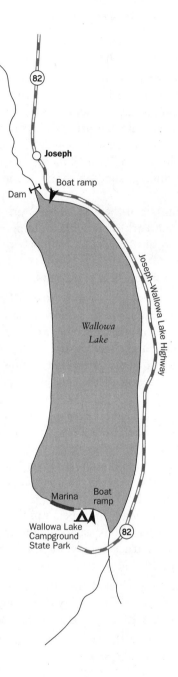

82

Joseph

Boat ramp

Dam

Joseph–Wallowa Lake Highway

Wallowa Lake

Marina

Boat ramp

Wallowa Lake
Campground
State Park

82

88 Imnaha River

Key Species: steelhead, rainbow trout

Best Way to Fish: bank

Best Time to Fish: steelhead, February through mid-April; rainbow trout, summer

Description: This Wild and Scenic River arises out of the Eagle Cap Wilderness in the Wallowa-Whitman National Forest and flows about 75 miles to its confluence with the Snake River, just north of the Hells Canyon Wilderness.

A good rainbow trout fishery, with the potential for producing fish up to 16 or 17 inches, the Imnaha sports a steelhead fishery as well. The Imnaha is open for steelhead fishing from January 1 to April 15 and from September 1 through the end of December. Only hatchery steelhead may be kept. There are spring Chinook in the Imnaha; however, no angling is allowed for them.

The best section of the river for fishing is from the community of Imnaha to the mouth, about a 20-mile stretch. There is some private land around town, but once you get below Horse Creek it is mostly USDA Forest Service land, so access is not a problem. A road follows most of this river segment.

Fishing Index: Bait, lures, and flies are all permitted on the Imnaha River. A likely approach is to drive the riverside road north from Imnaha and pick spots that look good, making sure that you are on public land before fishing. Steelheading here is similar to the Grande Ronde, except that it is not quite as good in the fall, making it a less desirable destination for anglers hoping to catch one on a fly. Spring steelhead fishing can be very good. Conditions to look for are high water, which brings the fish upriver, but not so high as to cause excessive turbidity.

Directions: Imnaha can be reached by driving east from Joseph on Oregon Highway 350 (Little Sheep Creek Highway) for about 30 miles. Dug Bar Road (which becomes Forest Road 4260) parallels most of the river north of Imnaha.

For More Information: Oregon Department of Fish and Wildlife, Enterprise District Office and Wallowa-Whitman National Forest

Imnaha River

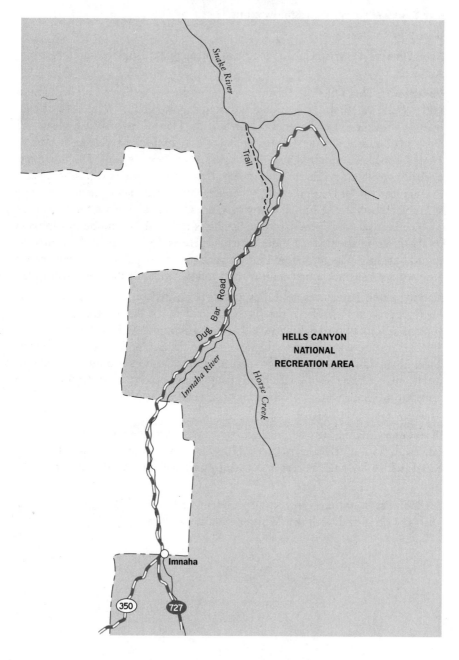

Snake River

Trail

Dug Bar Road

Imnaha River

Horse Creek

HELLS CANYON
NATIONAL
RECREATION AREA

Imnaha

350 727

Appendix: Sources of Additional Information

USDA Forest Service

Deschutes National Forest
USDA Forest Service
1645 Highway 20 E.
Bend, OR 97701
(541) 388-2715

Fremont National Forest
HC 10, Box 337
Lakeview, OR 97630
(541) 947-2151

Malheur National Forest
431 Patterson Bridge Road
John Day, OR 97845
(541) 575-1731

Ochoco National Forest
1645 Highway 20 E.
Bend, OR 97701
(541) 388-2715

Umpqua National Forest
Diamond Lake Ranger District
2020 Toketee Ranger Station Road
Idleyld Park, OR 97447
(541) 498-2531

Wallowa-Whitman National Forest
P.O. Box 907
Baker City, OR 97814
(541) 523-6391

Winema National Forest
2819 Dahlia Street
Klamath Falls, OR 97601
(541) 883-6714

Bureau of Land Management

State Office
1515 S.W. 5th Avenue
Portland, OR 97201
(503) 952-6000

Prineville Office
3160 N.E. Third Street
Prineville, OR 97754
(541) 416-6700

Rand Visitor Center
(541) 479-3735

Oregon Dunes National Recreation Area

Siuslaw National Forest
855 Highway Avenue
Reedsport, OR 97467
(503) 271-3611

Siskiyou National Forest
200 N.E. Greenfield Road
Grants Pass, OR 97526
(541) 471-6724

Siuslaw National Forest
4077 Research Way
Corvallis, OR 97333
(541) 750-7000

Umatilla National Forest
2517 S.W. Hailey
Pendleton, OR 97801
(541) 278-3716

Oregon Department of Fish and Wildlife

Portland Headquarters
2501 SW First Avenue
Portland, OR 97207
(503) 872-5264
Web Site: www.dfw.state.or.us

Northwest Region
7118 N.E. Vandenberg Avenue
Corvallis, OR 97330
(541) 757-4186

Southwest Region
4192 N. Umpqua Highway
Roseburg, OR 97470
(541) 440-3353

High Desert Region
61374 Parrell Road
Bend, OR 97702
(541) 388-6363

Northeast Region
107 20th Street
La Grande, OR 97850
(541) 963-2138

Marine Resources Program
2040 S.E. Marine Science Drive
Newport, OR 97365
(541) 867-0300

Central Point District
1495 E. Gregory Street
Central Point, OR 97502
(541) 826-8774

Columbia Region
17330 S.E. Evelyn Street
Clackamas, OR 97015
(503) 657-2000

Charleston District
4475 Boat Basin Boulevard
Charleston, OR 97420
(541) 888-5515

Gold Beach District
742 Airport Way
Gold Beach, OR 97444
(541) 247-7605

Enterprise District
65495 Alder Slope Road
Enterprise, OR 97828
(541) 426-3279

Hines District
237 S. Hines Boulevard
Hines, OR 97738
(541) 573-6582

John Day District
305 N. Canyon Boulevard
Canyon City, OR 97820
(541) 575-1167

Klamath Falls District
1850 Miller Island Road
Klamath Falls, OR 97603
(541) 883-5732

Lakeview District
101 North D Street
Lakeview, OR 97630
(541) 947-2950

Mid-Coast District
2040 S.E. Marine Science Drive
Newport, OR 97365
(541) 867-0300

North Coast District
Rt. 1, Box 764, House 2
Astoria, OR 97103
(503) 338-0106

Ontario District
3814 Clark Boulevard
Ontario, OR 97914
(541) 889-6975

Pendleton District
73471 Mytinger Lane
Pendleton, OR 97801
(541) 276-2344

Prineville District
2042 S.E. Paulina Highway
Prineville, OR 97754
(541) 447-5111

Salem District
4412 Silverton Road N.E.
Salem, OR 97305
(503) 378-6925

Springfield District
3150 East Main
Springfield, OR 97478
(541) 726-3515

The Dalles District
3701 West 13th Street
The Dalles, OR 97058
(541) 296-4628

Tillamook District
4909 Third Street
Tillamook, OR 97141
(503) 842-2741

Fish Hatcheries

Alsea Fish Hatchery
29050 Fish Hatchery Road
Alsea, OR 97324
(541) 487-7240

Elk River Fish Hatchery
95163 Elk River Road
Port Orford, OR 97465
(541) 332-7025

Fall River Hatchery
15055 South Century Drive
Bend, OR 97707
(541) 593-1510

Klaskanine Fish Hatchery
Route 1, Box 764
Astoria, OR 97103
(503) 325-3653

Leaburg Fish Hatchery
90700 Fish Hatchery Road
Leaburg, OR 97489
(541) 896-3294

Nehalem Fish Hatchery
Rt. 1, Box 292
Nehalem, OR 97131
(503) 368-6828
(503) 368-5670 (river information)

Salmon River Fish Hatchery
575 North Bank Road
Otis, OR 97368
(541) 994-8606

Sandy Fish Hatchery
39800 S.E. Fish Hatchery Road
Sandy, OR 97055
(503) 668-4222

Wizard Falls Fish Hatchery
Camp Sherman, OR 97730
(541) 595-6611

Oregon Parks and Recreation Department

State Office
1115 Commercial Street, N.E.
Salem, OR 97310-1001
(503) 378-8587

Detroit Lake State Park
(503) 854-3346

Joseph H. Stewart State Park
(541) 560-3334

Lake Owyhee State Park
(541) 523-2499 ext. 3

Milo McIver State Park
(503) 630-7150

The Cove Palisades State Park
(541) 546-3412

Wallowa Lake State Park
(541) 432-4185

Indian Tribes

The Confederated Tribes of Warm
 Springs
(541) 553-3233

Umatilla Indian Reservation
(541) 276-4109

Tackle Shops and Resorts

Crane Prairie Resort
(541) 383-3939

Crescent Lake Resort
(541) 433-2505

Cultus Lake Resort
(541) 389-3230

East Lake Resort
(541) 536-2230

Elk Lake Resort
(541) 382-1019

Lake of the Woods Resort
(541) 949-8300

Lake Stop Grocery
(503) 357-4270

Odell Lake Resort
(541) 433-2540

Paulina Lake Resort
(541) 536-2240

Rocky Point Resort
(541) 356-2287

The Fly Fisher's Place
151 West Main Avenue
Sisters, OR 97759
(541) 549-3474

Access and Shuttles

Private Boat Launch, Necanicum
  River
Johnson Construction Company
(503) 738-7328

Coos River Access
North Pacific Security
1170 Newport Street
Coos Bay, OR
(541) 267-5915

Williamson River Shuttle Service
Williamson River Anglers
(541) 783-2677

Index

s

Upper Klamath Lake 196–98

Upper Rogue River 97–100

W

walleye
  best bets for 25
  best sites for 108–11
  species information 25

Wallowa Lake 243–44

Wallowa River 239–40

white crappie 212, 227–29

whitefish, mountain. *See* mountain
  whitefish

white-striped bass
  best bets for 22
  best sites for 205–7
  species information 22

white sturgeon. *See* sturgeon

Wickiup Reservoir 170–72

wild fish, identifying 4–6

Willamette River, Lower 116–20

Willamette River, Middle Fork
  131–33

Williamson River 185–89

Wilson River 46–48

Wood River 189–92

Y

Yaquina Bay and Yaquina River
  57–59

Yellowjacket Lake/Delintment Lake
  209–11

yellow perch
  best bets for 23
  best sites for
  northwest Oregon 66–68
  species information 22
  Willamette Valley 120–22

Youngs Bay and Lower Columbia
  River 28–31

About the Author

An Oregon resident for twenty-five years, author Jim Yuskavitch lives on the east slope of the Cascades, just outside the small town of Sisters. He is a full-time writer and photographer who specializes in natural history and the environment.